African Spirituality in Black Women's Fiction

African Spirituality in Black Women's Fiction

Threaded Visions of Memory, Community, Nature, and Being

Elizabeth J. West

LEXINGTON BOOKS
Lanham • Boulder • New York • Toronto • Plymouth, UK

Published by Lexington Books
A wholly owned subsidiary of The Rowman & Littlefield Publishing Group, Inc.
4501 Forbes Boulevard, Suite 200, Lanham, Maryland 20706
www.rowman.com

10 Thornbury Road, Plymouth PL6 7PP, United Kingdom

British Library Cataloguing in Publication Information Available

Library of Congress Cataloging-in-Publication Data

The hardback edition of this book was previously cataloged by the Library of Congress as follows:

West, Elizabeth J., 1957–
African spirituality in Black women's fiction : threaded visions of memory, community, nature, and
being / Elizabeth J. West.
p. cm.
Includes bibliographical references and index.
1. American fiction—African American authors—History and criticism. 2. American fiction—Women authors—History and criticism. 3. Spirituality in literature. 4. African American women authors—Intellectual life. I. Title.
PS153.N5W39 2012
813.009'3827008996073—dc23
2011036294

978-0-7391-6885-1 (cloth : alk. paper)
978-0-7391-7937-6 (pbk. : alk. paper)
978-0-7391-6886-8 (electronic)

Printed in the United States of America

For my parents, Wessie Cistrunk Martin and Cleo Martin.
And for Thomas West, who was like a father.

Contents

Acknowledgments

I am deeply grateful for the support of more than a few sources and persons in my efforts to bring this study to fruition. The 2002 award of a research fellowship from the American Association of University Women (AAUW) was the earliest and most resolute expression of belief in the importance and promise of this project. Their support granted me the extended months needed to complete the earliest draft of the manuscript. As a participant in the ROOTS 2003 NEH Summer Seminar (also supported by Virginia Foundation for the Humanities and University of Virginia), I benefitted greatly from the intellectual sharing and feedback from fellow participants. I thank Dr. Joseph Miller for his directorship of ROOTS: he structured a setting for the sharing and debating of ideas that broadened my understanding of Africa and the Atlantic World. Two summer research grants from Georgia State University also freed me to move toward completion. In the summer of 2011 through the Faculty Learning Community Retreat sponsored by GSU, I was fortunate to have the feedback from fellow participants, Dr. Cora Presley, Dr. Mary Zeigler, Dr. Kameelah Martin-Samuel, and Dr. Consuela Bennett. Their careful reading helped me fine-tune the introductory chapter. I am grateful to my colleague, Dr. Carol Marsh-Lockett, for both her scholarly feedback and her encouragement. Dr. Vivian May and Dr. Beth Feri have been both intellectual sounding boards and cherished friends—I thank them in both regards. The graduate students I have mentored have been an invaluable resource and inspiration. I owe special thanks to Jill Goad, an energetic and committed graduate research assistant, who assisted me in the nuts and bolts preparation of the manuscript.

Though they are the least connected to the scholarly side of bringing this book to form, my family has been my greatest inspiration. It is the Cistrunks' deep belief in education and learning that has fueled and sustained my love of academia and desire to know more. I thank my husband and children for being interested enough in my work to occasionally inquire, but more importantly for being ongoing reminders to me that we have to close the books to be able to experience the stuff that makes them.

Chapter One

From Africa to America

I. ENCOUNTERS OF AFRICAN SPIRITUALITY AND ANGLO CHRISTIANITY

The place of western Christianity in African American culture has been considered in the works of countless scholars across numerous disciplines. Scholarship has shown that the adoption of Christianity by blacks in the United States was central in shaping African American culture. Similarly, the case for Christianity's import in African American literature has also been made. Lacking, however, is a similar depth of scholarship that examines African spirituality in black fiction. This work addresses this shortfall, specifically in the field of African American women's literature. Informed from the onset by spiritual principles of continental Africa, black women writers have shaped a literary history that reflects these origins. While these principles do not connect to any single African source, "[s]pirituality, as depicted in black women's literature and film, is recognizably African/Black . . . [and] its contours are shaped by the core ethical and philosophical values around which several traditions cohere within the African cultural domain" (Ryan 23). That core is a shared African cosmology rested in the belief that all world entities emanate from a "cosmic oneness," or spirit which can be described as "the undifferentiated, formless, underlying factor that drives the universe . . . [and] suffuses all objects" (Rahming 2, 4). This concept of spirit is not singular to African thought, but it contrasts western Christianity which does not recognize spirit as present in all entities, particularly inanimate entities. Understanding spirit as formless yet manifested in form, African spirituality rests in the belief that all entities—formed and formless, interconnect and that the degree to which humans understand and honor this interconnectedness speaks to and shapes their fortunes in the material world.

1

Africans in the new world fashioned a worldview that, while informed by their pre–Middle Passage cosmology, had to necessarily undergo transformations. These transformations occurred alongside the birth and evolution of African American Christianity. Understanding the evolution of African spirituality in African American culture thus calls for some attention to the evolution of African American Christianity. Early in their struggle for freedom, black activists adapted Christianity to their rhetoric of liberation. The adoption of Christianity by blacks, however, required significant rhetorical negotiations, for it was a doctrine delivered in a discourse that alienated and vilified blackness. Before the Revolutionary War, Anglo America was shaping a racialized Christian rhetoric that proclaimed the African's subservient relationship to the superior and divinely chosen white race. While the Puritans had come to America to seek religious asylum from Britain's tyranny, they sought

> not to break with old Europe, but to bring about the logic and fullest extent of a hegemonic Protestantism and cultural civilization. . . . [T]hose bold pioneers brought the same view of blacks as demonic, evil, inferior, and sinful that their European mother churches had propagated . . . thus the Pilgrims set in motion a theology—a conscious religious justification—laden with signs of ordained racial hierarchy. (Hopkins 15)

Even for Cotton Mather, early Puritan leader and proponent of Christianizing Africans, the underlying presumption of African inferiority could not be contained. In his 1706 publication, "The Negro Christianized," Mather advocates Christianizing blacks, but his interest in Africans does not originate in a philosophy of racial equality or abolitionism: "While he reminds his readers parenthetically that it is not yet proved that the slaves are not descendants of the biblical Ham, he leaves room for doubt, which reinforces . . . a persistent conceptual link in the text between skin color and moral degradation" (Nelson 26). The speculation about the connection between Africans and the biblical curse of Ham (Ham's son, Canaan) would continue in American racial discourse well beyond Mather's own century. By the dawn of the Civil War it was commonplace in written and oral discourses to hear Africans referred to as the children of Ham.[1]

By the early 1800s, the writings of African Americans demonstrated that at least among the literate, blacks identified themselves in biblical terms born out of Anglo racial discourse. Among whites, the Bible became a commonplace reference for either justifying America's exploitation of blacks, or asserting a racial hierarchy that seated blacks as inferiors. Ironically, in a process that amounted to Africanizing their Christianity, early blacks appropriated Christianity to proclaim their humanity and ultimate divine redemption. In general, blacks who learned to read, quickly discovered that they had been provided the means to interpret the Bible for themselves. The result was a dynamic negotiation of scripture and experience that came to define the religious legacy of black Christians in the United States. Blacks would take biblical stories of suffering and bondage and make them their own, and as Phillis Wheatley illustrates in her poem "On Being Brought from Africa to America" (published in her 1773 collection of poems), blacks would begin to demonstrate their thorough understanding of misrepresented biblical stories. While Wheatley's work is oftentimes dismissed as self-denigrating, this poem, in fact, exemplifies a carefully constructed critique of Anglo Christianity. Her reminder to whites that blacks are worthy of redemption undermines both their exclusionary presumptions of divine providence as well as their racialized interpretation of scripture: "Remember, Christians, Negroes, black as Cain, / May be refin'd, and join th' angelic train." Linking blacks to the biblical Cain, Wheatley ostensibly accepts a myth that has become popularized in eighteenth-century Anglo Christian discourse. Proclaiming that blacks are the descendants of the biblical Cain who was cursed for murdering his brother, Abel, this Anglo biblical myth maintained that blacks were destined to suffer because they were from the cursed line of Cain. Wheatley's assertion that blacks "may be refin'd" and ultimately redeemed reveals that she was acquainted with the biblical text (Genesis 4.1–16) in its entirety, understanding that though God had initially cursed Cain, God later answered his plea for mercy. In kind, God would also answer the African's plea and, like Cain, Africans would be restored to God's grace.

Wheatley's detractors have been quick to indict her poetry for its presumed silence on slavery and racism. This criticism may resonate with those who privilege activism that is overt. Wheatley's style is more often subversive, however, requiring readers to discursively ascertain her meaning. Wheatley's covert criticism of white Christian racism has been contrasted with the more explicit challenge offered by her well known male contemporaries, Benjamin Banneker and Prince Hall as well as nineteenth-century black activists who would succeed her. While Banneker has been best remembered for his achievements in science and his role in surveying the nation's capital, his 1791 letter to Thomas Jefferson has been hailed as a hallmark in African American literary protest. Banneker's letter challenges the dehumanizing assessment of black intellect and spirit posed by Jefferson in his *Notes on The State of Virginia* (1787). Addressing members of his Masonic lodge in 1797, activist Prince Hall mirrors Banneker in his open and explicit critique. Identifying slavery as a cruel and tyrannical system, Hall employs biblical scripture to remind his fellow blacks of their historical link to Christianity. His recollections of African connections in the Bible—Moses's Ethiopian father-in-law, the Ethiopian eunuch who is converted by the apostle, Philip, and the meeting between the Queen of Sheba and the wise King Solomon—affirm a black biblical experience that predates the conversion of Africans in America.

The defiance exemplified in Banneker's and Hall's writings spilled over into nineteenth-century black activism, as black writers followed Wheatley and Hall with their recollections on the African's pivotal place in biblical history. In his 1829 *Appeal*, activist, David Walker represents this continuum. He vehemently rejects white claims to racial superiority and challenges whites to identify the biblical scripture that supports the racial myth that ties Cain to blacks: "I have searched the Bible as well as they . . . and have never seen a verse which testifies whether we are the seed of Cain or of Abel. Yet those men tell us that we are of the seed of Cain and that God put a dark stain upon us, that we might be known as their slaves!!!" (71–72). Whereas Wheatley inferred that whites had misinterpreted this scripture, Walker defiantly rejects their reading and admonishes them for their barbarous treatment of blacks. Walker trusts his own independent reading of the Bible and delivers Jeremiac warnings of the destruction to come if whites continue to enslave and abuse blacks. Like many of his contemporaries, Walker engages in biblical typology, enlisting biblical stories that mirror the plight of blacks in America and transforming these into stories of black experience. This practice would become a cultural legacy in black Christian rhetorics of liberation. The story of Joseph who is sold into bondage by his brothers, the story of Moses who delivers his people from bondage in Egypt, and the story of Christ who delivers man from sin are among those biblical tales passed along for generations as stories that prefigure the plight and deliverance of blacks in bondage.

African American heroes/heroines would be likened to prophets and their stories paralleled with those of biblical victims. This merging of histories played out not only in black writing, but in well-known, real-life events as well. For example, slave insurrectionist Gabriel Prosser saw himself as the black Sampson called to a divine mission:

> Gabriel believed that God had marked him from childhood to be a deliverer of his people. Throughout the summer of 1800 he frequently made this divine election known to several men with whom he associated. He interpreted to them the various parts of Scripture that he believed referred to the condition of the Negro in slavery and the necessity of rising up against the Philistines—the slaveholders. The exploits of Sampson in Judges 15 had particular significance to Gabriel as he laid careful plans to sow destruction throughout Henrico County and lead the slaves to the establishment of a new black kingdom in Virginia with himself as ruler. (Wilmore 54)

Similarly, Denmark Vessey, leader of the 1822 slave revolt in South Carolina, employed the biblical story of Joshua in Jericho in his recruiting campaign (Wilmore 59). One of the most well-known legacies of deliverance, Harriet Tubman's repeated journeys South to guide slaves to freedom, came to be a legend couched in the story of Moses, the biblical deliverer. Tubman became known as the Moses of her people, who, like Moses, could have ignored the plight of her people in bondage, but instead risked her own life and safety to deliver those left behind. By the mid-1800s black leaders had begun to rally around two particular scriptural references: the image of Jesus Christ as deliverer became symbolic of the cry for black deliverance from slavery, and the promise of Psalm 68:31 that "Princes shall come out of Egypt; Ethiopia shall soon stretch out her hands unto God."

Throughout the nineteenth century, Psalm 68:31 would be the subject of countless numbers of sermons by black preachers (Wilmore 121). The identification of African people with biblical predecessors had, by the end of the nineteenth century, become commonplace. Many black preachers identified the ancient Egyptian and Ethiopians as the ancestors of new world blacks, and often they specifically identified those biblical figures who were themselves black. This practice made the Bible an easy adaptation for blacks, despite a racist public discourse that continually painted them as subhuman. While the Bible had been used for centuries by many whites to justify the enslavement of blacks, blacks had themselves learned to use the Bible to recreate themselves and to validate their humanity. Although blacks had used Christianity as a liberative tool, Christianity's otherworldliness often imposed a cultural rhetoric that at times lulled black communities into complacency: in particular

> [d]uring the 1920s and 1930s most black churches retained a basically rural orientation and retreated into enclaves of moralistic, revivalistic Christianity by which they tried to fend off the encroaching gloom and pathology of the ghetto. As far as challenging white society, or seeking to mobilize the community against poverty and oppression, most churches were too otherworldly, apathetic, or caught up in institutional maintenance to deal with such issues. . . . The large, social action-oriented, institutional church was always the exception rather than the rule. (Wilmore 161)

It was not until the surge of civil rights activism in the 1960s that the black church once again came to the forefront of black activism.[2] The Civil Rights Movement gave rise to a new generation of activist clergy, most notably Dr. Martin Luther King, Jr., and it gave the black church renewed liberationist momentum. This movement issued in a body of black scholars and theologians, men and women, whose explorations of the place of the church in the worldly struggles of African descent people in America continues to the present.

Just as their black theological predecessors, many contemporary black theologians assume that the inquiry into African American Christianity "on the one hand draws from the African American experience, history, and culture and on the other hand turns to divine revelation, Scripture, and the church's tradition" (Coleman 180). From the 1960s to the present black theologians have in general been more concerned with questions of theology as they pertain to Christianity; however, a number of black scholars and thinkers, including some theologians, have turned their attention to the question of how an African-rooted worldview has influenced the spiritual history of blacks in America. While whites assumed that blacks were mere heathens who arrived in America with no religion and who were either unfit for Christianity or only fit to know Christianity as a faith of bondage, blacks arrived on American shores out of centuries old philosophical and religious traditions. Africans transported to America brought with them many shared as well as many dissimilar practices and beliefs, for they were people of varying group affiliations. Out of the language of slavery the monolithic label of African would emerge as the representative term for all slaves in the Americas. Although slaves from Africa consisted of people captured from many different communities and nation states, in the New World they became known simply by the generic term, African. More recently, scholars of African history and culture emphasize the need to recognize Africa as a continent of diverse population groups. I employ often used generalizations such as Africa, African, and Africanity to refer to the diverse populations from Africa delivered into slavery in the New World; however, I do so not under the presumption of black universality or a monolithic blackness. I acknowledge the distinctness of black population groups on the African continent, and I use these generalized terms as a semantic encapsulation that refers to sub-Saharan Africa and its populations that are the source of common metaphysical beliefs and practices found throughout black societies in the New World.

While blacks transported to America represented diverse groups, slavery became the common denominator that would define their experience in the new world. Blacks would transform beliefs and practices from their native home to install a common culture that represented a blending of groups and ideologies. The question of African influence in American and African American society remains an ongoing debate with some scholars suggesting that blacks lost memory of and connection to their pre–Middle Passage worldview. In large part, this argument has hinged on the supposition that African American cultural practices and beliefs had no ties to continental Africa. But as historian Lawrence W. Levine explains, such conclusions defy logic:

> To insist that only those elements of slave culture were African which remained largely unchanged from the African past is to misrepresent the nature of culture itself. Culture is not a fixed condition but a process: the product of interaction between the past and present. Its toughness and resiliency are determined not by a culture's ability to withstand change, which indeed may be a sign of stagnation not life, but by its ability to react creatively and responsively to the realities of a new situation. (5)

Recognizing African influence in African American culture as a dynamic defined by transformations, we arrive at a more informed understanding of black culture in America, including understandings of black spirituality. This is a theoretical position that grounded the works of one of America's first black anthropologists, Zora Neale Hurston. Hurston was interested in black folk culture, and she was especially interested in black religion and spirituality. She traveled extensively throughout the American south as well as the Caribbean, conducting field studies that offered evidence of African cultural practices and beliefs among blacks in the Americas. Regarding new world Afro-Christianity, Hurston argued that, "in fact, the Negro has not been Christianized as extensively as is generally believed. The great masses are still standing before their pagan altars and calling old gods by a new name" (*Writings by Zora Neale Hurston* 95). In her anthropological work as well as in her fiction Hurston demonstrated that black spirituality was the product of more than black Christian experience, and that black folk religion did not hold Anglo Christian religion as its sole model or its authoritative core. She maintained that "there is a great respect for the white man as a lawgiver, banker, and the like, but the folk Negroes do not crave his religion at all" (*Writings by Zora Neale Hurston* 98). In her 1931 article "Hoodoo in America," Hurston planted the seed of inquiry into the study of black folk culture and African retentions/transformations. She highlighted the similarity between American "hoodoo" and conjure and folk practices of blacks in the Caribbean, drawing the connection between these diasporic African peoples and their West African ancestors. Decades after Hurston's work, scholars from a range of disciplines have undertaken and continue to engage in more detailed study of African carryovers in African American culture as well as the culture of blacks throughout the Atlantic world. Works such as Joseph Murphy's *Working the Spirit* (1994), Henry Louis Gates Jr.'s *Signifying Monkey* (1988), Judylyn Ryan's *Spirituality as Ideology in Black Women's Film and Literature* (2005), Jocelyn Moody's *Sentimental Confessions: Spiritual Narratives of Nineteenth-Century African American Women* (2001), Yvonne Chireau's *Black Magic: Religion and the African American Conjuring Tradition* (2003), Will Coleman's *Tribal Talk: Black Theology, Hermeneutics, and African/American Ways of "Telling the Story"* (2000), and Naana Opoku-Agyemang's (et al.) anthology, *Africa and Transatlantic Memories: Literary and Aesthetic Manifestations of Diaspora and History* (2008), demonstrate that in a range of disciplines—history, religion, sociology, and literature for example—the significance of African influence in American and African American culture has been established.

Although Charles A. Cerami's biography of eighteenth-century black scientist Benjamin Banneker reminds us that carryovers of traditional African thought may be evident in African American scientific achievements, the strongest evidence of surviving African-rooted practices has persisted in the cultural arenas of African American religion, writing, dance, music, and language.[3] Call and response and ring shouting are among the most widely documented spiritual practices that have been traced back to pre–Middle Passage West Africa. Call and response, the interactive speaker-audience dynamic found in black music, black conversation, and black preaching, has also been maintained in African American culture, and to date, still highlights the dynamic and creative art of communication among African descent people.[4] Call and response has notably survived in the religious performances of African Americans: from the choir's musical call to the preacher's sermonic call to the congregation, a successful spiritual message requires clear and open expressions of consensus between the messenger(s) and the congregation. Failure to achieve this level of interaction amounts to "bad preaching," for "black preaching depends upon its connections with the congregations' experiences and their visible assent, their response to the call. Interdependence is an essential condition for effective preaching" (Towsend-Gilkes 129).

Dating back to slavery, blacks gathered for spiritual ceremonies that conveyed "a rhythmic call and response way of being in the world. . . . In a sense, the highly charged and seemingly ecstatic singing and dancing were ways of giving thanks to life and invoking a new tempo, opportunity, and presence among them. Movement and sound became acts of freedom" (Hopkins 120). In fact, movement and sound defined black life long before the Middle Passage. The ring shout, a religious ceremonial dance that was especially maintained among rural blacks in the south, is evidence of the importance of movement and sound in African based spirituality and the retention and transformation of pre-colonial spiritual rituals: "the connection between the religious forms of the ring shout dance (of enslaved African Americans in secret worship) and the memory of the drum (of their West African ancestors) displayed the vital sacred relation between black theology and the indigenous religions of West African communal practices" (Hopkins 142). As drums became systematically outlawed in America, blacks "performed the memory of the drum into a ring shout" (Hopkins 143).

Across diverse disciplines, scholars have demonstrated that specific cultural practices, artifacts, stories and rituals among African Americans (as well as those that have been absorbed into the larger culture) originated among West African people long before European contact with sub-Saharan Africa. Tracing the origins of highly recognizable American and African American inheritances such as African American language, artifacts such as the banjo, the numerous folktales of America's south, and America's popular music roots has revealed tangible Africanisms that have survived in America, influencing black culture and also informing the larger/white society.[5] While a significant body of work has been published on physical manifestations of Africanisms in American and African American culture, much remains to expand our understanding of African metaphysical influences. We may better understand African-rooted spirituality by recognizing the interconnectedness of the physical and the spiritual in this worldview. African ancestors of blacks in America sang and danced not for the mere sake of artistry or enjoyment, but rather as a means to spiritual ends. For them, God was served through acts that recognized the benevolence of God and the spirits: "African religion and spiritualism thus emphasized a celebration of human life. To live fully and robustly, to be esteemed by the community, was basic to African thinking and was incorporated into Africans' particular ontology" (Washington 73).

Because traditional African religion and philosophy were not articulated in written treatises as was customary for Europeans, and because it served their purpose not to acknowledge Africans as having a meaningful culture, Europeans presumed that Africans transported to the Americas lacked a real religion and philosophical worldview. This claim is clearly posited by one of America's most celebrated icons; in his *Notes on the State of Virginia*, Thomas Jefferson presumes that "in general, their [blacks'] existence appears to participate more of sensation than reflection . . . in imagination they are dull, tasteless, and anomalous" (in *Heath Anthology* 903). Jefferson's words capture the sentiment that would inform Anglo interpretations of African spirituality and philosophy in his own time and that are no less alive today. Early white statesmen and writers engaged in superficial observations and speculations about African behavior, and in general they found little need to consider that Africans had held to a religious/philosophical worldview before their contact with Europeans. In general, even those who sympathized with blacks maintained that it was through their contact with whites that blacks had begun to understand the world beyond the immediate and corporeal. It was not until a century after Emancipation that black scholars would in significant numbers challenge longstanding racialized rhetorics of black epistemological and ontological thought.

Works focusing on traditional African religions have served as the foundation for many comparative studies of African and African Diasporic worldviews. African religious scholar, John S. Mbiti has contributed much in this regard: his 1970 publications, *African Religions and Philosophy*, and *Concepts of God in Africa* have served as the theoretical foundation for many studies. Mbiti's work has been notable for its comprehensiveness, that is, its exploration of both the physical and the metaphysical in African spirituality among sub-Saharan Africans. His insightful exposition on African religion and philosophy defies the Eurocentric premise that Africans lacked these key markers of culture and civility. Mbiti explains that "African knowledge of God is expressed in proverbs, short statements, songs, prayers, names, myths, stories and religious ceremonies," logical modes of transmission in societies whose sacred traditions and beliefs are not committed to writing (*African*

Religions and Philosophy 38). The sacred and the secular are not separate
realities for African peoples; therefore, African spirituality, African philosophy, and African cultural practices are not functionally independent or separate. Particularly when speaking of pre–Middle Passage Africa, one can inter-
changeably use the terms African spirituality and African worldview.
Pre–Middle Passage African societies were not splintered by distinctions of
secular and sacred, thus their worldview and their spiritual view were one
and the same. For Africans, life is religion, life is philosophy, expressed in
the acts and words that are passed on from generation to generation: "Because traditional religions permeate all the departments of life, there is no
formal distinction between the sacred and the secular, between the religious
and non-religious, between the spiritual and the material areas of life.
Wherever the African is, there is his religion" (Mbiti *African Religions* 2).
This has been no less the case for African Americans. Although blacks have
written much during their time in America and, while blacks have been
subject to a dominant culture that awards the highest authority to the written
word, black culture remains highly oral. Like their continental counterparts,
blacks in America have nurtured a religiosity that is anthropomorphic and
this-worldly, but also decidedly spiritual.

In his frequently referenced study of African American religious history,
A Fire in the Bones, Albert Raboteau underscores this shared perspective
between continental Africans and blacks in America:

> The crucial factor linking the two traditions was a conviction that authentic
> worship required an observable experience of the divine presence. "It ain't
> enough to talk about God, you've got to feel Him moving on the altar of your
> heart," as one former slave explained. . . . In a society chronically split be-
> tween body and spirit, African-American ritual exemplifies embodied spirit
> and inspired body in gesture, dance, song, and performed word. . . . Contrary
> to the depersonalizing pressures of slavery and racial oppression, the person is
> of ultimate value as image of the divine. (190)

This explains the historically central place of music, oratory, and dance not
only in the black church but also in African American culture at large. In
traditional African religion as well as in African American culture, the spirit
of the divine, of the ancestors, of the community is manifested in act. The
divine rules that guide humankind are not recorded as abstract written treatises, but again, are performed and spoken, giving them perpetual life. One
must then delve into the many acts, rituals, and stories in black culture to
understand the worldview that defines black spiritual sensibilities.

II. AFRICAN SPIRITUALITY AND AFRICAN AMERICAN WOMEN

In the history of African American literature, we find a legacy of women's writings that draw on the physical and experiential to explore matters of spirituality. This tradition of spiritual musings is guided by four principles central to pre–Middle Passage African cosmology: 1) the value of memory to both individual and group well-being; 2) the belief that community represents the essence of human existence and being; 3) the view that nature— both animate and inanimate—represents divineness; and 4) belief in the interconnectedness of worldly and otherworldly beings. These principles are integral to black epistemological and ontological thought, pre– and post–Middle Passage and are central to shaping a tradition of spiritual explo- ration in black women's writing. African American women writers from Wheatley to Morrison integrate these themes in their work, signaling the early maintenance and integration of an African worldview among displaced Africans and the important role of women as carriers of culture. Dating back to slavery, black women were purveyors of spiritual tradition: "Black women were the carriers of the culture and tradition both within their families and the hush harbors of slave worship. When slavery ended, northern missionar- ies, white and black, rushed to the South and intended to make good Chris- tians out of the former slaves. These missionaries discovered Christians en- gaged in distinctive religious practices that they were reluctant to relinquish" (Towsend-Gilkes 79). Black women were central to the process of merging African spirituality with Christianity, including the early slave religion that historians call the "invisible institution." The invisible institution, the "exten- sive religious life [of the slaves] that thrived outside the institutional church," consisted of the slaves' own biblical and experiential spiritual interpretations (Raboteau *Canaan Land* 43). Slaves did not simply digest Christianity as whites fed it to them, and again, they did not simply abandon their precoloni- al cultural practices and beliefs. They were, for the most part, led by slave preachers of the invisible institution. While these preachers were male like their counterparts in the regular church, slave women "authorized authority nonetheless. Some served their communities as experts in the healing arts, combining the use of herbal medicine with prayer and religious ritual to assist the sick, the dying, and women experiencing childbirth. Others acted as 'spiritual mothers,' respected for their spiritual wisdom and gifts of insight, including the ability to explain people's dreams and to advise them on the state of their souls" (Raboteau *Canaan Land* 47).

Whether in the conventional church or the invisible church of slave soci- ety, black women found themselves early on alienated from the role of preacher. Despite an ongoing tradition that frowned on women as preachers, the history of black religion is not wholly absent of women preachers. The glossing of black women preachers in historical accounts of black religion has occurred in part because "with the exception of a very few women . . . most black preaching women who pursued a ministry between 1800 and 1970 are virtually unknown," but despite this obscurity, "legions of women . . . enjoyed great visibility and had long careers in the ministry" (Collier-Thomas xv). Black women preachers Julia A. J. Foote, Harriet A. Baker, Jarena Lee, and Mary J. Small are among those who were pioneers for later generations of black women. Perhaps not altogether accidentally, some black women, such as Jarena Lee and Julia Foote, were part of the nineteenth-century holiness tradition which "played a central part in the struggle of women, particularly black women, to preach. . . . Preaching women who embraced the holiness doctrine asserted that they did not need the Church's sanction, because their ministry was authorized by a power beyond the Church, namely God, who spoke to them through the Holy Spirit" (Collier-Thomas 12). The African spiritual belief that one can be taken over by and receive divine instruction from a holy spirit was maintained in African American culture, including African American Christianity. This doctrine allowed women to subvert male authority in the church, and it was founded on a spiritual concept—the power of the Holy Ghost/Holy Spirit—a direct contribution to American Christianity from America's slave community (Collier-Thomas 13). Whether these women knew that they were drawing from their African heritage is not indisputably evident; it is nonetheless important that they did, for their connection to this and other long-lived African spiritual beliefs illustrates the survival of African spirituality among diasporic blacks.

Claiming the holy spirit as the authority calling them to evangelism, black preaching women have been present from the earliest accounts of black religious experience to the present; they have, however, had a history of struggle. Even in the black church, black women would not be granted ordination rights until the twentieth century—in the African Methodist Episcopal (A.M.E.) Church, which was founded in response to white religious bigotry, women would not gain ordination rights until 1948 (Collier-Thomas 27). Their alienation notwithstanding, black women still assumed leadership roles in black religious circles: "black women emerged as worship leaders, preachers, catechizers, exhorters, prayer warriors,[6] singers, teachers, and storytellers—all authoritative agents of the black religious tradition" (Towsend-Gilkes 101 02). These were roles that mirrored black women's spiritual place in traditional African culture. Blacks who arrived on American shores via the Middle Passage were the product of spiritual traditions that held to the primacy of both male and female in the world. This is a common view held by many sub-Saharan populations from which Africans were shipped to the Americas. Among these, the Dahomeans, whose religion was the precursor to voodoo of the Americas, maintain a veneration of the supreme power and the deities as male/female dualities. From a Dahomean tale of creation, life begins with Nana Buluku, an androgynous being who is the source of all life (Coleman 3–4). Among the many deities, or vodun, we also find beings who are sexual dualities. For example, "Aido Hwedo, like so many other vodun, is both female and male, with separate bodies as well as two distinct person-ae. The female serpent lives in the sky, the male under the earth. Together, they signify that the air and earth are conjoined or interdependent" (Coleman 13). Male-female interdependence was acknowledged in African societies, and in spiritual rituals and practices men and women played significant roles: "African religious systems, regardless of how patriarchal they were, exalted both the male and female in their various collective expressions of the holy (the cult)" (Towsend-Gilkes 97).

Though many black churches would adopt the sexist practices of their white Christian counterparts, often excluding women from leadership roles in the church, black women made their presence known and they found ways to gain authority in their churches. Throughout the history of the black church "the African-American gospel-bearers who refused to permit the Black male clerical establishment's insistence on male dominance and female subordination to overrule the higher calling of God in their lives were many" (Martin in *A Troubling in My Soul* 20). These women represent a preacherly and spiritual tradition that has been recorded in the writings of both African American men and women writers. Among black male writers, James Baldwin and Langston Hughes stand out for their representations of prayer warriors: "James Baldwin's character, Praying Mother Washington, is such an example. Langston Hughes incorporates the prayer warrior tradition into his novel *Not Without Laughter* in the character of Aunt Hagar. The link between black women and the prayer tradition is firm and well recognized in letters and folklore" (Towsend-Gilkes 135). Similarly, in black women's writing we can trace a tradition of spiritual narratives that reveals black women's determined place in the religious world of their communities. Early black women's spiritual narratives reveal the spiritual legacy that has been maintained and passed on by black women to the present.

In "Spirit Matters: Re-Possessing the African-American Women's Literary Tradition," Anne Dalke explains the relationship between early spiritual narratives and later fictional works by black women:

> In their celebration of the agency of spirit, in their literary construction of a world which transcends the limitations of the everyday, nineteenth-century spiritual autobiographies lay part of the groundwork for the non-realistic, sometimes surrealistic, prose by twentieth-century African-American women. The spiritual journals provide rich background for, and an additional way of understanding, works such as Zora Neale Hurston's *Their Eyes Were Watching God*, Alice Walker's *The Color Purple*, Toni Cad Bambara's *The Salt Eaters*, and Toni Morrison's *Beloved*, which certainly draw on the literary

modes of realism and naturalism, but which also energetically explore the
spiritual life. (3)

Dalke draws an insightful connection between Rebecca Jackson's nineteenth-century journal (1830–1864, posthumously published in 1981 under
the title *Gifts of Power*) and writings by contemporary black women. She
acknowledges that few modern authors have read Jackson's work, but she
echoes Toni Morrison who has argued that, "the absence of self-conscious-
ness hardly negates the existence of a tradition" (11). She thus argues that
"Jackson's belief in an expanded universe, her reliance on the authority of
experience, and her self-conscious record of her history of self-ownership, -
empowerment, and –exploration all suggest that she, and other women writing in this genre, offers a rich legacy for the writing of at least four twentieth-
century writers: Hurston, Walker, Bambara, and Morrison" (11). Dalke's
supposition and her subsequent analysis significantly illustrate key thematic
preoccupations that can be traced from Jackson to her twentieth-century
successors. In this study, I begin with Dalke's supposition, that there is a
traceable and significant African American women's literary tradition—one
that draws on specific cultural sensibilities of blacks in America. I expand on
this supposition looking at how specific metaphysical sensibilities in black
women's fiction represent a tradition of African rooted spirituality among
African descendants in the United States. In particular, I examine the literary
evolution of African American women writers negotiating an inherited
African worldview in a society that has historically devalued ideas that
Africans held most deeply.

III. FOUR AFRICAN SPIRITUAL PRINCIPLES AT WORK

The importance of memory and the act of remembering, in both continental
African and diasporic African societies, has been conveyed in numerous
recent historical and anthropological studies as well as countless fictional
works by African and African-descent authors. From centuries-old African
rituals that invoke ancestral spirits to African American religious testimonies, black people have maintained cultural practices that call on the community to remember. A cultural and communal act, remembering preserves
metaphysical order. Among African people specific funereal and ancestor
rituals are performed to recognize the presence of those departed spirits that
continue to influence the conditions of those who still live in the union of
mind and body. These rituals underscore the connection between memory
and well-being: the stable relationship between worldly and other-worldly
beings depends on a reciprocity of acts between them. It is the otherworldly
beings, God, ancestors, divinities, and spirits who must be worshiped and
venerated to ensure the fortunes of those in the corporeal world. As the most

immediate entities connected to the interests of those living, the ancestors must be awarded due attention because they "bless, protect, warn, and punish their living relatives depending upon how much their relatives neglect or remember them" (Ray 103). This act of remembering the ancestors must continue "so long as someone is alive who once knew the departed personally and by name . . . while the departed is remembered by name, he is not really dead: he is . . . the living-dead" (Mbiti 32). The living-dead exemplify a level of existence that spans both the world and the other world. Higher otherworldly beings, gods and divinities, must also be remembered through rituals, for they too can change the fortunes of humans according to how well they have been remembered. Among continental Africans, rituals offer a connection to the spirits who are called up through the act of remembering; and like their diasporan counterparts, African descendants in the United States sustained this cultural worldview. They were able to do so in part because they renewed these views and practices in the New World, and also because "the ongoing influx of fresh arrivals from Africa to North America reinforced indigenous African religions and philosophical outlook (claims of ultimate truth, knowledge, and meaning) from 1619 to 1807" (Hopkins 115). While early African Americans may not have openly acknowledged remembering as an African carryover, blacks have nevertheless integrated remembering into much of black culture. In folktales, in parables, in songs, in dance, and in sermon, the act of remembering is integral, and through this act the spiritual and historical connectedness of the group is confirmed.

Remembering is most meaningful and most powerful when it is a group experience. In contrast to idolization of the individual that is central in western societies, traditional African societies have maintained the primacy of the community. That is not to say that the value of the individual is minimized, but rather that the spirit of the individual is sanctioned through his or her place in the community. John Mbiti explains this relationship of interdependence in African culture:

> Only in terms of other people does the individual become conscious of his own being, his own duties, his privileges and responsibilities towards himself and other people. When he suffers, he does not suffer alone but with the corporate group; when he rejoices, he rejoices not alone but with his kinsmen, his neighbours and his relatives whether dead or living. . . . The individual can only say: "I am, because we are; and since we are, therefore I am." (141)

Belief in the primacy of community would be maintained among African descendants in America; however, just as continental African communities have been threatened by an invasive European worldview, blacks in America have battled to maintain a culture consistent with their traditions and beliefs. While their belief in a community-based existence has contributed to their survival in America, "this community or collective consciousness has, since slavery, lived in constant tension with the impulse toward individualism that the dominating culture values, rewards, and encourages Americans to develop" (Williams 137). Many blacks have bought into America's dominant rhetoric of individualism, especially as a philosophy of economic prosperity; however, their belief in community has continued to be expressed in their spirituality. Blacks may invoke America's discourse of individuality in the marketplace, but in the church, in matters of the spirit, black cosmology is still grounded in the premise that "the spirit moves individuals in particular ways, but never alone. The individual cannot manifest the spirit without the assistance of the community" (Murphy 173–174). Whether raising the spirit/ holy ghost on Sunday mornings, guiding initiates through conversion, celebrating marital unions, waiting with those who are transitioning into the spirit world, or celebrating group bonds in family reunions, blacks have maintained the significance of community in life and death events.

Through memory and community African Americans shaped themselves into a distinct people in America. Maintaining community rituals and practices, they have been able to preserve significant African-rooted ontological beliefs. For generations Africans designed their communal and individual lives in response to their understanding of the natural world. African belief that God is manifested in nature and that life consists of an interdependent relationship between humans and spiritual beings survived the Middle Passage. In traditional African thought there is "a mystical power in the universe. This power is ultimately from God, but in practice it is inherent in, or comes from or through physical objects and spiritual beings. That means that the universe is not static or 'dead': it is a dynamic, 'living' and powerful universe" (Mbiti 264). The earth, the planets, the moon, the heavens are integral living parts of God's world and, are not unrelated to the fortunes of humankind. In fact, the physical world is a union of the physical and the spiritual; therefore, in traditional African cosmology "the weather and natural phenomena are generally associated with divinities or personified as such. Major objects of nature, like the sun, mountains, seas, lakes, rivers and boulders, are also attributed to have or to be spiritual beings or divinities" (Mbiti 98).

The similar reverence of water among traditional Africans and African Americans has been noted in numerous works. In *Myth of the Negro Past*, Melville Herskovits notes this commonality: he reports that in "the religious patterns of West Africa . . . [among] the river cults . . . the river spirits are among the most powerful of those inhabiting the supernatural world, and . . . priests of this cult are among the most powerful of tribal priestly groups" (232). While there are no identical river cults among blacks in the United States, there are clear signs of a derivative reverence for water that has been translated into African American Christianity. Herskovits offers an example of the transformation of traditional African water worship to black Baptist religion. He explains,

> Negro Baptists do not run into the water under possession by African gods. Their water rituals are those of baptism. Yet it is significant that, as the novitiate whose relation has brought him to the running stream or the tidal cove is immersed, the spirit descends on him at that moment if at all, and a possession hysteria develops that in its outward appearance at least, is almost, indistinguishable from the possession brought on by the African water deities. (234)

Similarly, the practice among Africans of the Congo and blacks in America to construct graves in close proximity to trees illustrates African nature carryovers in America (Thompson 172). Among many African people, animals are thought to have spirits and some, like the snake and the dog, are assumed to have mystical powers that can influence human life. The carryover of West African concepts of the mystical powers of animals is especially evident in Voodoo and African American folktales. Like inorganic natural entities, animals can cause harm or good.

The spirits must be appeased if they are to watch over the living; the living must remember the dead in ritual and in living. The necessary closeness of the living and the departed highlights an African cosmology of life and death that is anathema in western Christian orthodoxy. Africans draw no clear line between the living and the dead: thus, life and death, beginning and ending, are not separable as they are in western cosmology. Life and death are interdependent states of existence in traditional African thought, and this relationship is evident in the African's view of the circularity of nature. Plants, animals, the earth and the universe at large work in unison to provide a world that is unending. Life, then, is not the linear experience that is imagined in western philosophy. Just as plants feed animals that eventually die and transform into nourishment that spawns new life, the living are transformed through death and return as spirits that can return in many forms to influence and intervene in the physical world: "Belief in afterlife was integral to traditional African religion. . . . Death was a journey into the spirit world, not a break with life or earthly beings. The idea of perpetuity of life through time, space, and circumstance was common to African religious culture" (Washington 81). Time is circular in the African mind and it is born out of action. Moreover, there is little concern for what is known in western cosmology as future, for "[t]ime has to be experienced in order to make sense or become real. A person experiences time partly in his own individual life, and partly through the society which goes back many generations before his own birth" (Mbiti 23). From religious ceremonial dances that call for clockwise circular movement (Coleman 46), to villages with houses arranged in a circle and houses that are themselves circular (Mbiti 140), the circularity of life is reaffirmed in African culture through rituals and everyday communal acts. The case is similar among African-descent people in America: the ring shout, for example, illustrates the carryover of African ceremonial dance that calls for circular movement that culminates in spirit possession.

African Americans would name their religion Christianity, but they did not simply empty themselves of the religious legacy of their ancestors. Black Christianity has been defined in part by a conflicting philosophical and experiential coexistence between western interpretations of Christianity and African belief systems. However, Christianity did not appear wholly foreign to Africans: much of African spiritual beliefs and practices could be easily reconfigured into a Christian cosmos. For example, African notions of death and time have been shaped into a black Christian rhetoric that serves the cultural worldview of blacks and allows them to proclaim themselves Christians. Christianity's promise of resurrection, of God's deliverance after death, is not so removed from traditional African beliefs in the transformation of the soul after death. Christianity's ideology of resurrection can be interpreted as a theology of circularity, echoing African views of death as a transition to another state of being.

Just as Christian converts throughout history, blacks have taken liberty with incidental theological details to shape Christianity into a religion more representative of their culture. One such incidental detail was the matter of African concepts of physical and supernatural beings. African belief in worldly and supernatural beings was maintained in the worldview of the slaves and passed on to subsequent generations. This is evident again in the many folktales, narratives and cultural practices of African Americans. While black Christian converts were required to denounce their cultural notions of the supernatural for the God/Jesus/Holy Ghost trilogy, blacks maintained a belief in the supernatural and the interrelatedness of humans and otherworldly entities. Therefore, even when blacks converted to Christianity, the church held a different place in black society than it did among whites. Because of the church's central place in black culture, "sacred-secular distinctions are complicated" (Moss 18). Blacks in America maintained the African belief that spiritual and material beings are connected entities. In traditional African religious ontology God is held as the supreme power, but unlike Christian ontology which has God working primarily alone (with the exception of Jesus who was offered as salvation for humankind), Africans maintain a cosmological view that has God, spirits, ancestors and humans in an ongoing relationship. God, spirits, and ancestors can be found in our world, and they must be appeased if humans are to find prosperity.

Human relationship with the supernatural is not simply to prepare for life after death as it is in Christian thought; rather, human relationship with the supernatural is to make the human experience in the material world fulfilling. The ancestors are then remembered so that they will watch over the living; the spirits are appeased so that they will not cause harm, and God is worshipped and acknowledged as the source of all that is. In African religion "an ontological balance must be maintained between God and man, the spirits and man, the departed and the living. When this balance is upset, people experience misfortunes and sufferings, or fear that these will strike them" (Mbiti 76). The renewal or affirmation of human connectedness to the supernatural occurs ritually through ceremonies, but spiritual interveners are called upon when people experience troubles or circumstances that require contact with the spirit world.

Spiritual interveners may be priests or priestesses, seers, prophets, oracles, mediums or diviners, and they can be men or women. These religious interveners have specific responsibilities and roles: the duties of the priests include "making sacrifices, offerings and prayers, conducting both public and private rites and ceremonies, giving advice, performing judicial or political functions, caring for the temples and shrines where these exist, and above all fulfilling their office as religious intermediaries between men and God" (Mbiti 88). The seers and prophets primarily "act as ritual elders, to give advice on religious matters . . . receive messages from divinities and spirits through possession and dreams and . . . pass on the information to their communities. Oracles are generally the mouthpieces of divinities and spirits, and tend to be connected with divination" (88). Mediums and diviners make connections between the living-dead and humans. Mediums, who are usually women, make these connections through spirit possession (Mbiti 224). In traditional African societies women who serve as spiritual leaders often find their gift an eventual source of independence: this is exemplified among the Olokun of West Africa whose priestesses tend to leave their husbands' houses and establish their own living quarters when their income allows (Ben-Amos 130).

African concepts of the relationship between humankind and the supernatural have not been sustained among diasporic Africans without revision. This has been the case, in part out of necessity, as many blacks in the Americas were required to conceal cultural beliefs that were African in origin, but it has also been the result of blacks adjusting their worldview to address their experience. African Americans were unable to maintain a fully conscious African cultural worldview, and thus much that they retained was transformed and oftentimes abridged. The detailed distinction of supernatural entities that we find in traditional African culture is not so consciously maintained among African Americans. Distinctions between the living-dead, the divinities, and the spirits have not been directly carried over into African American cosmology. However, the general supposition that there are human and spirit entities and that communications are and must be maintained between these entities has survived the Middle Passage and Christian conversion. The transformation of this traditional African religious belief in African American culture represents an important cultural dynamic, for in a similar manner much of traditional African culture was transferred and transformed in America. Recent scholarship has shown that the centuries-old contention that Africans arrived in America with little if any meaningful culture, and that upon arrival in America they had been effectively disconnected from their past, misrepresents the central influence of African culture in African American life. We now understand that Africans did not give over their worldview to a European one, even with the cultural terrorism that they endured in the slave system. Historian Michael A. Gomez poignantly makes this point:

> To appreciate the fact that Africans continued to practice their own beliefs in large numbers, one has only to afford them the same consideration and assumptions regularly afforded Europeans. That is, it should be expected that people from any given background would have strong propensities to preserve as much of their cultural patrimony as possible. (249)

Africans came to America with ways of understanding and experiencing the world. African American religious history does not begin with Christianity: it originates in the traditional African worldview that the slaves merged with European Christianity and transformed into AfroChristianity. AfroChristianity represents, then, "the voluntary acceptance of what the slavemaster thought was his Christianity by his human property" (Hopkins 109). This acceptance was possible "both because a fundamental structure in West African religions was somewhat compatible to a (reinterpreted) slave Christianity and because the malleability of African American chattels' creativity wove together select portions of mainstream biblical teachings with remnants of the West African worldview" (Hopkins 109).

Perhaps in the purely spiritual scheme of things the determination of African or European origins in black spirituality is inconsequential; however, because we find ourselves in a world of white privilege that claims all cultural worth to be of European/Anglo origin, resulting in an epistemological erasure of others, the matter of origins is, in fact, significant. It is imperative that we record the historical influence of "others" both to their own culture and to the dominant culture. Understanding and acknowledging the importance of African thought in African American culture and American culture at large brings us to a more accurate picture of America's history—cultural and religious. That early blacks in the United States contributed to worship practices and ideologies of the spirit that have survived among white as well as black religious groups can be both inspiring and unsettling information: [7] inspirational because it suggests that spiritual enlightenment can survive corporeal victimization. On the other hand, this historical fact can be unsettling because it highlights America's historical racial pathology, often manifested in the conviction that goodness must be painted as white before it can be confirmed and marketed as good. Whether we ever acknowledge the contributions of Africans to American society at large is yet to unfold; however, many contemporary fictional works explore connections between traditional African thought and African American culture.

Scholars have demonstrated that studies of African and African American cosmologies should consider that these worldviews are born out of a vision of the world as a religious place, a vision that sees all of life as religious. Just as their African ancestors did not separate the secular and spiritual, African Americans developed a cosmology that saw all life entities as interconnected. In her work, "Secret and Sacred: Contextualizing the Artifacts of African American Magic and Religion," Laurie A. Wilkie explains that more accurate accounts of African American religious history will follow studies that recognize "the importance of magical and religious systems in African American communities," and studies that "interpret these data in a diachronic manner" (81). Wilkie maintains that the place of the spiritual in African American culture must be considered to more fully understand the lives of African Americans (81). To consider black spirituality diachronically requires a look back to the antecedents of what has evolved into contemporary black religion(s) and an inquiry into the process(es) that shaped contemporary black spirituality. Wilkie proposes the use of a model employed by George Brandon in his 1993 study, *Santeria from Africa to the New World*. Brandon identifies a three-stage process that can be employed to trace the development of Santeria: "a formative, a persisting, and a transformative period" (3). While Brandon's focus is the historical and sociological dynamic that gives birth to Santeria in the New World, his model offers a critical method that can help us better understand the evolution of the spiritual in black women's fiction. Brandon defines the first stage of his macro level three-stage process as follows:

> In terms of religion, a formative period is when a religion is beginning to assume a different physiognomy than previously, through exposure to other religions, internal developments, economic or political catastrophe, and so forth. What marks this period is exposure, innovation, recoil, or seeking . . . these developments eventuate in a period of conflict over a small number of alternatives, followed by a taking of positions and the working out of these alternatives until one or more of them becomes a major direction of change" (3). This stage is followed by the period of persistence which occurs when "[t]hose alternatives that survive assume a form which is recognizable and whose recognizability can be successfully and consistently reproduced. (3)

Finally, the transformative stage is "simply another version of the formative stage, with the form that exists during the persisting stage as its point of departure" (3).

Drawing on Brandon's three-stage model, including his supposition that the model represents a cyclical process, this work examines the evolution of African spirituality in black women's fiction to the Harlem Renaissance. Again, as iterated early in this chapter, manifestations of African spirituality—particularly the physical and experiential—are readily found in African American culture and have to significant degree been the subject of literary scholarship. The focus of this study, however, is the evolution of an African spiritual cosmology in black women's fiction. Black women's fiction was born out of black women's autobiography; therefore, a study of black women's fiction must consider how it was informed by this genre. This study begins, however, with America's pioneer black poetess, Phillis Wheatley, whose work represents the springboard for African American women writers negotiating Africanity and western ideology. Chapter 2, then, focuses on Wheatley's poetry in the context of the religious stage that Brandon calls the formative period. This formative period is marked by the encounter between African-rooted spirituality and western Christianity. Wheatley is a particularly appropriate example, given her personal history. Sold into slavery around age six or seven, Wheatley was young, but not so young that she would retain no memories of her native home in West Africa. [8] Though there are only few occasions in her writings that directly refer to her African homeland, Wheatley's metaphysical worldview can be connected to West African cosmology. Chapter 3 turns to Wheatley's literary successors, whose compositions are in prose but also represent the formative period. Even though these early black authors call on the trappings of the conversion narrative, they are not limited to this source. Carla Peterson argues that, in fact, early black women writers and orators "appropriated many different cultural discourses ranging from a reliance on Africanisms to the adoption of standard literary conventions in order to become producers rather than mere consumers of literary expression" (22). Examining specifically the writings of early nineteenth-century itinerant preachers Jarena Lee and Rebecca Cox Jackson and activist Maria Stewart, we witness the tension between Africanity and Christianity in early narrative productions by black women. Though they identify Christianity as their religion, they propel themselves into male dominated public space through the assumption of a traditional African belief in the power and primacy of the spiritual voice and the workings of the spirit without regard to gender.

The period of persistence follows the formative period and this application of Brandon's model is marked by slave and spiritual narratives and the birth of African American full length fiction in the mid-1800s. Chapter 4 considers the transition from slave and spiritual narratives to the birth of the novel in African American women's literary tradition. While this era marks a solidification of black Christianity with writers compelled to demonstrate their adaptation to western Christianity, their works harbor signs of remaining African sensibilities. As Brandon notes in his discussion of Santeria, religious transitions are fluid. Hence, while these narratives are scripted in Anglo Christian rhetoric, African sensibilities are retained and translated into African-American Christianity. Four extant works of the mid-1800s illustrate the transition from autobiography to fiction, a shift that perhaps provided the narrators greater literary license. These "novelized autobiographies"—a term coined by Carla Peterson to describe the hybrid nature of early African American fictional works—allowed writers to extend their imagination beyond the confines of the predictable structure of the slave or spiritual narrative. To Peterson's classification of Harriet E. Wilson's *Our Nig* (1859) and Harriet Jacobs's *Incidents in the Life of a Slavegirl* (1861) as novelized autobiographies, I add the recently recovered and published (2002) work of Hannah Craft, *Bondswoman's Narrative* (circa 1850s), and Elizabeth Keckley's 1868 memoir, *Behind the Scenes.*

Chapter 5 covers the second half of the period of persistence: the post-Reconstruction era to the Harlem Renaissance. During this period works such as Harper's *Trial and Triumph* (1888) and *Iola Leroy* (1892), and Pauline Hopkins's *Contending Forces* (1900) exemplify the solidification of a Christianized African cosmology that is found in fiction as well as nonfiction. Only in the crevices can one find ambivalence or rejection of the deep-rooted AfroChristianity of late 1900 and early twentieth-century black society. Such a deviation is revealed in the writings of Alice Dunbar-Nelson, specifically her 1895 collection, *Violets and Other Tales* and *The Goodness of St. Rocque and Other Stories* (1899). Dunbar-Nelson's writings exemplify again the fluidity of religious transformation; her works demonstrate the existence of an underlying resistance to public accord. While Christianity was the dominant religious allegiance of African Americans, Dunbar-Nelson's work shows that it did not escape rejection and scrutiny. In her writings, Dunbar-Nelson conveys a skepticism of Christianity that is unconventional for black women authors at the close of the nineteenth century.

At the dawn of the twentieth century, blacks maintained a general acceptance of Christianity as their religious foundation. However, the close of World War I and the birth of the Harlem Renaissance marked the transformative period in the treatment of spirituality by black women authors. Chapter 6 examines the beginnings of this shift as evinced in Jesse Fauset's novels. Many scholars have read Fauset's novels as simply sentimental musings on black middle class desire. While trappings of sentimental fiction are apparent in Fauset's writings, she nevertheless interrogates black middle class life, especially its Christian element. Her novels fall short of outright condemnation; however, they suggest that beneath the black Christian exterior lurks an indifference to Christianity and the church. In Fauset's novels, Christianity is an institution acknowledged by the community, but its influence in the lives of blacks is negligible.

Chapter 7 follows with the ground-breaking novels of Nella Larsen and Zora Neale Hurston. These novels exemplify a transformative period, a period representing a heightened and openly expressed tension between African and Western Christianity. The Harlem Renaissance marks a noted beginning of transformation in black women authors' imaginations of the spiritual. Nella Larsen's novel, *Quicksand*, is of particular interest because Larsen's commentary on Christianity is the outgrowth of that begun in the novels of Fauset. Going beyond Fauset's portrait of the church as a superficial influence in black life, Larsen paints the church as an accomplice in the historical victimization of blacks. However, like Fauset, Larsen does not imagine an alternative to the church, especially one that might originate in an African spiritual legacy. In the writings of their contemporary, Zora Neale Hurston, this will not be the case. In particular, *Jonah's Gourd Vine* and *Their Eyes Were Watching God* highlight the priority blacks give to the spiritual practices and perceptions of their African ancestors. While *Jonah's Gourd Vine* does not offer a triumphant protagonist like Janie Crawford, the novel nevertheless affirms the place of African spirituality in its fictional black community. In *Their Eyes Were Watching God* Hurston suggests that Christianity ill serves blacks, and the novel returns to an African rooted understanding of the world that brings Janie home and leaves her at peace. Hurston's novels pave the way for a discourse that privileges an African worldview, with an unquestionable dismissal or invalidation of Christianity. *Their Eyes Were Watching God* represents the birth of a tradition in which black women writers explore tensions between Africanity and Christianity, and unlike their fictional foremothers, offer a resounding affirmation of the African spirit as central to the African New World self.

NOTES

1. In *White on Black: Images of Africa and Blacks in Western Popular Culture*, Jan Nederveen Pieterse (New Haven, CT: Yale University Press, 1992) summarizes the history of the Curse of Ham myth: "In the Church of Augustine the curse of Ham or Canaan was regarded as an explanation of slavery, but not of blacks, simply because slavery at the time was 'colourless.' The association of the curse of Canaan with blackness arose only much later in medieval Talmudic texts. In the sixteenth century it became a Christian theme and by the seventeenth it was widely accepted as an explanation of black skin colour. From here it was but a small step to the interpretation of the curse of Canaan as an explanation of and justification for the slavery of black Africans" (44).

2. See Gayraud S. Wilmore's *Black Religion and Black Radicalism* (pp. 167–219) for more thorough discussion of the rebirth of black Christian activism in the 1960s.

3. In his 2002 biography, *Benjamin Banneker: Surveyor, Astronomer, Publisher, Patriot*, Charles Cerami traces the African influence in Banneker's scientific theories and observations.

4. For further explanation and example of call and response see *Call and Response: The Riverside Anthology of the African American Literary Tradition* and Dolan Hubbard's "Call and Response: Intertextuality in the Poetry of Langston Hughes and Margaret Walker," in *Langston Hughes Review* 7 (Spring 1988): 22–30.

5. For more on "white Africanisms," see John Edward Philips's essay "The African Heritage of White America," in Joseph E. Holloway's *Africanisms in American Culture* (Bloomington: Indiana University Press).

6. In Cheryl Towsend Gilkes's *If It Wasn't for the Women*, she explains that prayer warriors are "church mothers who have a mighty gift of prayer," and that "men with such gifts are usually deacons" (134).

7. Works such as Noel Ignatiev's "The Revolution as an African-American Exuberance" (in *Eighteenth-Century Studies* 27.4), David R. Roediger's *Wages of Whiteness* (Verso Press), and John Edward Philips's "The African Heritage of White America" (in Joseph E. Holloway's *Africanisms in American Culture*) provide more thorough discussion of African influences in American culture.

8. See John C. Shields's biographical sketch of Wheatley in the *Oxford Companion to African American Literature*. Shields makes the case that while Wheatley may not have articulated a memory of her home as her contemporary, Venture Smith in his narrative, her correspondences to Obour Tanner, and some of her verses indicate that she had not forgotten her native land.

WORKS CITED

Ben-Amos, Paula Girshick. "The Promise of Greatness: Women and Power in an Edo Spirit Possession Cult." *Religion in Africa: Experience and Expression.* Eds. Thomas D. Blakely, Walter E. A. vanBeek, Dennis L. Thomson. Portsmouth, NH: Heinemann, 1994. 118–134.

Brandon, George. *Santeria from Africa to the New World: The Dead Sell Memories.* Bloomington: Indiana University Press, 1993.

Coleman, Will. *Tribal Talk: Black Theology, Hermeneutics, and African/American Ways of "Telling the Story."* University Park: Penn State University Press, 2000.

Collier-Thomas, Bettye. *Daughters of Thunder: Black Women Preachers and Their Sermons, 1850–1979.* San Francisco: Jossey-Bass Publishers, 1998.

Dalke, Anne. "Spirit Matters: Re-Possessing the African-American Women's Literary Tradition." *Legacy. A Journal of American Women Writers* 12.1 (1995). 1 16.

Gomez, Michael A. *Exchanging Our Country Marks: The Transformation of African Identities in the Colonial and Antebellum South.* Chapel Hill: UNC Press, 1998.

Herskovits, Melville J. *The Myth of the Negro Past.* 2nd ed. Boston: Beacon Press, 1990.

Holloway, Joseph E., ed. *Africanisms in American Culture.* Bloomington: Indiana University Press, 1990.

Hopkins, Dwight N. *Down, Up, and Over: Slave Religion and Black Theology.* Minneapolis: Fortress Press, 2000.

Hurston, Zora Neale. *The Sanctified Church.* Foreword by Toni Cade Bambara. New York: Marlowe & Co., 1981.

———. *Writings by Zora Neale Hurston from the Federal Writers' Project.* Ed. Pamela Bordelon . NY: WW Norton & Co., 1999. 94–111.

Jefferson, Thomas. *Notes on the State of Virginia.* in *The Heath Anthology of American Literature.* Vol. I. 2nd ed. Ed. Paul Lauter et al. Lexington, MA: D. C. Heath and Company, 1994. 894–909.

Johnson, Clifton H., ed. *God Struck Me Dead: Religious Conversion Experiences and Autobiographies of Ex-Slaves.* Philadelphia: Pilgrim Press, 1969.

Levine, Lawrence W. *Black Culture and Black Consciousness: Afro-American Folk Thought from Slavery to Freedom.* New York: Oxford University Press, 1977.

Martin, Clarice J. "Biblical Theodity and Black Woman's Spiritual Autobiography." Ed. E. M. Townes. *A Troubling in My Soul: Womanist Perspectives on Evil and Suffering.* Maryland, NY: Orbis Books, 1993. 13–35.

Mbiti, John S. *African Religions and Philosophy.* 2nd ed. Rev and enlarged. Portsmouth: Heinemann Press, 1990.

Moss, Beverly J. *A Community Text Arises: A Literate Text and A Literary Tradition in African-American Churches.* Cresskill, NJ: Hampton Press, Inc., 2003.

Murphy, Joseph M. *Working the Spirit: Ceremonies of the African Diaspora*. Boston: Beacon Press, 1994.

Nelson, Dana D. *The Word in Black and White: Reading Race in American Literature 1638–1867*. New York: Oxford University Press, 1993.

Peters, Erskine. "The Poetics of the African-American Spiritual." *Black American Literature Forum* 23.3 (1989): 559–578.

Peterson, Carla. *Doers of the Word: African-American Women Speakers and Writers in the North (1830–1880)*. New Brunswick, NJ: Rutgers University Press, 1998.

Raboteau, Albert J. *The Canaan Land: A Religious History of African Americans*. New York: Oxford University Press, 2001.

———. *A Fire in the Bones: Reflections on African-American Religious History*. Boston: Beacon Press, 1995.

Rahming, Melvin B. "Theorizing Spirit: The Critical Challenge of Elizabeth Nunez's *When Rocks Dance* and *Beyond the Limbo Silence*." *Studies in the Literary Imagination* 37.2 (Fall 2004): 1–19.

Ray, Benjamin C. *African Religions: Symbol, Ritual, and Community*. 2nd ed. Upper Saddle River, NJ: Prentice Hall, 2000.

Ryan, Judylyn S. *Spirituality as Ideology in Black Women's Film and Literature*. Charlottesville: University of Virginia Press, 2005.

Thompson, Robert Farris. "Kongo Influences in African-American Artistic Culture." In *Africanisms in American Culture*. Ed. Joseph E. Holloway. Bloomington: Indiana University Press, 1990. 148–184.

Townsend-Gilkes, Cheryl. *If It Wasn't for the Women*. New York: Orbis Books, 2001.

Walker, David. *Walker's Appeal in Four Articles*. New York: Arno Press, 1969.

Washington, Margaret. "Gullah Attitudes toward Life and Death," in *Africanisms in American Culture*. Ed. Joseph E. Holloway. Bloomington: Indiana University Press, 1990. 69–97.

Wilkie, Laurie A. "Secret and Sacred: Contextualizing the Artifacts of African-American Magic and Religion." *Historical Archaeology* 31. 4 (1997): 81–106.

Williams, Delores S, ed. *Sisters in the Wilderness: The Challenge of Womanist God-Talk*. Maryknoll, NY: Orbis Books, 1993.

Wilmore, Gayraud S. *Black Religion and Black Radicalism*. Maryknoll, NY: Orbis Books, 1986.

Chapter Two

Wheatley as Beginning

Note: This chapter's section on the poetry of Phillis Wheatley (pp. 27–42) is reproduced with permission from an earlier chapter publication, "Making the Awakening Hers: Phillis Wheatley and the Transposition of African Spirituality to Christian Religiosity," in *Cultural Sites of Critical Insight*. Eds. Angela Cotton and Christa Acampora. NY: SUNY Press, 2007. 47–66.

The Great Awakening of the 1700s has been identified as a watershed event in the history of African American Christianity and civil rights activism. In contrast to the early Puritan cosmology maintaining that only a small (and presumably white) elect would be saved in the final days, the Awakening promised salvation to all and opened the floodgates to new groups of converts. Blacks, who had for the most part, been ignored, excluded, or given incidental consideration in Puritan religious reflection, could now appropriate the language of Christian salvation to proclaim their humanity and their rights in the eye of the divine authority. The Bible, Christianity's guiding text, became the written authority for African American calls for equality and justice as well as a guiding spiritual force for a disenfranchised black population. Exemplified in these early writings is an African American typology of scripture much like that of the Puritans a century earlier. They mark the beginning of a tradition in African American arts and letters and political activism. Interpreting their struggles in America as the reenactment of key biblical stories of struggle and suffering, these black writers gave history and religious legitimacy to their cause. Phillis Wheatley's hallmark 1773 published collection of poems exemplifies the birth of a tradition of black writers who would transform an Anglo Christian discourse of black denigration into a language of self-affirmation.

Wheatley's often criticized poem "On Being Brought from Africa to America" illustrates this literary manipulation. Wheatley's use of understatement and her seeming acquiescence in this poem leads many readers to dismiss it as self-denigrating. Her use of the word "brought" to represent the horrific transportation of Africans to the Americas can be read as an appeasement to her white audience. However, in its entirety, the poem asserts the place of Africans in biblical history as well as affirms their place at the gates of redemption. With Wheatley's call to her Christian/white audience to remember that "Negroes, black as Cain, / May be refin'd, and join th' angelic train" (7–8), she appropriates the pro-slavery myth that links blacks to the cursed Cain of the Genesis story. Wheatley demonstrates her own interpretive astuteness, however, as she proclaims the salvation of blacks on the basis of the very story that whites had used to justify black enslavement. Wheatley knows that in its entirety the story of Cain is a redemptive one, for he is ultimately restored to the good graces of God. She therefore maintains that blacks, like their presumed ancestor Cain, will be similarly redeemed.

Wheatley's discursive appropriation of scripture occurs early in the history of AfroChristianity but is not a singular effort. Jupiter Hammon, slave and poet, also emphasized that God's universal redemption was extended to Africans as well as whites. In his poem "An Evening Thought: Salvation by Christ with Penetential Cries," Hammon reminds readers that God alone is the source of salvation and that he extends his offering to all people: "Salvation comes by Jesus Christ alone, / The only Son of God; / Redemption now to every one, / That love his holy Word" (1–4). Hammon and Wheatley, and countless black interpreters of biblical scripture who would follow them, embraced the message of spiritual inclusiveness born out of America's Great Awakening. Trusting their own abilities to interpret scripture and history, they adopted biblical stories and doctrine to tell the story of black experience in America.

While scholars have recognized The Great Awakening as a pivotal event in the history of African American Christianity, too often African metaphysical influences in black Christianity have been overlooked. For more than a century before The Great Awakening, particularly during the first century of African enslavement in Colonial America, when slaveholders did not generally concern themselves with the religion of their slaves, slave communities were able to transform much of their traditional culture into their new world. Hence, the slave work songs, field hollers, folktales and cultural rituals of Africans in America were an outgrowth of their African heritage. This African legacy first informed the oral tradition of the slaves and, as Adisa A. Alkeluban explains, served as the foundation for African American rhetoric. [1] It is important to recognize, then, that the Afro-Christian enthusiasm of The Great Awakening was not born out of an African spiritual void, but rather was the result of a particular social dynamic. The meeting of traditional African spirituality and the Awakening's revivalism exemplifies the formative period defined in George Brandon's model (discussed in chapter 1 of this work). Again, in Brandon's words, this period is marked "when a religion is beginning to assume a different physiognomy than previously, through exposure to other religions, internal developments, economic or political catastrophe, and so forth" (3). By the time of the Awakening, this is clearly the cultural dynamic at work in African American society. Unable to live uncompromisingly under the cosmology that defined traditional African life, Africans in America faced the task of reshaping their worldview.

Phillis Wheatley's 1773 collection of poems, notably religious/spiritual in nature, marks a comprehensive reflection on the formative experience that called on blacks to reimagine their spiritual worldview. And as Katherine Clay Bassard suggests, "early black women's writing community begins with Phillis Wheatley's seven-year correspondence with Obour Tanner, her confidant and a fellow enslaved African woman" (515). Wheatley's ongoing correspondence with Tanner, who lived in the neighboring state of Rhode Island, challenges the notion espoused by some scholars that she was isolated and removed from the experiences and conditions of fellow slaves. Moreover, her friendship with Tanner suggests that the community of black women writers was born in early America with the likes of Wheatley and Tanner and perhaps black women whose correspondences are yet uncovered, or worse, permanently lost. Their correspondences suggest that real and fictionalized black women, finding greater salvation in each other than in the church, can be found in the writings and relationships of early black women writers. While Trudier Harris insightfully points to the primacy of religion and community in contemporary black women's writings, we must consider the legacy that informed this contemporary convention.[2] Black women surviving in a community of women is no cultural accident, but rather a continuation of an African-rooted cosmology that sanctioned community as sacred, and as a result of gender divisions, empowered women to collectively aid and support each other. Wheatley's efforts to maintain a relationship with Tanner through letter writing, the only avenue available to them, hints at her desire to remain connected to an African community. And her greeting to Tanner as friend and sister in the seven extant letters that Wheatley wrote her, underscores the deep alliance between the two despite the miles that separated them. Wheatley's own poem titled "To S.M. a Young African Painter, on Seeing His Works," Jupiter Hammon's 1778 poem, "To Miss Phillis Wheatley," and her now highly anthologized portrait by African American artist Scipio Moorhead (S.M.) attest to the bonds that existed among black New Englanders.[3] These intertextual works also contradict simplistic historical glossing of Wheatley as "not concerned with the problems of blacks or the country" (Franklin 94).

In her life and her poetry Phillis Wheatley reveals the spiritual struggle of early generations of African Americans to shape a cosmos in a foreign land. She embodies the formative experience of blacks reimagining the world through the convergence of Anglo Christianity and African spirituality. While it is tempting to read her poetry as a surrender of Africanity to a dominant, white supremacist discourse, Wheatley's poetry is the narrative of a young African renegotiating the self in a white cosmos. A young, native-born African encountering a foreign religion/cosmology as the result of personal and cultural trauma, Wheatley symbolizes the early struggles of blacks to reconcile an African world view to an antagonistic western cosmology. To salvage a self in this environment, Wheatley, like Africans at large in America, struggled to validate and redefine herself through a language and worldview that deemed blackness synonymous with abjection. Wheatley's success was the result of her intellectual shrewdness and also a conviction of self-worth that survived the Middle Passage. Like other Africans forced into bondage, Wheatley did not completely lose connections to her African roots. This connectivity, albeit held by the thinnest of threads, is evident in her poetry, which represents one clearly aware of one's African self. The affirmation of Africanity that emerges in her writing suggests that though she was young and deprived of an immediate community of fellow blacks, Phillis Wheatley employed language to affirm her place as African and human.

In a number of her poems, Wheatley asserts her African identity, reminding her white audience that she defies their presumptions about blackness and humanity. She is African and literate, as she reminds readers in the poem "To Maecenas." This poem, which serves as the prologue and invocation for the 1773 collection also ties Wheatley and Africanity to both history and intellectualism. With her reflection on the ancient poet Terence, a Roman slave born in Africa, Wheatley hints at her own poetic genius. Like Terence, Wheatley is a native African taken and made a slave in a distant land, and like Terence, Wheatley masters the language and art of her non-African captors. Her recurring reference to herself in her poetry as the "Afric muse," hints at a need to reassure herself that she can be both black and literate/intelligent. This ongoing struggle for self-justification is layered with what is perhaps a more subconscious struggle to reorient her spiritual cosmos. We cannot say with certainty that Wheatley's assertions of African selfhood represent a conscious or deliberate struggle against personal and national erasure; however, her writings do suggest that at the very least in her subconscious mind, Wheatley attempted to reconstruct herself in a way that would validate her/Africans in the larger/western cosmos. More concretely, we find in Wheatley's poetry and correspondences a connection to an African worldview that survived her Christian conversion. While many readers presume that the infusion of Greek and Roman classics in her poetry is the result of the Neoclassical influence in early American writing, Wheatley's fascination with the classics was also informed by meaningful parallels between the mythological cosmos of these ancients and her native Africans.[4] Consequently, converging classical Greek and Roman images with her poetic interpretations of Christianity may have served as a means to white wash, but salvage, her African memories. For example, Greek and Roman representation of spiritual entities as gods of natural forces was consistent with traditional African spiritual concepts of nature forces. Hence, Wheatley's poetic expressions of awe at the power of the sun, the moon, and other natural forces may have been reflections on African spiritual concepts of nature. Similarly, Wheatley's constant call to the muses for artistic inspiration may also have been triggered by memories of her native culture.

While John Shields argues convincingly that "her [Wheatley's] grasp of the possibility of using the sublime as a principle of freedom exceeds that of her predecessors and anticipates Kant, English romanticism, and American transcendentalism" (257), an exploration of the origins of Wheatley's notions of the aesthetic must also consider the likely influence of traditional African beliefs and practices. It is plausible that Wheatley's "use of her imagination to create 'new worlds'" (Shields 256), points to rituals of African spiritual possession that she likely witnessed as a young child in Africa. Spiritual possession is an act through which the subject, as well as the community, enters a different or new world, one that can provide participants a new way of seeing themselves and the world around them. Poetry was clearly the medium through which Wheatley was lifted to a new world, a world in which she could claim her humanity and reflect on her African past. Wheatley's writings demonstrate a negotiation of key African cosmological ideas and the dominating rhetoric of Colonial American Christianity. In particular, Wheatley struggles to define the place of memory in art and life; she attempts to seat African notions of nature and being into Christian discourse; and she constructs a self that is centered not in her individuality, but by her connection with community.

Wheatley's most evident conscious musing on memory is found in the poem "On Recollection." Here, she defines memory as both a source of creative inspiration for the poet and a spiritual beacon that guides humanity. Speaking of memory in the language of classical Greek, Wheatley hails it as "Mneme, immortal pow'r," and in her request for mneme's artistic inspiration, Wheatley highlights the African concept of reciprocity between spirit and human. "Assist my strains, while I thy glories sing" (4), she pleads. This reciprocity of grace echoes the African dynamic of spirit and human interdependency that Joseph M. Murphy describes. Murphy details a relationship in which the spirit bestows blessings onto humans but only as humans celebrate and acknowledge the greatness of the spirit. [5]

"On Recollection" emphasizes the power of memory as it manifests itself in dreams. In traditional African cosmology spirits speak to humans most often through possession and dream visions. Wheatley echoes the latter as she connects the power of spirits and their message transmissions to dream visions or prophesies:

> Mneme in our nocturnal visions pours
> The ample treasure of her secret stores; . . .
> And, in her pomp of images display'd,
> To the high-raptur'd poet gives her aid,
> Through the unbound regions of the mind,
> Diffusing light celestial and refin'd. (9–10, 13–16)

When the lessons of memory are heeded, memory, like traditional African spirits, is a source of human empowerment and good fortune; however, when memory's message is disregarded, misfortune follows. In contrast to the western construct of memory as a human act that simply chronicles past events, Wheatley defines memory as a spirit or energy that resides in humans. Memory guides and comforts when we hear its message:

> Sweeter than music to the ravish'd ear,
> Sweeter than Maro's entertaining strains
> Resounding through the groves, and hills, and
> Plains. (22–24)

On the other hand, Wheatley warns that when we fail to heed memory's guidance, it leaves us desolate:

> But how is Mneme dreaded by the race,
> Who scorn her warnings, and despise her grace?
> By her unveil'd each horrid crime appears,
> Her awful hand a cup of wormwood bears.
> Days, years mispent, O what a hell of woe!
> Hers the worst tortures that our souls can know. (25–30)

The power of memory in human fortune is thus a double-edged sword: memory, like most African spiritual forces, holds the power to both bless and curse. Equally notable is the picture of memory as a conduit between worlds. It is not an image that Wheatley draws overtly, but rather one that is intimated in her reflection on the swiftness of time passing in her own first eighteen years:

> Now eighteen years their destin'd course have Run,
> In fast succession round the central sun.
> How did the follies of that period pass
> Unnotic'd, but behold them writ in brass!
> In Recollection see them fresh return. (31–35)

Although the eighteen years have passed rapidly, they can be called to life again through memory. This notion that memory/recollection can converge the past and the present echoes a central African spiritual view that will survive generations of AfroChristianity and emerge as a conscious presence in the works of twentieth-century black women writers.

While "On Recollection" speaks to memory's grace as well as its terror, the poem "To the Honourable T.H. Esq; on the Death of his Daughter" employs memory for its power of consolation. To this father who has suffered the loss of a child, Wheatley recommends that he give himself over to memory/recollection to arrest the pain. While the poem ends with the often offered elegiac promise of a meeting in the next world, Wheatley first speaks of the consolation found in remembering:

> While deep you mourn beneath the
> Cypress-shade
> The hand of Death, and your dear daughter laid
> In dust, whose absence gives your tears to flow,
> And racks your bosom with incessant woe,
> Let Recollection take a tender part,
> Assuage the raging tortures of your heart,
> Still the wild tempest of tumultuous grief,
> And pour the heav'nly nectar of relief. (1–8)

We can only speculate whether Wheatley's concept of memory as spirit is born out of a conscious connection to her African heritage; however, her musings on the nature and authority of memory remain a powerful testament to the survival of African spirituality in the African American psyche. While some scholars have argued that Wheatley and others like her, who were captured and transported to America at a young age, would not have retained any meaningful connections to their African homelands, the evidence of an African worldview in her writing rebuts this position. Wheatley's conflation of memory and spirit do not originate in the religious discourse of her Christian mentors; on the contrary, this concept is more likely the fusion of Wheatley's African heritage and her education in Greek and Roman classics. Memory, a spiritual force that must be fed by human sacrifice or acknowledgment, bears greater similarity to African, rather than Christian spirituality.

The importance of memory in Wheatley's ontological view is also evident in the act of remembering. Along with her cognitive negotiation of memory, Wheatley engages in memory as an act or means of spiritual connection. Her frequent references to her African origins arguably represent a subversion of white authority, but they can also illustrate the act of remembering and reaffirming the African self. In a world in which whiteness is validated and Africanity/blackness is negated, Wheatley remembers with self-satisfaction that she is African and that there is worth and humanity in Africanness. This memory act is most striking when Wheatley interjects the self in poems where the focus is otherwise not the self. The often anthologized poem "To the University of Cambridge, in New England" illustrates this point. This poem, ostensibly an admonishment of and reminder to America's young, promising thinkers, begins with a brief autobiographical reflection. Wheatley reminds these great minds that she is but a humble African standing before them:

> While an intrinsic ardor prompts to write,

> The muses promise to assist my pen;
> Twas not long since I left my native shore
> The land of errors, and Egyptian gloom:
> Father of mercy, 'twas thy gracious hand
> Brought me in safety from those dark abodes. (1–6)

Following this self-reflection, the body of the poem reminds listeners that no matter how great their worldly accomplishments, their ultimate test is a measurement of their spiritual achievements. It is God's final judgment that speaks to their real worth. On one level, this autobiographical reflection serves as a biting proclamation of Wheatley's/Africans' equal status before God, but it also serves as a ritual of self-acknowledgement and self-affirmation. Interjecting these moments of remembering her African self, Wheatley echoes traditional African belief in the necessity and the power of remembering. Wheatley understands—whether consciously or unconsciously—that remembering renders the spirit alive and whole. We find further evidence of this insight in the poem of praise "To the Right Honourable William, Earl of Dartmouth, His Majesty's Principal Secretary of State for North America, & c" and the elegiac poem "To His Honour the Lieutenant-Governor, on the Death of His Lady." Here again, Wheatley engages in moments of remembering that seem outside the focus of the poems. It is a one line moment that is easily overlooked in the elegiac poem "To His Honour the Lieutenant-Governor." Here, as is typical of her elegiac poetry, Wheatley offers the Christian message of salvation and eternal life to console one who has lost a loved one. Proclaiming that death is not the ultimate victor, Wheatley reminds this grieving husband that his lost wife has been delivered into the eternal kingdom:

> There sits, illustrious Sir, thy beauteous spouse;
> A gem-blaz'd circle beaming on her brows.
> Haul'd with acclaim among the heav'nly choirs,
> Her soul new-kindling with seraphic fires,
> To notes divine she tunes the vocal strings,
> While heav'n's high concave with the music rings. (19–24)

Wheatley's reminder to this man of prominence (emphasized by her salutation, "illustrious Sir") that Christianity's promise of eternal life leaves no room for grief seems otherwise typical of eighteenth-century American elegies; however, it is in the closing lines of this stanza that his grief seems so remarkably unfit.[6] Just as she presumes she can advise the Cambridge scholars, Wheatley reminds this respected figure that it is she, a simple African, who brings him this all important message: "Nor canst thou, Oliver, assent refuse/ To heav'nly tidings from the Afric muse" (27–28). The subversion of white male supremacy does not reside far beneath the surface in this passage: given that the interjection of a line calling attention to her African identity adds no meaning to the elegiac theme, one can reasonably argue that Wheatley's contrasting image of her humble African self with the powerful white male figure highlights their equality before the ultimate judge—God. This subversive moment also shows Wheatley once again, in the act of remembering. Out of this experience of remembering, Wheatley displaces white hegemony and presence and unapologetically claims a black space.

The brevity of Wheatley's self-reflective line in "To His Honour the Lieutenant-Governor" is a striking contrast to her more revealing self-reflection in the poem "To the Right Honourable William, Earl of Dartmouth." This poem ostensibly pays tribute to the Earl of Dartmouth for his sympathetic view of America's call for freedom from British rule:

> Hail, happy day, when, smiling like the morn,
> Fair Freedom rose New-England to adorn:
> The northern clime beneath her genial ray,
> Dartmouth, congratulates thy blissful sway. (1–4)

Whether he is, in fact, a sympathizer is of little consequence to the poem's secondary, yet provocative discourse. Wheatley's praise for William's recognition of the colonists' rightful desire for freedom is tied to her secondary narrative of the African's natural desire for freedom: "Should you, my lord, while you peruse my Song, / Wonder from whence my love of Freedom sprung" (20–21). Here again Wheatley interjects self into a work whose purpose seems unrelated to her own personal narrative. The focal shift from the colonists' and the honorable William's love of freedom to Wheatley's love of freedom opens the discourse to the self-reflection/remembering that follows:

> I, young in life, by seeming cruel fate
> Was snatch d from Afric's fanc'd happy seat:
> What pangs excrutiating must molest,
> What sorrows labour in my parent's breast?
> Steel'd was that soul and by no misery mov'd
> That from a father seiz'd his babe belov'd:
> Such, such my case. And can I then but pray
> Others may never feel tyrannic sway? (24–30)

Overlaying her own personal narrative of desire with that of the colonists' desire for freedom, Wheatley makes an unmistakable plea for the cause of enslaved Africans, positing both their humanity and their equality. In addition to the more political argument offered in these lines, Wheatley engages in the spiritual act of remembering and affirming the self. Wheatley's brief autobiographical reflection in this poem represents a rare moment in her extant writings: here, she remembers her homeland beyond the western construct of a generalized paganism. She offers a more personal vision of a happy homeland where her loving parents were left devastated by her abduction. Wheatley may not have actually seen her parents' faces as she was

taken from her home; however, through memory and imagination she recon-
structs and relives this moment. The image of her father, suffering the loss of
"his babe beloved" quells the colonial discourse that painted Africans as a
people with no meaningful past. This account of Wheatley's early life reminds readers of the sadness imprinted into the mind of one so young. However, despite the "cruel fate" she endured at being "snatchd from her happy
home" and the subsequent suffering of her parents, the memory of her childhood consoles and confirms her.

In addition to the scattered reflections on memory and the acts of remembering in her poetry, carryovers of African spirituality are evident in repeti-
tions. In particular, Wheatley's recurring use of sun imagery and the preva-
lence of elegies among her poetic works point to traditional African concepts
of nature and being. The recurrence of sun imagery in Wheatley's poetry has
been noted by a number of scholars, and much has been made of the fact that
"[a]ll that she is known to have recalled to her white captors about her native
land is the fact that 'her mother poured out water before the sun at his
rising'" (Shields 241). While one can make the simplistic connection between Wheatley's familiarity with Greek classics and the early American
elegiac tradition to explain her frequent use of sun imagery and the significant number of her poems that focus on death, scholar John Shields argues
that

> [t]he animistic emphasis on death among the people of her native Africa may
> help to explain Wheatley's celebration of death in her numerous elegies . . .
> [and] the fetishistic emphasis on material objects—where in the case of sun
> worshipers the focal point is, of course, the object worshiped—may have so
> pressed itself upon Wheatley's memory as never to have been far beneath her
> conscious mind; this memory may indeed have served her as a powerful
> source of consolation. (242)

Evidence of this lay in Wheatley's indiscriminate reference to sun imagery:
in her elegies, in her occasional poems, in her religious contemplations, in
her poems of praise, and in her reflections on nature, Wheatley found a place
for sun imagery.

In light of the commonly held belief among precolonial Africans that
nature is the manifestation of God's power, Wheatley's preoccupation with
God's most marvelous natural wonder—the sun—is understandable. Among
African people, the sun is sacred: according to Mbiti numerous African societies maintain that "(s)unshine is one of the expressions of God's providence" (53). He points out the Akan, who refer to God as "the Shining One,"
and the Ankore, whose name for God means Sun (Mbiti 53). The connection
that Mbiti draws between the African's concept of the sun and God's benevolence is one that Wheatley draws in her works. In three meditative poems,
"Thoughts on the Works of Providence," "An Hymn to the Morning," and

"An Hymn to the Evening," Wheatley reveals a sacred reverence for the sun that exemplifies Mbiti's findings. "Thoughts on the Works of Providence" is ostensibly a meditation on the Christian God; however, Wheatley's conflation of Christianity's God and the god of her African homeland whose being is manifested in nature (in particular, the sun), demonstrates the religious duality that Wheatley negotiates. It is worth noting that in this poem reflecting on providence, Wheatley combines terms that predate Mbiti's observation by more than two centuries. Mbiti's explanation of the African's concept of the sun as providential and benevolent is exemplified in Wheatley's work. She opens with the image of the rising sun and suggests that this is the sign of God's benevolence:

> Arise, my soul, on wings enraptur'd, rise
> To praise the monarch of the earth and Skies,
> Whose goodness and beneficence appear
> As round its centre moves the rolling year,
> Or when the morning glows with rosy charms,
> Or the sun slumbers in the ocean's arms:
> Of light divine be a rich portion lent
> To guide my soul, and favour my intent.
> ("Thoughts on the Works of Providence" 1–8)

God, the monarch of the earth and skies, is the center/the sun, around which all life revolves: "Ador'd for ever be the God unseen,/ Which round the sun revolves this vast machine" (11–12). This Wheatley reiterates within the first half of this 131 line poem:

> Creation smiles in various beauty gay,
> While day to night, and night succeeds to day:
> That Wisdom, which attends Jehovah's ways,
> Shines more conspicuous in the solar rays:
> Without them, destitute of heat and light,
> This world would be the reign of endless night. (29–34)

As the poem progresses, we find that Wheatley's meditation on providence is a reflection on the manifestation of God in nature. While the sun is the central sign of God's presence, it is all of nature that signals God's presence and God's goodness:

> But see the sons of vegetation rise,
> And spread their leafy banners to the skies.
> All-wise Almighty Providence we trace
> In trees, and plants, and all the flow'ry race;
> As clear as in the nobler frame of man,
> All lovely copies of the Maker's plan. (69–74)

God is "Almighty Providence," "the Maker," ever-present in the world. Implicit in this view of God is the assumption that all is divine, for everything is a manifestation of God. God has not simply created a world and a promise for one particular people, but rather answers the needs of all. God, who is "Love," who is "Nature's constant voice," has made the wonders of nature, "To nourish all, to serve one gen'ral end,/The good of Man . . ." (127–128).

The significance of the sun in Wheatley's spiritual cosmos is evident in her corresponding poetic contemplations on nature, "An Hymn to the Morning," and "An Hymn to the Evening." Though the two works reflect on two contrasting extremes of the day, both highlight the sun as central and powerful. Morning is marked by the gentle west wind, the songs of birds, and early on by the shade and protection offered by trees:

> The morn awakes, and wide extends her rays,
> On ev'ry leaf the gentle zephyr plays;
> Harmonious lays the feather'd race resume.
> Dart the bright eye, and shake the painted Plume.
> Ye shady groves, your verdant gloom display
> To shield your poet from the burning day. (7–12)

This pastoral scene is interrupted, however, by the emergence of the sun in the eastern sky. The powerful sun will become the overwhelming presence in the day, nullifying the protection offered by the early shade:

> See in the east th' illustrious king of day!
> His rising radiance drives the shade away—
> But Oh! I feel his fervid beams too strong,
> And scarce begun, concludes th' abortive song. (17–20)

The quest of "the king of day," the sun, over the "gentle zephyr" may also be read as a subversive assertion of the might of the east (Africa) over the west (Anglo) in Wheatley's cosmology. It is a trope that she draws again in "An Hymn to the Evening," as she contrasts the west wind and the sun of the east:

> Soon as the sun forsook the eastern main
> The pealing thunder shook the heav'nly plain;
> Majestic grandeur! From the zephyr's wing,
> Exhales the incense of the blooming spring. (1–4)

While the evening is a magnificent showcase of artistry—"Through all the heav'ns what beauteous dies are spread!/ But the west glories in the deepest red" (7–8)—it is still the sun that Wheatley paints as the controlling force. It is he (God/the sun) who both "gives the light" by which humans make their way through each day and who "draws the sable curtains of the night," allowing for human solace and rest (11–12). Contrasted against the eastern sun that answers human need at both sunrise and sunset is the "deepest red" of the west that perhaps is synonymous with the deep red of human blood. The picture of a west that "glories" in a deep red hue is not so distinct from the picture of a western society whose wealth/glory is tied to the spilling of African blood across thousands of ocean miles.

A physical entity and a metaphor for her eastern home, the sun is a medium through which Wheatley connects with Africanity. By carefully converging her African-rooted reverence for the sun with her adopted Christian concepts of an omnipotent God, Wheatley maintains a lifeline to African spirituality. This is exemplified in the elegy "On the Death of the Rev. Mr. George Whitefield. 1770." Here, as in her other elegies, Wheatley grounds her consolation in the Christian discourse of the eternally blissful hereafter, but she also draws on her deeply rooted concept of the divine sun to explore the meaning of life and death. Focusing on death and the sorrow of loss, Wheatley employs sun imagery as a metaphor for both life and death. The sun signifies the warmth and brightness that fills our carnal existence, and it also signifies the light of the hereafter. God, as light, prevails in the carnal and the spiritual world: while death may bring darkness and sadness, it also brings the light of eternity. Therefore, Wheatley can represent the death of preacher and slave sympathizer George Whitefield as both sunset and a bright vision. She speaks of Whitefield himself as the sun that will no longer rise: "Unhappy we the setting sun deplore, / So glorious once, but ah! It shines no more" (9–10). This picture of death as the fading light is later eclipsed by the final image of Whitefield in heaven. Here, in the eternal hereafter, Whitefield, the setting sun, has been restored to a shining light:

> But, though arrested by the hand of death,
> Whitefield no more exerts his lab'ring breath,
> Yet let us view him in th' eternal skies,
> Let ev'ry heart to this bright vision rise. (42–45)

Wheatley's use of sun imagery to speak of death can be found in other elegies. In the elegy "On the Death of the Rev. Dr. Sewell. 1769," she cites Sewell among the "happy dead" (2), and describes him in his eternal image as having "brighter lustre than the sun" (35). Similarly, "To a Clergyman on the Death of his Lady," a poem offering consolation to one mourning loss, she invokes the sun's radiance as a metaphor for eternal light/life. Here, she paints a picture of eternity that is frequently drawn in Colonial American Christian discourse. Wheatley describes the deceased in a peaceful, angelic world that has welcomed her for eternal rest:

> There sits thy spouse amidst the radiant throng,
> While praise eternal warbles from her tongue;
> There choirs angelic shout her welcome round,
> With perfect bliss, and peerless glory crown'd. (5–8)

In a 14-line monologue (lines 17–30), the deceased explains to her mourning husband that she now enjoys eternal life, and at the conclusion of her testimony, she "turn'd from mortal scenes her eyes, / Which beam'd celestial radiance o'er the skies" (31–32). Again, with words that invoke images of the sun—"beam'd" and "radiance"—Wheatley paints death as an illuminated and vibrant state. The repeated connection Wheatley draws between death and the life sustaining sun echoes an African cosmology that sees death as simply an entry to a new life medium. Just as the memory of her mother in Africa greeting the morning's rising sun connected Wheatley to her African homeland, the remembrance of the sun's central power and its eastern location may have symbolized her vision of an ultimate return to her spiritual home in the bliss of the hereafter.

The connectedness of nature, God, and humanity in Wheatley's poetry evinces an African spiritual view that survived the Middle Passage and Anglo Christianity. Wheatley's vision of a physical world that is the manifestation of God's greatness echoes an African understanding of humankind as intricately connected to all that God has created. This extends to Wheatley's concept of human connectedness, as we see exemplified in the many poems in her collection that honor those she deems part of her extended family/community. Again, as her ongoing correspondence with friend Obour Tanner demonstrates, community is important to Wheatley. Her overwhelming concern for her friends as well as those she admires from afar who have suffered the loss of loved ones or themselves succumbed to death is exemplified by the fact that more than half the poems in her 1773 collection are personal addresses. While many scholars have painted Wheatley as a young black woman isolated from the larger slave community as well as dominant white society, Wheatley's poetry and her correspondences suggest the contrary. Wheatley felt a particular connection to whites who were sympathetic or that she thought capable of being sympathetic to the principle of African rights and humanity. Hence, her eulogy to George Whitefield, well-known sympathizer of Africans in bondage, celebrates his vision of a God who offers grace to all and focuses more on the ideology of the man than the man himself. "He pray'd that grace in ev'ry heart might dwell" (20), she says of Whitefield. She credits him with having indiscriminately called sinners to Christ:

> Take him my dear Americans, he said,
> Be your complaints on his kind bosom laid:
> Take him, ye Africans, he longs for you,
> Impartial Saviour is his title due. (32–35)

Whitefield's recognition of the African's equality in the eye of God renders him part of Wheatley's spiritual community as his position affirms her own self-worth and equality. Wheatley's many eulogies serve to connect her to a community of Christians and reflects an African worldview that maintains death as a human transition that must be acknowledged and experienced by the community. In traditional African societies the individual does not face death alone, but rather is attended by members of the community to help in the crossing-over experience. The death event must be followed by ceremony that celebrates the life of the departed and the entrance into the world of the spiritual. While her eulogies may be read for their Puritan influenced notions of the deliverance from suffering to the heavenly hereafter, they may also be interpreted as Wheatley's transformation of a traditional African spiritual ritual to a written form. Her eulogies represent a written enactment of the African celebration of the dead—again, an act that calls on the community to remember and to celebrate.

NOTES

1. See Alkeluban's essay "The Spiritual Essence of African American Rhetoric," in *Understanding African American Rhetori: Classical Origins to Contemporary Innovations*. Eds. Ronald L. Jackson and Elaine B. Richardson. London: Routledge, 2003. 23–42.

2. See Trudier Harris's essay "From Exile to Asylum: Religion and Community in the Writings of Contemporary Black Women," in Mary Lynn Broe and Angela Ingram's 1996 collection *Women's Writing in Exile*.

3. See Ann Allen Shockley's 1988 text, *Afro-American Women Writers 1746–1933: An Anthology and Critical Guide* (page 19), for discussion of Wheatley and S.M. See chapter 4 in John Hope Franklin's *From Slavery to Freedom* for discussion of blacks in Colonial America.

4. In her essay "Classical Tidings from the Afric Muse: Phillis Wheatley's Use of Greek and Roman Mythology" (*CLA* 35.4 June 1992), Lucy Hayden's focus is Wheatley's adoptions and revions of Greek and Roman mythology; however, she suggests in passing that Wheatley's recurring Greek and Roman allusions may have been the result of their similarities to the gods of her native Africa.

5. See page 7 of Murphy's *Working the Spirit* and chapter 1 of this work for discussion of traditional African concepts of spirit and humanity.

6. Wheatley's elegies have been discussed by a number of scholars. Some have argued that elegies, as well as her poetry in general, reflects a conciliatory/submissive ideology, while others have explored the satiric and subversive nature of her writing to suggest that we must read her poetry as self-affirming. See Phillip M. Richards's article "Phillis Wheatley and Literary Americanization" (*American Quarterly* 44.2) and James A. Levernier's "Phillis Wheatley and the New England Clergy" (*Early American Literature* 26.1) for an overview of twentieth-century criticism of Wheatley's work, including her elegies.

WORKS CITED

Bassard, Katherine Clay. "The Daughters' Arrival: The Earliest Black Women's Writing Community." *Callaloo* 19.2 (1996): 508–518.

Brandon, George. *Santeria from Africa to the New World: The Dead Sell Memories*. Bloomington: Indiana University Press, 1993.

Franklin, John Hope, and Alfred A. Moss, Jr. *From Slavery to Freedom: A History of African Americans*. 7th ed. New York: McGraw-Hill, Inc., 1994.

Hammon, Jupiter. "An Evening Thought: Salvation by Christ with Penetential Cries." 1760. in *Call and Response: The Riverside Anthology of the African American Literary Tradition*. Eds. Patricia Liggins Hill et al. New York: Houghton Mifflin Company, 1998. 74–76.

Mbiti, John S. *African Religions and Philosophy*. Garden City, NY: Anchor Books, 1970.

Raboteau, Albert J. *Canaan Land: A Religious History of African Americans*. New York: Oxford University Press, 2001.

Shields, John, ed. "Phillis Wheatley's Struggle for Freedom in Her Poetry and Prose." *The Collected Works of Phillis Wheatley*. New York: Oxford University Press. 1988. 229–270.

Wheatley, Phillis. *The Collected Works of Phillis Wheatley*. New York: Oxford University Press. 1988.

Chapter Three

African and Christian Encounters in Early Black Women's Writings

The survival of Africanity in Phillis Wheatley's writings represents the undercurrent of a traditional African worldview that would be transformed, but not extinguished. Among Wheatley's nineteenth-century literary successors, however, the voice of Africanity would become more submerged in dominant Anglo Christian rhetoric, especially espoused in spiritual autobiographies and essays. In the writings of early nineteenth-century black women writers we see the formative period winding into the dawn of the persisting period. In this latter part of the formative period the exposure of Africanity to Anglo Christianity results in an emerging African American cosmology that muffles its African voice and assumes the discourse of Christianity. While traditional African rituals and ideologies would remain part of black oral culture, African American writing would depict a world that had given itself over to a Christian cosmology. We see this evinced to different degrees in the spiritual writings of Maria Stewart, Jarena Lee, and Rebecca Cox Jackson—itinerant black women preachers whose spiritual callings directed them beyond the realm of the domestic. Laurel Bollinger argues that these black women preachers validated their roles as public figures on the cultural association of maternity and womanhood that prevailed in early America (359). While Bollinger demonstrates how Stewart, Lee, and Jackson negotiate this paradigm, she fails to explore the cultural origins of their claims to spiritual authority. Clearly, the early nineteenth-century religious fervor of the Second Great Awakening set the stage for black Christian evangelism. However, black spirituality was rooted in pre-Christian African belief systems that valued women as spiritual leaders. Stewart, Lee, and Jackson are inheritors of a spiritual tradition of black women leaders, but it was an unconscious connection. These black women articulated a Christian worldview that made no claims to Africanity. In particular, "Lee and Stewart grounded their sermons and spiritual writings in biblical discourse" (Peterson 23), a practice that would become commonplace for nineteenth-century black women writers.

By the dawn of the nineteenth century, the black church had been born and the institutionalization of black Christianity could more readily take root. It also marked the closing of the formative period, in part the result of the changing nature of the black population. America's black population was becoming increasingly American born: fewer blacks were native-born African like Wheatley, with a direct memory of their African homeland. Christianity would emerge in the persisting period as the dominant religious rhetoric of black written discourse. In particular, literate blacks and blacks in the north led the transition from an African worldview to an Anglo influenced AfroChristianity. Christianity would win out in the public/published discourse on black spirituality, and blacks in America would articulate a belief in Christianity predicated on an erasure of their African past. In increasing numbers blacks published written personal accounts and commentaries on race and slavery, and one of the most utilized literary conventions they adapted was the well-known conversion narrative. Black writers integrated this convention into their evolving written tradition to tell their stories and to make the case for their humanity. Black women writers were particularly drawn to this narrative alternative, in large part because speaking publicly under the guise of speaking for the divine, allowed women greater acceptance in public space.

It is under the presumption of spiritual/divine inspiration that black women launched a literary legacy of voices in search of a language to render African American humanity reality. Again, this quest would oftentimes entail a tenuous negotiation of an Anglo Christian discourse that at the very least, negated blackness, but more often demonized it. Many black writers responded to this challenge by acquiescing to a rhetoric that claimed Africa pagan and yet to be civilized, but these writers alternatively appropriated biblical language and myths to prophesy the rise of a great black nation. Jarena Lee was among those early black writers who drew from conventions of the Anglo Christian conversion narrative to proclaim her equality and salvation. Thirty years Wheatley's junior, Lee was born in 1783, a year before Wheatley died and twenty years before Maria Stewart was born. Lee's narrative, *Religious Experience and Journal of Mrs. Jarena Lee* (1849), begins with the anticipated confession of a preconversion state of sin and ignorance, and her story culminates in the account of her religious conversion that brings her into the Christian fold. Unlike the blueprint Puritan conversion narrative, however, Lee's narrative tells the story of one who did not have a familial connection to Christianity. She confesses, "My parents being wholly ignorant of the knowledge of God, had not therefore instructed me in any degree in this great matter" (3). The failure of Lee's parents to instruct her in Christianity may well have been their lack of interest or belief. In fact, while Lee recounts with great satisfaction the conversion experience of her son, she does not share an account of a conversion experience for either parent. It is not clear then, when and how her "aged mother" came to be "happy in the Lord," as Lee claims to have found her during one of her rare visits (80). Lee's personal emergence into Christianity and her years as itinerant messenger reflect the process by which blacks in America adopted Christianity. As exemplified in Lee's personal experience, Africans underwent a spiritual transformation that necessitated a negotiation of Africanity and Christianity. Lee's narrative illustrates how the language of Christianity evolved into the discourse of African American spirituality. Unlike Wheatley, Lee was not a first generation African in America; therefore, the African-rooted concepts that inform her spirituality highlight the cultural dualism that shaped AfroChristianity in America.

Jarena Lee's narrative offers no conscious recollection of Africanity: although her parents were not active proponents of Christianity, they either left her no link to an African past (they may have themselves been consciously disconnected) or Lee may have chosen not to acknowledge any African connection. Perhaps her diatribes on the evils of dancing are born out of a desire to disconnect herself from Africanity. On three occasions in her narrative, she condemns dancing as an unholy act. In her account of a woman who underwent conversion at one of her many prayer meetings, Lee reports that after the convert's spiritual enlightenment she "ceased her carnal amusements; quit dancing and went to praying, at which time she arose on her feet and said that she never saw that dancing was wrong before now" (69). Similarly, Lee recounts a woman who had "formerly kept a dance house," but was converted, "and afterwards joined the church . . . [and] appeared very serious" (84–85). On a third occasion Lee found herself at a preaching engagement where she was challenged by those in opposition to a woman preacher. Among her detractors was a group "preparing to have a dance rather than come to hear preaching" (94). According to Lee, as they boasted of inviting the Elder to attend the dance, "God laid his heavy hand upon the man that was to play the fiddle for them; he fell sick on the floor; but he was determined to carry it out, and sent for another man, and he refused, and at last this Goliah-like man was glad to send for the Elder to come and pray for him" (94).

Lee's criticism of dance is likely a response to the colonial New England festivities that took place among poorer whites and blacks. Poor and working class whites and blacks in Colonial New England regularly engaged in community celebrations that included dancing, music, and drink.[1] These were activities that the more affluent and learned looked upon with disapproval. Dance and music among blacks in early America was in great part connected to cultural practices and rituals that survived the Middle Passage. These survivals were often associated in white racist discourse as evidence of black savagery. In Lee's nineteenth-century Christian and Anglo-social orientation, the marker of one's humanity and civility meant shedding one's pagan past. She represents the rising Afro Christian rhetoric of nineteenth-century America that would orient itself in an Anglo biblical worldview. Dance was a reminder of the African's non-Christian, and hence uncivilized past, and by the preachings of these early black Christian leaders, blacks had to abandon this act. Lee's criticism of dance symbolizes her break with African tradition and her transition to a Christian self. Her Anglo Christian understanding of dance as evil represents the Calvinist origins that inform her notion of the carnal world. She echoes the Calvinist notion of man's evil nature, describing herself prior to conversion as "a wretched sinner," and humanity in general as "the fallen sons and daughters of Adam" (3, 43). This view of humanity clearly contradicts the view of traditional Africans who deem man a manifestation and a worthy recipient of God's goodness. The Calvinist vision of humanity suffering in this world while awaiting the next is consistent with early Christian American criticisms of such reckless jollity as dance and music.

The dominating biblical doctrine that informs Lee's religiosity can lead readers to hastily read the narrative as confirmation of an absent African spirituality. But as in the case of Lee, her contemporaries, and those who would carry on the tradition of AfroChristianity, the prevailing deference to Christianity as the religious anchor for African Americans often coexisted with unacknowledged retentions of African spirituality. In general this coexistence was possible because African carryovers were not specifically identified as African, and in fact, were often couched in Christian practices and discourse. This was particularly evident in Lee's belief in vision and prophesy—a belief common to both Africans and Christians. Similarly, the convergence of the Christian Holy Spirit and African spiritual possession, and the parallel Christian and African-rooted justification of women spiritual leaders are also found in Lee's narrative. The primacy and authority that Lee awards visions and the Holy Spirit is consistent with traditional African spirituality. Lee's visionary experiences and her belief in the Christian Holy Spirit are consistent with African spiritual beliefs in the transmutability of states of being. The interaction of the carnal and the spiritual worlds, that is, the ability for beings to cross over states of existences, was a commonly accepted concept among precolonial Africans. Lee echoes African beliefs in spirit possession and spiritual revelations that are transmitted via human vessels. Just as oracles in African societies are used by spirits to speak to those in the material world, Lee is used by the spirit. The spirit speaks through Lee to her congregations and instructs her in matters specific to her own life. This is the case when she finds herself unhappy in the community of Snow Hill where her husband pastors. When a voice in a dream vision instructs her that her husband is answering a divine call, Lee becomes more patient and accepting of their place in this community (13). And when her son undergoes conversion at a time when she is away on one of her many missions, his experience is made known to her "by revelation of the spirit" (72).

Throughout the narrative, Lee reminds readers that the power of speech granted her at religious meetings and gatherings is solely the spirit of God/ the Holy Spirit speaking through her. It is this claim that also serves as the foundation for her presumption to preach. She explains early in the narrative that she took up the call to preach not by some self-will, but rather by God, who commanded her to go out and preach (10). She frequently references the Bible to give authority to her call. In one such instance she draws on the image of Mary, the mother of Christ. However, rather than emphasizing Mary's maternal role, Lee proclaims Mary a preacher, and asserts that "she preached the resurrection of the crucified Son of God" (11). To an elder "averse to a woman's preaching," Lee retorts, "If an ass reproved Balaam, and a barn-door fowl reproved Peter, why should not a woman reprove sin?" (23). Again, she rests her authority in a Christian legacy, but she is the successor in a cultural tradition of women leaders that predates Afro-Christian experience.

Evident also in Lee's Christian worldview are African cultural concepts of community and the interconnectedness of carnal and spiritual entities. Maintaining the primary importance of fellowship and community among Christians, her story is not simply the story of an individual, but rather a "testimony and prophecy [that] speaks from and to a particular faith community" (Hubert 45). At a time when the national rhetoric of the self-made man was emerging as the portrait of Americanness, community was a controlling force among blacks in America. Whether slaves or members of the small free black population, blacks in America had by the eighteenth century come to view themselves as a common people, a community. Again, Wheatley's sustained long distance relationship with friend Obour Tanner illustrates the central place of community in the psyche of New World Africans. The deference to community that we find among early black women would prove a significant influence in the history of black self-help in America. For many, like Wheatley and Lee, whose circles included ties to a white and Native American Christian community, this would include a multiracial community. Lee preached to white, Native American, black, and racially mixed congregations; however, it was particularly among black Christians that she experienced the deepest sense of community. She explains this inclination with the story of her entrance into the fold of Rev. Richard Allen's congregation. She recalls that upon her return to Philadelphia, she attended "the English Church," but soon realized "that there was a wall between [her] and a communion with that people" (4). Upon the recommendation of a Methodist acquaintance, Lee visited Allen's church and decided that she had found a spiritual home: "During the labors of this man that afternoon, I had come to the conclusion, that this is the people to which my heart unites" (5). While Lee suggests that the nature of her connection to this group was their Methodism, it is noteworthy that she left the "English Church," which was pastored by an Englishman, and came into conversion in the company of a black congregation, led by a black pastor. It was three weeks later that Lee was "gloriously converted to God, under preaching, at the very outset of the sermon" (5). In a fashion reminiscent of African spiritual rituals, Lee, in the company of community—fellow congregates—found herself leaping to her feet and, without reservation, speaking to the congregation (5).

The importance of community and spiritual-carnal connectedness in Lee's religious world is further evident in her recollections of death vigils. Like their African ancestors, blacks in America formed societies that maintained the responsibility of the community to individuals in this world as they crossed over into the other world. The practice of waiting with those departing as they enter the spirit world remained central to black communal life. This is illustrated in the story Lee tells of a young "colored" man who had agitated and mocked the churchgoers of his community, but who, when fallen deathly ill, was watched over by Lee and others in the community (15). Although the young man sought to "disturb and ridicule" the congregants, his sister called on the church community to save his soul before death. After the minister of the community failed to make headway with the man, it was a coalition of praying black women that succeeded in converting him at his deathbed:

> We found the Rev. Mr. Cornish, of our denomination, laboring with him. But he received but little satisfaction from him. Pretty soon, however, brother Cornish took his leave; when myself, with the other two sisters, one of which was an elderly woman named Jane Hutt, the other was younger, both colored, commenced conversing with him. . . . He said but little; we then kneeled down together and besought the Lord in his behalf, praying that if mercy were not clear gone for ever, to shed a ray of softening grace upon the hardness of his heart. He appeared now to be somewhat more tender, and we thought we could perceive some tokens of conviction, as he wished us to visit him again.(16)

Two days later the young man called for Lee, and it was Lee and five others sitting vigil who sang and prayed the young man into the next world. After watching his "happy and purified soul" depart, Lee recalls that the room was filled with an overwhelming bliss: "I was filled with the power of the Holy Ghost—the very room seemed filled with glory. His sister and all that were in the room rejoiced" (17).

In another account of a death vigil, Lee paints a similar picture of a community grounded in the conviction that the worth of all human life must be acknowledged. She tells the story of "[o]ne poor colored man," who after boasting that the wave of cholera that was invading nearby communities was no match for him, became suddenly stricken (64). Deciding that his case was hopeless, "by 8 o'clock P.M., the Doctors requested some colored Methodist family to let him die in their house, which was cheerfully acceded to, and he died about 12 o'clock, and was buried before day-light the same morning" (64). Lee parallels this story with that of a rich man who also died of cholera, making the point that the wicked, whether rich or poor, meet a "dreadful end." The moral of Lee's story notwithstanding, a secondary message is revealed. As in traditional African cosmology, African American spirituality maintains the importance of each human life and the necessity to acknowledge the worth of each person as he or she departs this world. This poor, outcast, disease-stricken man was received by the community that would not abandon him on his journey into the spirit world. Despite his boastful and depraved nature and his material destitution, the community "cheerfully" received him rather than leave him to face death alone.

The notion of community and spirit that anchored Lee's worldview was again connected to a legacy of African spirituality to which she did not draw a conscious alliance. The African spiritual legacy that informed Lee's religiosity was more evident in her acts than her espoused ideology. In the act of taking up preaching, watching over the dying, and engaging in community affirming practices, Lee exemplifies the African influence in African American spiritual life. In the structure of the narrative itself, Lee demonstrates a concept of space and time that is African rooted. Carla Peterson explains that Lee's narrative reveals a nonlinear, interspacial worldview: "the linearity of chronological time is disrupted from the beginning, as the first pages of the narratives [that is, both 1836 and 1849 versions] repeatedly circle back around Lee's moment of conversion, so that, although the autobiography progresses by means of metonymic accumulation of words, sentences, and paragraphs, it also insistently looks back to that single conversionary moment" ("Secular and Sacred Space" 51). Peterson further explains that Lee's "capacity to facilitate communication between cosmic planes is . . . applicable to sacred space not only in Christianity but in African and African American religions as well, in which life and death are perceived as a continuum, death often being envisioned as a door between two worlds or the crossing of a river" (52).

Lee's consciously constructed Anglo Christian cosmology did not totally disconnect her from remnants of an African rooted cosmology; she called on images and concepts of Africanity that lived in her memory. Like Wheatley, Lee conveys an awe of nature that she connects with the divine. The power of the sun and the power of God are one: in her account of the revelation of her mission to preach, she describes a dream in which the morning sunrise became hidden by a cloud, but after a third of the day the sun rays burst through (14). According to Lee "the bursting forth of the sun . . . was the recovery of [her] health, and being called to preach" (14). Similarly, Lee later recalls a preaching engagement that ended in a great spiritual moment for all who attended, and this was confirmed by members who reported that "they saw the glory of God like a sun over the pulpit, and a face shone after it, thus the battle was the Lord's" (88–89). This convergence of the Christian God with the sun—one of nature's most powerful images—echoes traditional African concepts of the sun as divine and is reminiscent of Wheatley's expressions of reverence for the sun. Lee's account of her conversion experience further hints at an African-rooted influence in her recollection of having been "permitted to have [a view] of Satan, in the form of a dog" (6).[2] This connection between Satan and dog echoes a commonly held view in traditional African societies that animals can house spirits—good and evil.

Rebecca Cox Jackson, Lee's contemporary and also a self-proclaimed preacher, reports a divinely inspired call to spread God's message, and "[i]t is precisely her self-claimed ability to function as God's pen that connects Rebecca Jackson to other nineteenth-century African-American autobiographers" (Connor 26). Jackson's writing exemplifies the conviction of black women who maintained the primacy of the inner voice, that is, the spirit speaking and revealing through the human medium. Again, however, early black women preachers grounded this presumption not in an African spiritual pretext, but rather a Christian one. In the case of Jackson, that presumption is further articulated through her interpretations of Shakerism. Like Lee, Jackson is called to Christianity through Methodism, but she later finds Shakerism more consistent with her spiritual sensibilities. In particular, Jackson called on true believers to be celibate: this position gained her considerable disfavor among fellow Methodists, but she found this belief congruent with Shaker doctrine. In Shakerism Jackson found acceptance in her conviction that God sanctioned women as well as men to preach and lead in the church. With the divine figure, Mother Ann Lee, as the Shaker icon of Christ's revelation, Jackson found a religious group that did not withdraw from the notion that women, too, were instruments of God's divine manifestations. Jackson's conversion, then, is a two-stage event: she first experiences her conversion to Christianity, and years later she experiences the visions that lead her to the Shaker community. In both cases, Jackson comes into her conversion through divine revelation: she is visited by a divine spirit that brings her to a greater understanding of God and her divine mission in this world.

Jackson opens her narrative recalling the experience that culminated in her Christian conversion. She is brought to her revelation in 1830 during a frightening thunderstorm. As the storm is lifted, so is her fear and her past transgressions, and she has become a follower of Christ. She gives the following account of that moment: "I then felt a desire for all the world to come and love God for Christ's sake. I thought by faith I saw the blessed Jesus who placed my case before the Father, pleading for all sinners" (72). This spiritual conversion leads to her call not only to preach, but also to serve as a spiritual medium, relaying messages from the divine, and stringently following commands from the divine. Jackson's conversion to Shakerism comes after a series of visions and spiritual visitations that occur over several years. Before attending her first Shaker meeting in the fall of 1836, she had already experienced spiritual visits that instructed her to dress in the plain fashion of the Shakers. She had already seen images of the Shaker holy mother, and she had already come to know that she was to live a celibate life.[3] Therefore, upon her first visit with the Shakers, Jackson felt an immediate connection, one that she interprets as divinely ordained: "When they [Shakers] came in, the power of God came upon me like the waves of the sea, and caused me to move back and forth under the mighty waters. . . . They all took their seats. They all set alike. They all were dressed alike. They all looked alike. They all seemed to look as if they were looking into the spiritual world" (139). Swept into the world of Shakerism, Jackson reinterprets her 1830 conversion experience as a prophesy of her entry into the Shaker fold. She explains that though she was called to Methodism as a child, she had always found it a disingenuous and worldly religion. She now interprets her 1830 conversion through the Shaker cosmology that pays deference to the inner voice that brings each person to his or her spiritual revelation: "that morning in 1830 when it pleased God to speak to my outward ear by thunder and lightning and also to my spiritual ear by the silver trumpet, the seven thunders uttered their voices into the seven senses of my soul" (167).

In a later (1854) account, Jackson further elaborates on her 1830 conversion in a section she calls "Mystery of the Thunders Revealed." Citing biblical precedence for her visionary conversion, she reports, "[t]he thunders that called me out of Egypt in 1830 not only pealed literally on my outward ear. But it thundered spiritually out of Mt. Zion, to the awakening of my poor soul from her long sleep in the grave of nature. And now I can see and understand the meaning of the seven thunders that John heard, when the Almighty Angel cried and they uttered their voices" (243). Jackson then explains that the mystery of the seven thunders unlocks the door to the New Jerusalem but can only be revealed to those who have experienced a true conversion. Hence, John was forbidden to write down the mystery revealed by the seven thunders because "every soul should find out that mystery by obedience to their call in the day of the revelation of that mystery" (244).[4] Consistent with Shaker doctrine Jackson believed that each soul is guided by the divine spirit; therefore, she trusted the inner voice that told her of John's vision. This inner voice revealed to her that John had seen a vision of the second coming of Christ: "John had a clear view of the female spirit of Christ, that was to dwell in the Second Eve, who was to stand with the Second Adam in the work of the regeneration" (245). Jackson's vision is consistent with the Shaker belief that Christ had come again in the form of the blessed mother (the Second Eve) who represented the female in Christ. In contrast to the skepticism Jackson faced from many of her Methodist superiors, among the Shakers, she found acceptance of her visionary gifts and her role as a preacher. Jackson had found herself under particular scrutiny in the African Methodist Episcopal Church which sought to legitimate their church in part, by duplicating the dry, stoic services of the colonial white churches. Religious practices that were associated with Africanisms were shunned; therefore, individual and arbitrary claims to spiritual contact were suspect, and religious meetings that deviated from church ritual were censured. As a Shaker, Jackson found freedom from the stringent world of the A.M.E. Church. Among Shakers, Jackson found a world that more closely paralleled her religiosity while sustaining her Christian identity.

Rebecca Jackson draws no connection to a pre-Christian or African inheritance. Her silence is nonetheless revealing, for she and her black Christian contemporaries demonstrate that despite their efforts to distance themselves from their African past, early African Americans sustained in practice, if not in conscious discourse, links to an African spiritual past. While Jackson links her spiritual self to a Christian tradition, some of her strongest religious sentiments hint at a pre-Christian legacy: most notably, "[a]spects of Jackson's parabolic visions can be attributed to the influence of a distinctively African-American religious sensibility which does not separate the sacred from the profane" (Connor 33). Like her African ancestors, Jackson maintains that the spiritual/the divine cannot be separated from the carnal, and her resolve to follow her inner voice speaks to this conviction.

For Jackson, there is no otherworldliness that alienates the spirit from the carnal; the spirit informs the material world and the spirit manifested as the inner voice must be obeyed. Throughout her narrative, Jackson invokes biblical divines and events to validate this conviction; however, her recollection of her mother's similar spiritual gift hints at a spiritual legacy of non-Christian origin. In a rare preconversion remembrance in her more than three decades autobiographical account, Jackson recalls a premonition experienced by her mother. At the age of ten, Rebecca Jackson experienced a dream vision that according to her mother was the revelation of her father's death. From this dream, her mother "had a presentiment of her death" (which occurred four years later) and a further revelation that Rebecca Jackson would outlive her siblings (240). The relation that Jackson repeatedly draws between her visionary gifts and her Christian conversion are compromised by this memory. Jackson shares few memories of her childhood: she portrays herself as having emerged into her spirituality from a tabula rasa. While she tells us that she came into Methodism as a child, she does not portray herself as one whose spiritual evolution was informed by community or family. This portrait of Jackson's self-generating spiritual self is momentarily eclipsed by the story of her mother, whose visionary powers preceded and presaged hers. While Jackson's inner voice may be that of a Christian divine, the gift to receive the voice of the divine is a legacy that predates her Christian experience.

Although Jackson repeatedly links the authority of her inner voice to biblical and Shaker doctrine, the accounts of her spiritual experiences fall generally into precepts of traditional African spirituality. Much of Jackson's narrative focuses on Shaker doctrine and her conviction that this religion conveys God's true message. The notion that the individual is called by the divine and that God makes known his will to each person was a Shaker belief that Jackson found consistent with her own notion of the spirit. This is a belief, however, that can be traced to traditional African thought centuries before the Middle Passage. Blacks came to America believing that humans live in constant contact with the spiritual. From this supposition Africans maintained that the boundary between the spirit and the carnal world could be readily crossed by those in the flesh as well as those in the spirit world. Whether Jackson came to this view through cultural practices in her home or community is not clear; however, her preoccupation with connecting to the spirit world is arguably derived from the influence of traditional African spirituality. Jackson's belief in the personal influence of the inner voice extends further to the belief that the spirit residing in the human body can leave the body and travel. Her narrative, then, recalls both her worldly and her otherworldly travels. She transcends physical boundaries, and in her account of her otherworldly travels, she

> describe[s] an inner world to which few of us, with modern, secularized consciousness, have sustained or frequent access. She was able to capture states of consciousness in which waking personality, with all its quirks and defenses, drops away. Laws of nature are violated with ease, particularly in her accounts of visionary dreams. She soars, lifts, leaps easily into the sky, flies through the air, looks down from a great height, and can see things never visible from such a perspective before. She is given sudden, integrating flashes of understanding about the nature of the physical universe in visual form. She can leave the physical body behind, hold conversations with the angels, tour symbolic landscapes, and reenter the body again. (Humez 42)

Jackson's accounts of out-of-body experiences are not far removed from the African American folktale of the flying Africans—the mystical account of those enslaved Africans in America who through supernatural powers could fly back to Africa. Like these mystical Africans, Jackson can leave the world that physically binds her. She leaves her body and this world—oftentimes when she is to receive a divine revelation. This is the case in 1831 when Jackson, doubting the authenticity of her inner voice, is stricken ill. In her near-death experience she leaves her body several times, making three trips to the banks of the River Jordan and crossing over. On these journeys, a voice reveals to her that she has been called by the divine. When she awakens from her sick bed, her doubt is lifted and she feels assured that her inner voice is indeed the voice of the divine (111–112).

In her account of an out-of-body experience in 1850, Jackson highlights the thematic and panoramic range of her cosmic travels. She submits that she was "instructed concerning the atmosphere and its bounds" (220). She likens the upper atmosphere to the sea, which is "smooth and gentle when undisturbed by the wind"; however, when agitated by the power of the sun and moon, the atmosphere "rages like the sea and sends forth its storms upon the earth" (220). That the purpose of Jackson's spiritual journeys varies from messages of spiritual empowerment to travels beyond human capabilities signals the unlimited power of the spirit. Again, while this is a concept espoused in Shakerism, it is also central to African notions of being. Shakerism provides a theological home for the African-rooted beliefs that Jackson's Methodist and Shaker contemporaries would have dismissed were they thought to originate in an African belief system.

In addition to her recollections of out-of-body experiences, Jackson's accounts of spirit possession and visitations from the dead further exemplify her belief in the connectedness of the spirit and carnal worlds. Just as traditional African cosmology draws a connectedness between the spirit and the human body as well as the spirit and the natural world, so too does Jackson. For Jackson, spiritual revelations are usually presaged by some act of nature: in most instances her visions are brought on by a thunderstorm—a natural act that is considered a spiritual omen in many African societies. Reminiscent of Jackson's 1830 conversion, this pivotal experience begins with the onset of a thunderstorm, and Jackson's journey to redemption is cataloged by the progression of the storm. The beginning of the storm marks Jackson's fear; as the storm rolls on the thunder and lightning unveil her fear and shame, driving her to near desperation (71–72). At the very edge of despair, however, Jackson recalls that "the cloud bursted, the heavens was clear, and the mountain was gone. My spirit was light, my heart was filled with love for God and all mankind. And the lightning, which was a moment ago the messenger of death, was now the messenger of peace, joy, and consolation" (72). Similarly, in 1843 Jackson has a dream that conveys to her that God has called her to serve her people. In this dream Jackson encounters a storm where "it began to rain, as if it were cotton" (178). The storm finds many people lost and in distress, but the rain of cotton gives way to flowers and Jackson finds at the dream's end that the lost people "were all colored people," and that she had been sent among them to deliver God's word

(179–180). This dream again follows a dream pattern in which Jackson receives a divine message after coming through a thunderstorm.

For Jackson, the interconnectedness of the spiritual and the natural world is confirmed not only in the transcendence of spirits and humans between those worlds, but is also evident in nature itself. Echoing the African cosmological view that all in the carnal world is a reflection of the divine, Jackson, like Wheatley and Lee, sees nature as a reflection of God. She finds that "things visible are representations of things spiritual" (232–233). Often in her narrative Jackson reflects on the beauty and awe of nature, finding a spiritual essence in both the animate and inanimate. Jackson's vision of God and nature as interwoven entities resonates with nineteenth-century Romantics who articulated a similar vision. We find this vision expressed throughout the works of America's most celebrated Romantic, Ralph Waldo Emerson. For example, in *Nature* (1836) he writes, "In the woods . . . all currents of the Universal Being circulate through me; I am part or participle of God" (695). Similarly, in *The American Scholar*, he explains that man's intricate relationship to God comes by way of nature, asking "What is nature to him [man/scholar]. Emerson answers "There is never a beginning, there is never an end, to the inexplicable continuity of this web of God, but always circular power returning into itself" (696). That Jackson's vision of nature and God resonates with that of Emerson and the Romantics should not be presumed evidence of their influence in this regard. Worth noting here is that the Romantics identified religious and philosophical systems of the East as the origins of their religious vision. Jackson's writing does not suggest that she has read or been influenced by writings of the Romantics; moreover, while she does note the period of her pre-Christian awakening as well as her stint with Methodism, she does not indicate that her journey to the Shaker faith entailed encounters with the New England Transcendentalists or their movement.

The recurring images of thunder and lightning and water in her visions parallel the commonplace use of these natural images in many African rituals and tales. Thunder and lightning are often the paradoxical source of both fear and deliverance in traditional African spirituality, and water is commonly connected to spiritual rebirth. Among Ifa divinities, for example, Sango, the god of thunder and lightning, "illuminates truth," and his lightning bolt "symbolizes his power to destroy and serve as punishment for wrongdoing and warning to do right" (Montgomery 54, 78). Just as in Ifa tradition, thunderstorms often portend ensuing revelations for Jackson: thunder and lightning set the stage for her first conversion experience, and it is during a thunderstorm in April 1845 that Jackson is "brought to the Judgment" (207), a visionary experience that allows her to witness the call of souls to the hereafter. Her dreams are often filled with journeys across bodies of waters: she makes several spiritual journeys to the biblical Jordan River. On other journeys she is directed to an unidentified inlet, such as the visionary small stream she found herself revisiting. It is at this stream that she looks out and sees a bucolic landscape that foreshadows the divine vision she will experience: "The water was clear as crystal, with little white stones at the bottom. I looked across some distance, and saw a beautiful arbor formed by the union of the branches of the trees, which were so interwoven as to form a beautiful arch. And beneath it stood the Mother of the New Heaven and Earth, the Queen of Zion, with her face toward me, as if waiting" (274). Jackson's narrative illustrates early African American negotiations of African spirituality and emerging AfroChristianity that resulted in a disregard for African influences. Anglo American views of Africanisms as signs of barbarity informed the practice of many literate blacks, including Jackson, to commit no ink to records of Africanity in their discourse. With her repeated reminders that her acts are answers to divine instruction, and with the claim that that divinity is the God of Christianity, Jackson asserts the legitimacy of her spiritual experience.

Rebecca Cox Jackson marveled at the heavens and the terrestrial landscapes as manifestations of God's power, and like her African foreparents, she saw the creatures of nature as harbingers of spiritual messages. For Jackson, as with many continental and diasporic Africans, this manifestation is evident in certain animals. Among many West African people the dog and the snake are connected to manifestations of spiritual presence, and more specifically in the case of the snake, the conjuration of spirits. The African folkloric representation of the dog as a low and sometimes evil creature and the snake as mysterious and powerful is echoed in Jackson's narrative. In several instances the dog and the snake appear in her dreams and they serve as symbols of the spiritual adversity that she must overcome. In one such dream in 1831, Jackson finds herself in a garden rich with blackberries. As she begins to pick the berries she discovers that she is surrounded by snakes, and "[e]very one had their mouth open, their stings out . . . ready to spring upon [her]" (94). She escapes their stings through her faith, but as she passes, she witnesses a dog being killed by the snakes. The blood of the dog splatters on her white apron, but she is able to shake the apron clean and escape the scene unscathed. Jackson explains the dream as God's affirmation that he will deliver her from her enemies so long as her faith remains. Jackson does not identify the role of the snake and the dog in her dream; however, the snakes clearly symbolize her enemies, and the dog represents the unsaved— those who will be consumed by evil because they do not have the protection of the divine. Jackson's representation of the snake as possessing supernatural powers points to African cosmology; however, her association of the snake with evil reveals a western influence. Among continental Africans, the snake is a reverential being: "in African tradition the snake represents the ancestors," and thus is not deemed a symbol of evil (Montgomery 97).

In two accounts of her real life confrontations with a vicious dog and a bed of venomous snakes, Jackson once again asserts that she is under the protection of the divine—particularly in the face of two symbolically evil creatures. In a garden where Jackson stopped to pray, she rose from her prayer met by a ferocious dog who had broken loose from his chain. The dog was, however, stopped in his tracks by an unexplained force: he looked at Jackson, "then turned around as if he had been turned by somebody, [and] went back from whence he came" (110). On another occasion, Jackson attends a camp meeting (made popular during the revivalism of the Awakening, especially among Methodists) where she encounters three venomous snakes as she prepares her tent site. At the amazement of those at the camp, she kills the three snakes with a shovel. She is told that this is an amazing feat since "it takes a smart man to kill one racer [venomous snake] at a time," and she had killed three (113). Again, Jackson suggests that her powers over such threatening creatures come from the grace of the divine—the Christian divine. Her claim to Christianity and Shakerism, however, does not discount the tie between the images of the snake and the dog in her writing and similar African folkloric images of these creatures as spiritually empowered.

The importance of the visionary, particularly the high status of women visionaries in many African societies, resonates in Jackson's writing. The numerous accounts of her visions and spiritual experiences are designed to substantiate her self-proclaimed role as spiritual medium and messenger of God. She eagerly accepts the Shaker interpretation of the supreme spirit as a manifestation of man and woman—an interpretation of the divine that, again, validates her claims of spiritual leadership, but also echoes traditional African interpretations of the divine. She is frequently visited by a female apparition that she identifies as the Shaker holy mother, the "female spirit of Christ" (245). She likens the holy mother to the spirit of the second coming of Christ as foretold by the apostle John:

> When John saw the male Spirit in Christ, he called it the Lion of the tribe of Judah. And when he saw the female Spirit, he called it the New Jerusalem, prepared as a Bride adorned for her husband, coming from God out of Heaven. . . . Here is the mystery of the City, and the seven thunders. By the Spirit of the Bride, which is the City into which we must enter through these twelve gates. And then we shall come into these twelve virtues, which are in Christ the Lamb; and Christ the Bride. (248–249)

Jackson, like her Shaker counterparts, will not displace Christ as the divine; however, she reimagines him as a duality that allows for a male/female divinity.

The supposition of a divine mother figure paves the way for women's spiritual leadership, a role familiar to Jackson before her conversion to Shakerism. Jackson's recollection of an encounter with an elderly woman who

once belonged to a Methodist praying band with her mother, is a reminder
that Jackson's understanding of the legitimacy of women spiritual leaders
predates her Shaker visions. When Jackson heals the old woman's blindness
and then sits in vigil at her deathbed, we are also reminded that black women
maintained a spiritual community reminiscent of traditional African communities. In America, as in Africa, they were called upon to tend to the needs of
those living and those transitioning into the spirit world. Rebecca Jackson
assumed this role on many occasions, and oftentimes she sat vigil over those
who were sick, after having had a premonition of their ensuing death. She
assumed the role of visionary and caretaker, which kept her intimately connected to those she served. This, too, echoed longstanding African communal
practices that bound people to each other through firm notions of the obligation of each person to his or her community. As Joseph Murphy and John
Mbiti point out in their contemporary works on African religions, the importance of community among African people has been longstanding. Mbiti's
emphasis on the African's integral notion of spirit and community is exemplified in Jackson's writing. Blacks may have out of necessity come to adopt
the western discourse of separate secular and spiritual realms: perhaps they
found it less difficult to reconcile their lives as slaves and marginalized
people if they could treat the world in which they interacted with whites as a
world separate from their real selves. Therefore, blacks in America could
save their African-rooted cultural practices and beliefs for the world they
shared beyond white dominance. While mid-nineteenth-century American
thinkers were embracing the Emersonian rhetoric of individualism, blacks
maintained the primacy of community. We see this exemplified in Jackson's
accounts of her ministry. Jackson is steadfast in her belief that she must
concede to the guidance of her inner voice; however, it is a voice that leads
her to commune with and to serve others. Jackson feels legitimated by her
service to others: as a healer, as a seer, and as a preacher, she serves the
larger community. And when she joins others, especially in the many camp
meetings she attends, Jackson experiences what Joseph Murphy describes as
the African and African American Diasporic practice of working the spirit,
that is, coming together as a community to praise and acknowledge the spirit
and to reap the reward of the blessings of the spirit.

Although blacks did not embrace Shakerism in significant numbers, this
did not alter Jackson's desire to commune among blacks. Her account of a
reconciling meeting with her contemporary, Jarena Lee, demonstrates the
importance she awarded community. Jackson recalls that there was a time
when Lee had been one of her "most bitter persecutors," but on this meeting
in January 1857 Lee and Jackson's girlhood friend, Mary Peterson, visit and
pray with her and the meeting leaves Jackson with an overwhelming sense of
validation. Lee, who according to Jackson, had been critical of her, now
prayed for her mission: "She [Lee] prayed that the Lord might open the door

for me to preach the Gospel, and also prayed for a blessing on my household" (263). Jackson recounts the following tide of emotion that concluded their visit:

> To my great surprise, when she was done I felt a gift to pray. And Mother blessed me with a weeping spirit, and with love. When done, I rose and went to her, and embraced, and kissed her. And I was filled with Mother's love. I then went to Sister Peterson and did the same, and then to Mary Jones. And when I put my hands on her and blessed her, a portion of Mother's weeping spirit fell upon her, and she wept freely. My heart was filled with gratitude to God for all His kindness to me, a worm of the dust. (263)

While Jackson describes herself as being filled with the spirit of the blessed Shaker Mother, her spiritual fulfillment comes from a communion with her nonShaker alliance, the Methodist, Jarena Lee. But Lee and Jackson's reconciliation is not simply grounded in a mutual Christian theology, but rather a cultural and communal bond that predates their Christian roots.

Jackson's need to connect to spiritual and community roots that predate her Shaker conversion is further evident in her desire to bring blacks into the Shaker fold. Through dream visions she is made aware of her calling to bring the Shaker doctrine to blacks. In 1857 she records an explicit dream of this kind. In this dream Jackson encounters black Shakers and converts who do not live and dress in the ways of the Shakers. They are alienated from and ignored by the larger Shaker community, and she is made to realize that it is her mission to guide the black converts into the larger Shaker community (268–270). A year after this dream and several years following a rift between Jackson and Shaker elders regarding her desire to work among blacks, a Shaker eldress calls on Jackson to return to Philadelphia to establish a black Shaker community. Though her Shaker group never reached numbers that would compare to the growth of other black Protestant churches in the mid-1800s, this mission proved her primary call and confirmed her convictions that women were significant emissaries of the divine and that the spirit speaks to and guides each person. Jackson would not compromise these principles, and while she contextualized these beliefs through Christian and Shaker discourse, they were beliefs that had been preserved across the Middle Passage and passed on by Africans in the New World.

In the writings of Maria Stewart, Lee's and Jackson's younger contemporary, we find a continuation of early black women responding to a call to lead and preach. Although Lee's junior by twenty years, Maria Stewart published her first pamphlet, "Religion and the Pure Principles of Morality, the Sure Foundation on which We Must Build" in 1831, preceding Lee's first autobiographical account by five years. Stewart's writing, however, demonstrates the generational transition of the spirit in black women's writing. Where we find clear links to Africanity in Wheatley's work and surviving connections in Lee's writings, in Lee's generational successor, Stewart, the connections to an African spirituality become less apparent. In contrast to Wheatley who addressed a white readership, Stewart represents the leap in literariness of blacks in a matter of a half century. By the middle of the nineteenth century, blacks had established publishing outlets that allowed them to speak to a community of black readers. Stewart addresses fellow black Americans with a message anchored in Christian discourse and framed by conversion narrative convention.

In the fashioned tradition of the Puritan conversion narrative, Stewart begins her narrative with an account of her pre-enlightened period, that time in her life before she knew God. She follows with the account of her spiritual enlightenment, her conversion, and her profession of faith: "I was born in Hartford, Connecticut, in 1803, was left an orphan at five years of age, was bound out in a clergyman's family; had the seeds of piety and virtue early sown in my mind . . . in 1826 was married to James W. Stewart; was left a widow in 1829; was, as I humbly hope and trust, brought to the knowledge of the truth, as it is in Jesus, in 1830; in 1831 made a public profession of my faith in Christ" (3).[5] Though the focus of this tract is not Stewart, she provides an introductory autobiographical account that validates her as author. She is thus qualified to speak on the subject of morality and religion because she is an authority by virtue of her Christian conversion. Stewart believes that God has called her for this mission, and this role of divine agent further explains her assumption of authority. To those who question her presumption to speak publicly she answers, "I am sensible to exposing myself to calumny and reproach; but shall I, for fear of feeble man who shall die, hold my peace? Shall I for fear of scoffs and frowns, refrain my tongue? Ah no! I speak as one that must give an account at the awful bar of God; I speak as a dying mortal to dying mortals" (6). Like Lee and Jackson, Stewart does not tie her claims to leadership to the tradition of African women serving as spiritual leaders, but rather in the dominant Christian discourse of mid-nineteenth-century America.

Stewart interprets the condition of blacks in America through biblical allusions that parallel their circumstances to ancient biblical people and times. Acknowledging the great numbers of non-christian blacks, Stewart, like her literary contemporaries, will not consider that blacks reluctantly embrace Christianity because they have an alternative worldview. Instead, she parallels their non-Christian status to that of the ancient Israelites who had turned away from God: "and when I see the greater part of our community following the vain bubbles of life with so much eagerness, which will only prove to them like the serpent's sting upon the bed of death, I really think we are in as wretched and miserable a state as was the house of Israel in the days of Jeremiah" (8). Here we see Stewart employing the often used Jeremiad of the Puritan tradition, a biblical trope that blacks would adapt to explain the threatening evil in America that was the result of slavery. Stewart represents that legacy of African American writers who shaped Christian doctrine into a rhetoric of racial uplift and deliverance and a platform to voice political discontent. Though Stewart sees the link between the biblical Jeremiac warning and the potential doom in her time, she is no less optimistic that African redemption has been prophesied in Psalms with the promise that Ethiopia shall stretch forth her hand unto God (11).

Maria Stewart's messages to her black audiences reveal her assumption of connectedness to those people now characterized as black in America's dominant white society. Throughout her writings, Stewart grounds her affirmations of racial equality and her call for the freedom of blacks in Christian discourse. Like her nineteenth-century contemporaries, Stewart does not draw on the memory of a precolonial African self; instead she has created self out of a Christian redemption story. She proclaims Christianity the path to salvation for blacks, and her personal crusade to spread Christianity among blacks demonstrates that while a dominant theme in early black discourse, Christianity had not yet become a stronghold of black life. Therefore, in her 1832 speech, "An Address Delivered Before the Afric-American Female Intelligence Society of America," we find Stewart chiding her audience for their lack of Christian conviction: "The only motive that has prompted me to raise my voice in your behalf, my friends, is because I have discovered that religion is held in low repute among some of us; and purely to promote the cause of Christ" (57). While Stewart sees herself as part of a black community, her sense of that community is not shaped by an inherited remembrance of Africanity but rather as blacks in the new world connected to biblical prophesy. Stewart's frustration is a reminder that "substantial fragments of African religion . . . continued through the antebellum period," thus diminishing a need for blacks, en masse, to embrace Christianity (Gomez 261).

Stewart believes in the spiritual redemption of her people, but she envisions this event through an Anglo Christian lens. She acknowledges an Africa that was once great, but she explains its demise in familiar Anglo Christian rhetoric. In "An Address Delivered at the African Masonic Hall," she argues that "poor despised Africa was once the resort of sages and legislators of other nations, was esteemed the school for learning, and the most illustrious men in Greece flocked thither for instruction. But it was our [Africans'] gross sins and abominations that provoked the Almighty to frown thus heavily upon us, and give our glory unto others" (65). Stewart's account of the African's fall from grace reflects an understanding of God's relationship to humanity that is informed largely by a Puritan/Calvinist view. She echoes the Calvinist view of humankind as inherently sinful rather than the traditional African view of humankind as deserving recipients of a benevolent God. In her warnings of the ultimate damnation that sinners will face, Stewart employs the fire and brimstone images frequently invoked in Puritan sermons. She espouses the Christian dichotomy of good and evil, explaining that the good will meet God's grace while the evil will meet God's wrath:

> The day is coming, my friends, and I rejoice in that day, when the secrets of all hearts shall be manifested before saints and angels, men and devils. . . . The dead that are in Christ shall be raised first. . . . Ah, methinks I hear the finally impenitent crying, "Rocks and mountains! Fall upon us, and hide us from the wrath of the Lamb, and from him that sitteth upon the throne." ("Address Delivered Before the Afric-American Female Intelligence Society of America" 57)

It is not without cultural precedence that Stewart asserts her qualification to speak publicly as a messenger of God. Like her black female contemporaries and those who would succeed her into the twentieth century, she does not connect this right to an African inheritance. Instead, just as Jarena Lee and Rebecca Cox Jackson, Stewart represents an African legacy of spiritual women leaders, but she will claim Christian precedence as her authority. She maintains that it is the will of Jesus that she act as voice for her people ("Lecture Delivered at the Franklin Hall" 51). In "Mrs. Stewart's Farewell Address to Her Friends In the City of Boston," Stewart recounts her conversion experience in greater detail than the brief account she offered two years earlier in her 1831 tract, "Religion and the Pure Principles of Morality . . ." In her lengthier recollection Stewart recalls a pivotal moment in which God spoke to her, assuring her that he would be with her. From that moment she knew that she was called to speak for God, and she explains, "thus far I have every reason to believe that it is the divine influence of the Holy Spirit operating upon my heart that could possibly induce me to make the feeble and unworthy effort that I have" (74). While Stewart credits Christianity's God as the authoritative source for her public calling, her role as divine medium calls attention to a tradition of black women answering the call. Stewart's spiritual narrative represents the transformation of African spirituality from the formative to the persisting period. African American women would maintain their precolonial roles as spiritual leaders; however, as Christianity became the defining religion for blacks in America, their spiritual roles would be defined through Christian discourse. With this transformation, African American women writers launched a literary tradition marked by an explicit erasure of African spirituality in African American culture.

From Wheatley's poetry to the writings of Jarena Lee, Rebecca Cox Jackson, and Maria Stewart we find manipulations of discourse that informed the written and public dismantling of African spirituality. These black women writers demonstrate the struggle for ownership—ownership of ideas as well as ownership of self. Transforming their African-centered worldview into Christian discourse, they were required, in part, to relinquish ownership of their beliefs, their origins, and their identities. While it may be of little moral consequence whether a people can identify the origins of their beliefs and customs if they are morally upstanding: it is, however, of considerable consequence when the foundations that ground a people are redefined as originating from their oppressors and when those people are in turn told that all that they know as good originates outside themselves. This is the dynamic at work in these early black women's writings. Fundamental African-rooted ideals that informed black life were necessarily reinscribed as Christian and western to be claimed as valid in western discourse. Therefore, early black writers struggled to frame such common African ideals as the transformation of the corporeal into the spiritual through death, the influence of the spirit in the material world, the primacy of community, and the dual gendered nature of the divine into a discourse that would not be identified as African in origin. While blacks were able to maintain numerous practices and beliefs from their African past, they could not openly claim ownership of them. The result, as illustrated in the works of these early black women writers, is the paradox of affirming oneself in the face of a self-erasing discourse. Hence, we see the beginnings of a splintered oral/written tradition: in their written tradition black women would progressively silence or fail to acknowledge the African origins of the black self in America. It would be through the oral and ritual traditions that blacks would maintain a clearer connection to their African selves. And as revealed in the writings of Lee, Jackson, and Stewart, the African spirit that defines their worldview is not one that they will openly claim, but rather is evident only through the echoes of Africanity that make their way through the silence.

NOTES

1. See chapter 2 in David R. Roediger's *The Wages of Whiteness* for a more thorough discussion of pre-1900 black and interracial festivals in New England.

2. In her essay "Secular and Sacred Space in the Spiritual Autobiographies of Jarena Lee," Carla L. Peterson notes this particularly African view of the dog. She explains that Lee's use of the dog to signify evil "not only reflects the low status of the dog in African folklore but relates more specifically to African American popular beliefs about animals. Many of these beliefs, according to Newbell Puckett, were African in origin. An omen of death, the dog . . . was often viewed as the devil himself in disguise" (53).

3. In a passage subtitled "My Release from Bondage," Rebecca Jackson recalls that in January 1836 she was commanded to tell her husband, Samuel, that she was called to serve God and could no longer serve him (147). This was a vow that facilitated the end of her marriage. In "Revelation of the Mother Spirit," Jackson recounts that in 1835 she saw "for the first time, a Mother in the Deity." She explains that this was for her "a new scene, a new doctrine" (153–154).

4. Jackson is referring to Revelation 10:1–4, in particular the fourth verse in which John writes, "And when the seven thunders had uttered their voices, I was about to write: and I heard a voice from heaven saying unto me, Seal up those things which the seven thunders uttered, and write them not."

5. In an 1833 address, "Mrs. Stewart's Farewell Address to Her Friends in the City of Boston," Stewart offers a similar, but lengthier account of her conversion experience.

WORKS CITED

Bollinger, Laurel. "'A Mother in the Deity': Maternity and Authority in the Nineteenth-Century African-American Spiritual Narrative." *Women's Studies* 29 (2000): 357–382.

Connor, Kimberly Rae. "Womanist Parables in *Gifts of Power*: The Autobiography of Rebecca Cox Jackson." *A/B: Auto/Biography Studies* 10.2 (1995): 21–38.

Emerson, Ralph Waldo. *The American Scholar*. 1837. in *Heath Anthology of American Literature*. Ed. Paul Lauter. New York: Houghton Mifflin, 2004. 694–706.

———. *Nature*. 1836. in *Heath Anthology of American Literature*. Ed. Paul Lauter. New York: Houghton Mifflin, 2004. 691–694.

Gomez, Michael A. *Exchanging Our Country Marks: The Transformation of African Identities in the Colonial and Antebellum South*. Chapel Hill: UNC Press, 1998.

Hubert, Susan J. "Testimony and Prophecy in *The Life and Religious Experience of Jarena Lee*. *Journal of Religious Thought* 54/55. 1/2 (Spring/Fall 1998): 45–52.

Humez, Jean McMahon, ed. and introd. *Gifts of Power: The Writings of Rebecca Jackson, Black Visionary, Shaker Eldress*. Amherst: University of Massachusetts Press, 1981. 1–68.

Jackson, Rebecca Cox. *Gifts of Power: The Writings of Rebecca Jackson, Black Visionary, Shaker Eldress*. Ed. Jean McMahon Humez. Amherst: University of Massachusetts Press, 1981.

Lee, Jarena. *Religious Experience and Journal of Mrs. Jarena Lee, Giving an Account of Her Call to Preach the Gospel (1849)*. in *Spiritual Narratives*. Introd. Susan Houchins. New York: Oxford University Press, 1988.

Montgomery, Georgene Bess. *The Spirit and the Word: A Theory of Spirituality in Africana Literary Criticism*. Trenton, NJ: Africa World Press, 2008.

Peterson, Carla L. *"Doers of the Word": African American Women Speakers and Writers in the North (1830–1880)*. New Brunswick, NJ: Rutgers University Press, 1998.

———. "Secular and Sacred Space in the Spiritual Autobiographies of Jarena Lee." *Reconfigured Spheres: Feminist Explorations of Literary Space*. Eds. Margaret R. Higonnet and Joan Templeton. Amherst: University of Massachusetts Press, 1994. 37–59.

Stewart, Maria W. *Productions of Mrs. Maria W. Stewart*. in *Spiritual Narratives*. Introd. Susan Houchins. New York: Oxford University Press, 1988.

Chapter Four

Africa Silenced

Christianity's Persistent Voice in Early Black Women's Novels

Frederick Douglass's *Heroic Slave* (1853), William Wells Brown's *Clotel*, (1853), and Harriet E. Wilson's *Our Nig* (1859) are regularly included in anthologies as texts that mark the birth of African American fiction. While these works may continue to be viewed as prototypes of the black novel, a comprehensive study of black fiction must consider the influence of the slave narrative to this tradition. The slave narrative represents a significant transition to the black novel; among its many influences in black fiction, this genre extended the discourse of the black author beyond the religiosity of the spiritual narrative. Spiritual enlightenment, conversion, and evangelism would continue as themes in the slave narrative. However, the slave narrative offered black authors an opportunity to move outside the scripted and predictable spiritual narrative to explore the individual experience of the narrative subject. The slave narrative developed into a predictable form—it told the story of the slave's journey to freedom, the story of the slave's spiritual/conversion experience, the story of the slave's travels, and particularly for women, it conveyed the narrative of domesticity. In many cases slave narratives were corrupted by the outside influences of transcribers who recorded the stories told by illiterate ex-slaves. Nevertheless, this unique American genre allowed blacks a written platform to record and preserve the impressions and experiences of those in bondage.

Slave narratives are windows that offer glimpses of slave life from firsthand experiences, and nineteenth-century abolitionists made particular propagandistic use of this genre, understanding the greater immediacy conveyed when slavery's story was told by slaves. Although a story of slavery in the

West Indies, the *Narrative of Mary Prince* (1831), one of the earliest published bondwoman's narratives, illustrates this point. The editor could have merely taken the transcribed account that Prince had dictated and summarized it in a propaganda tract. It is, however, the combination of the editor's narrative interventions and Prince's own account of her horrific bondage that makes the compelling argument against slavery. Similarly, in the 1850 *Narrative of Sojourner Truth*, the story of Truth's journey from slavery to freedom is conveyed through transcription. Truth's story is then overlaid with the voice of the transcriber, and thus we have the voice of the abolitionist mission interjected throughout the work. Despite the presence of another voice, Truth's story emerges and her words reveal a connection to Africanity that again speaks to its presence in early spiritual and slave narratives by black women. Like other early black women's spiritual narratives, Truth's *Narrative* is framed in Christian discourse, and the work reveals no deliberate suggestion of a connectedness between African spirituality and black Christianity.

Although contemporary scholars readily acknowledge the influence of African spirituality in Sojourner Truth's religiosity, Truth's transcriber/editor made no correlations between Africa and what she (the editor) recognized as Truth's sometimes uncharacteristic Christianity.[1] While Truth's narrative emphasizes her journey from bondage to freedom, the work reads much like the spiritual narratives of her contemporaries, Jarena Lee and Rebecca Cox Jackson. Just as Lee and Jackson's narratives report their emergence into spiritual enlightenment, noting their moments of doubt and backsliding and highlighting the actual moment of their conversions, Truth's narrative is similarly structured. Interwoven in the account of the perils she faced as a slave, Truth recalls the importance of God in her life from early childhood. She remembers that her mother ritually gathered the siblings in the evenings after work and spoke to them about "the only Being that could effectually aid or protect them" (3). This recollection echoes the African concept of god and nature that likely informed the spiritual teaching that Truth's mother imparted to her children. It was "under the sparkling vault of heaven" that Truth's mother would gather them and "point them to the stars, and say . . . 'Those are the same stars, and that is the same moon, that look down upon your brothers and sisters, and which they see as they look up to them, though they are ever so far away from us, and each other'" (4). This deference to god through nature would remain with Truth, as she continued into adulthood the practice of praying in the woods where she believed God could more readily converse with her (32).

Truth relates the wavering commitment that first marked her spiritual awakening. Reminiscent of conversion narrative accounts, she tells of her broken promises to God, of her attempts to bargain with God, and of the constant guilt that plagued her (33). Her subsequent account of a visitation from Jesus represents the moment of her Christian conversion (36–37). From this experience, she is on the path to Christian understanding and is led to the culminating moment of her life. She changes her name from Isabella to Sojourner, and having been "moved by the spirit . . . she leaves her home . . . [and] sets off on a journey of preaching and praying along the east coast" (58). Truth's call to preach echoes that of Lee and Jackson. All three women answer a voice, a call from within, that sets them on a road to serve God as he specifically instructs them. Just as Lee and Jackson would not connect their calling to a pre-Christian influence, neither would Truth. Truth would also frame her spiritual awakening through Christian discourse; however, as in the spiritual narratives of her contemporaries, Truth's narrative nonetheless reveals a spiritual legacy informed by Africanity. The survival of African belief in memory and community is evident in Truth's account of her parents' ritualistic rememberings:

> Bomefree and Mau-mau Bett [Truth's parents],—their dark cellar lighted by a blazing pine-knot,—would sit for hours, recalling and recounting every endearing, as well as harrowing circumstance that taxed memory could supply, from the histories of those dear departed ones, of whom they had been robbed, and for whom their hearts still bled. (3)

Like their ancestors, Truth's parents maintained the importance of sharing and passing on stories of those who had passed on to the spirit world. While they may not have articulated the objective of their rituals of remembering, they clearly were guided by a longstanding cultural tradition.

Though she declared herself Christian, Sojourner Truth was independent in her interpretations of God and biblical scripture, and her independent interpretations hint at African origins. Her obedience to the spirit's call to preach and her understanding that she could communicate with God reflect a spiritual worldview that predates New World black Christianity. This is evinced in what Truth's transcriber describes as Truth's conviction that "God . . . was to be worshipped at all times and in all places; and one portion of time never seemed to her more holy than another" (64). The transcriber's apparent awe at Truth's vision of the sacred suggests that this worldview is foreign to her own Anglo, Christian concept of God. Anchored in the presumption that all human experience is inextricably connected to the divine, Truth's vision of the divine echoes traditional African belief in the sacredness of all life. Hence, Truth found God in everything and as she made clear throughout her narrative, she always felt free to ask God for the smallest or the largest gifts as she imagined that he was part of every detail of her life.

The presence of Africanity in the slave narratives of Mary Prince and Sojourner Truth demonstrates the influence of African spirituality in early African American culture; and this is perhaps more remarkable because their stories are not written by their own hands. Prince and Truth's narratives suggest the presence of a consistent and sustained spiritual legacy that informed the lives of blacks in America—it is not insignificant that their transcribers would record a cultural cosmology that echoed that of black women writing their own narratives. The similar African carryovers in Prince and Truth's transcribed narratives and those spiritual narratives written by their black female contemporaries demonstrate a continuity across genres. Alternatively, however, this continuity is also evident in the Christian discourse that dictates the current of both slave and spiritual narratives. In both genres, the authors/subjects are bound by a prevailing and anticipated narrative of spiritual awakening that required a structured tale of one's emergence from spiritual darkness into light—that light in early American literature was synonymous with Christian conversion. While these women were telling their own stories, they were bound by cultural ideas and conventions that alienated and discounted the existence and the experiences of nonwhites. Black experience could be recognized as valid and worthy only when it could be framed in the discourse of whiteness—and in the case of the spiritual, whiteness was constructed out of a EuroAmerican interpretation of Christianity.

Early black authors—men and women—found themselves engaged in a constant struggle against a lexicon of self-denigration. By the mid-nineteenth century, however, the emerging black novel would pave the way for greater latitude in this discourse battle. An outgrowth of the slave narrative, the African American novel provided black authors a wider lens through which they could view and thus imagine themselves and their possibilities. As a fictional medium, the novel allowed black writers creative space—rather than being restricted to narratives of "truthful" events, authors could recreate and reimagine events, experiences, and people. This authorial control allowed writers greater control in navigating the intent of their literary productions. By ostensibly removing themselves from their narratives, black authors could explore unchartered and sometimes unsanctioned territories while minimizing the risk of personal indictment. The expansion of black writing into the novel did not occur as a distinct literary event—the black novel emerged as a fusion of genres that included the spiritual/conversion narrative, sentimental fiction, and the slave narrative. The slave narrative or autobiography, itself a fusion of sentimental, spiritual, and travel narrative conventions, has been identified by Carla Peterson as the foundation of the black novel. Peterson specifically identifies Harriet E. Wilson's *Our Nig* (1859) and Harriet Jacobs's *Incidents* (1860) as novelized autobiographies (*Doers of the Word* 146). Wilson and Jacobs's works represent the fusion of autobiography and fiction that marked early black fiction. While Wilson tells a story based on her life, Jacobs tells her life story, fictionalizing names and places, and perhaps taking some literary license in telling the story. Wilson's narrative is illustrative of a novel based on the life of a real person; alternatively, Jacobs's narrative is autobiography (the presumed truthful account of one's life) that is weaved with fiction, and both represent the beginnings of the African American novel—fictionalized autobiography.

Until Henry Louis Gates's recent discovery and posthumous publication of *The Bondwoman's Narrative*, an 1850s autobiographical novel by an obscure African American woman, Hannah Crafts, Wilson's *Our Nig* was the earliest known extant work of this genre. The date of the Crafts manuscript cannot be determined with certainty, but Gates estimates that it was written in the 1850s and may be the first novel written by a black woman. Like Harriet E. Wilson, Hannah Crafts is not a figure of notoriety, but her narrative adds to contemporary study of the emerging nineteenth-century fictional imagination of black women writers. Crafts's narrative is, therefore, included in this chapter's focus on these early fictional milestones. Along with the writings of Crafts, Wilson, and Jacobs, I consider Elizabeth Keckley's 1868 memoir, *Behind the Scenes*, an account of her years as seamstress to President Lincoln's wife, Mary Todd Lincoln. Keckley narrates both the autobiographical account of her slavery-to-freedom journey and the concurrent story of Mary Todd Lincoln's White House years. Although she gained her freedom years before the war finalized the emancipation of America's slave population, Keckley's story is told by one looking back at a historical moment. Unlike Crafts, Wilson, and Jacobs, who write during the prewar period, Keckley writes in the early aftermath of the war—those early years when blacks harbored high hopes of becoming equal members of the larger society. Hence, Keckley speaks rather candidly about the subject of her narrative— Mary Todd Lincoln. While Keckley proclaims that her purpose is to set the record straight and redeem Mrs. Lincoln concerning the public scandal that followed her in the aftermath of her husband's death, Keckley instead paints a picture of a literary antagonist whose shortcomings underscore the heroine's (Keckley's) exemplary character.

A year after Keckley's 1868 publication of *Behind the Scenes*, Frances E. W. Harper published the series novel *Minnie's Sacrifice*. Published over a period of months in the black periodical the *Christian Recorder*, *Minnie's Sacrifice* is the fictional tale of two black children born into slavery, but transferred north and raised as white. While the novel is a telling commentary on the ambiguity of race, it does not contribute significantly to the focus of this study. Harper tells us very little of black spirituality in this work, in large part because for more than half of the narrative, the main characters, Minnie and Louis, live outside the black community. In fact, it is not until chapter 18 of a twenty-chapter narrative that Minnie and Louis, having been told that they are in fact black, settle in a southern town where they live among and serve the population of newly freed blacks. For two chapters we see Minnie and Louis living as blacks. It is during this period that the narrator provides a brief look at religion among southern blacks. This is revealed through testimonials of black women in the community who convey to Minnie the stories of their spiritual trials. These stories confirm the place of Christianity in the experiences of these ex-slaves. While Minnie has been raised in a pious Quaker family, she realizes that this community of suffering blacks holds a rich spiritual legacy. So impressed by their stories, she confesses, "I can't teach these people religion, I must learn from them" (84). Harper does not reveal what Minnie might have learned, for Minnie dies shortly after this revelation, and the novel concludes in the next chapter. Harper hints that Minnie has discovered something different and special in the religion of southern blacks, but again the novel ends with only this hint.

Hannah Crafts's narrative is a fitting start to a study of black spirituality in African American women's novels. If Crafts's work is as Gates suggests the first novel by a black woman, it stands as a landmark in that regard. However, the work has greater implications because it was not published. In his introduction to the text, Gates explains this peculiar significance:

> Holograph, or handwritten, manuscripts by blacks in the nineteenth century are exceedingly rare . . . . to my knowledge no holograph manuscripts survive for belletristic works, such as novels, or for the slave narratives, even by such bestselling authors as Frederick Douglass, Frances Ellen Watkins Harper, or William Wells Brown. And because most of the slave narratives and works of fiction published before the end of the Civil War were edited, published, and distributed by members of the abolitionist movement, scholars have long debated the extent of authorship and degree of originality of many of these works. . . here we could encounter the unadulterated "voice" of the fugitive slave herself, exactly as she wrote it. (xiii)

As an "unadulterated voice" of slave experience, Crafts allows entry into the world of slave culture through a discourse from within: "Hannah Crafts writes the way we can imagine black people talked to—and about—one another when white auditors were not around, and not the way abolitionists thought they talked, or black authors thought they should talk or wanted white readers to believe they talked. This is a voice we have rarely, if ever, heard before" (xxiv). The tension between African spirituality and Christianity in Crafts's narrative is especially informative given the absence of editorial intrusions that influenced the voice of early published black authors. Crafts's work then can help us better understand the layers of spiritual discourse and practice in nineteenth-century black culture. She provides a point of reference from which we can better decipher sites of subversion and sites of submersion in black spiritual discourse. Her uncensored narrative suggests that, although informed by outside voices, her published contemporaries still offer a representative account of the dynamics of the spiritual in African American society. In her tale of a slave woman's flight to freedom, Crafts reveals the complex dynamic of African practices and beliefs that found legitimacy through the language of Christianity.

While Henry Louis Gates, Jr., refers to Hannah Crafts's narrative as a novel, Crafts claims to offer a "record of plain unvarnished facts" (Preface). She adds that "[b]eing the truth it [her narrative] makes no pretensions to romance, and relating events as they occurred it has no especial reference to a moral." Crafts does not explicitly identify her work as autobiography; however, the subtitle and the narrative voice suggests autobiography. Crafts's full title, *The Bondwoman's Narrative by Hannah Crafts, a Fugitive Slave Recently Escaped from North Carolina*, identifies her as author, and the first person voice of the narrator named Hannah suggests that author and subject are the same. As Gates has reported, however, he has been unable to confirm the oneness of author and subject or to definitively identify the author. Other noted scholars in African American literature have echoed Gates in his acknowledgement of the narrative's autobiographical and fictional qualities.[2] Crafts's narrative can be likened to Harriet Jacobs and Harriet Wilson's works—autobiographics that tell the story of bondage and freedom with greater literary license than spiritual narratives. Crafts's narrative moves outside the anticipated slave narrative account of the protagonist's journey to freedom. She weaves layers of stories: in the backdrop of the central narrative of Hannah's enslavement and liberation are subplots that follow the trials of other key charatcers.[3] In particular, the curse of the slaveholding DeVincent family and their portended demise and the tragic story of Lizzy are sustained plots that parallel the central slavery-to-freedom plot. Filled with biblical allusions and repeated credits to providence, these interwoven tales hang together in a master narrative that validates Christianity as the protagonist's spiritual center. Throughout the tale, Crafts openly criticizes what she deems the superstitious inclinations of slaves, and she concurrently heralds Christianity as the path to spiritual salvation. Despite her professions of Christian faith, however, Crafts's words reveal a protaganist who is not entirely uninfluenced by an African spiritual legacy.

Crafts prefaces a number of her chapters with biblical passages that hint at the central theme in the chapter. Her narrative begins with a quote from the biblical text "Song of Solomon": "Look not upon me because I am black: because the sun hath looked upon me" (5).[4] While Crafts will describe a slave society divided along intraracial and class lines, her allusion to the speaker's proclamation of blackness in "Song of Solomon" underscores her ultimate understanding that despite internal divisions and stations, slaves were a people bound by their common experience and their social identity. She describes herself as mulatto and distinguishes herself as a house servant, but she recognizes that "the African blood in [her] veins" would forever limit her possibilities (5–6). Solomon, one of the bible's most celebrated kings, cannot escape his connection to blackness; similarly, Hannah, who is literate and cultured, cannot escape. Although she finds herself inescapably bound to blackness, Hannah attempts to distinguish herself from what she deems the unlearned and uncultured mass of field slaves. In addition to the priority that she awards literacy and domestic labor, Hannah also identifies spirituality as a measure of social station. She considers herself superior to the larger number of illiterate slaves who work in the fields and submit to beliefs and practices that whites dismiss as superstition or merriment. This is illustrated early in the narrative with Hannah's account of an elderly white couple who taught her to read. Her remembrance of this couple is not simply their contribution to her quest for literacy, but also their Christian influence: "They gave me insight into many things. They cultivated my moral nature. They led me to the foot of the Cross. Sometimes in the evening while the other slaves were enjoying the banjo and the dance I would steal away to hold sweet converse with them" (10). Hannah links morality to Christianity, and in turn, infers that the slaves's non-Christian status is tied to their less moral nature—evident in their music and dancemaking. Ironically, Hannah's escape from slavery is not precipitated primarily by an unquenchable thirst for freedom, but rather her horror at being thrown into the company of field slaves. After Hannah's mistress accuses her of disloyalty, she banishes Hannah to field labor and marriage to one among that class. This is for Hannah a punishment of the severest kind: she submits that corporal punishment or sale at a public slave auction would have been more acceptable (206). She decides to flee rather than "be driven in to the fields beneath the eye and lash of the brutal overseer, and those miserable huts, with their promiscuous crowds of dirty, obscene and degraded objects" (207).

Just as early black women's spiritual narratives invariably included denunciations of or silences regarding practices and beliefs associated with Africanity, Hannah Crafts's narrator attempts to affirm her humanity by distancing herself from all that is perceived African. However, not unlike early black women authors of spiritual narratives, Crafts is unable to construct a protagonist who is wholly free of pre-Christian origins. In particular, the narrator's sustained preoccupation with superstition reveals her inability to break with what she defines the unfounded beliefs of an unlearned and non-Christian people. Hannah's numerous parallel constructions between her experiences and biblical accounts and her repeated references to providence as the guiding force in her fortunes signal her Christian predilection; however, the interwoven tale of the curse of Sir Clifford and his Lindendale descendants looms larger than her timely expressions of Christian allegiance. While she credits providence for leading her always to a safe recourse, Hannah weaves a more integrated tale of Sir Clifford's misdeed and the resultant disaster for succeeding inhabitants of the Lindendale estate. It is the disaster that besets Mr. Vincent of Lindendale that both ties the three main female protagonists and influences their fortunes. Mr. Vincent, the last descendant of Sir Clifford to reside at the plantation, meets a tragic end that has been anticipated since the curse launched by Sir Clifford's faithful but ill-treated slave, generations earlier. Strung from the stately linden tree after disobeying her master, Rose, a lifelong servant to Sir Clifford's family, utters the curse that will for generations haunt the inhabitants of Lindendale: "I will hang here till I die as a curse to this house, and I will come here after I am dead to prove its bane. In sunshine and shadow, by day and by night I will brood over this tree, and weigh down its branches, and when death, or sickness, or misfortune is to befall the family ye may listen for ye will assuredly hear the creaking of its limbs" (25).

It is not, then, by any intervention of a watchful, providential Christian power that the persecuted servant is comforted, but rather the mystical hand of nature. As witness to atrocities and medium of prophecy, the linden tree highlights the symbolic role of the tree in many African belief systems. Alexis Brooks-DeVita explains that the tree as "symbol of life, death, and afterlife" can be traced from continental African societies to diasporic African communities (*Mythatypes* 33). Just as the dying servant portends, the linden tree will survive as an omen of ill fortunes, and Hannah's narrative will repeatedly return to this tree as the signal of misfortunes to come. In addition to its significance as the symbol of nature's mystical hand in human experience, Brooks-DeVita explains in a subsequent work that the tree as mythical figure also connects to the recurring construct of "the woman-as-tree symbol of spiritual motherhood" in black women's writings ("The Tree of Terror" 6). In this sense, the linden tree stands as the avenger mother figure, watching and waiting for the fruition of Rose's curse.

Even with the anticipated mirthful event of Mr. Vincent's marriage in the opening chapter of the narrative, "the linden creaked and swayed its branches to the fitful gusts" (17), hinting at the yet unveiled, but imminent tragedy. That Mr. Vincent's young bride is in truth one of African ancestry becomes a secret that binds her to Hannah and Lizzy, her two handmaids. Just as the creaking linden foreshadows, the newlyweds share only a fleeting moment of bliss. Threatened with exposure, the young mistress flees with Hannah. Hannah survives their eventual capture; however, unable to escape the curse of Lindendale, Mr. Vincent and his mistress die. With Mr. Vincent dead, Lizzy falls into the hands of the next inhabitant of Lindendale. While Mr. Cosgrove is not a descendant of Sir Clifford, he nevertheless falls victim to the curse. Accidentally causing the death of his estranged wife, he lives in unending torture. But Cosgrove's misfortune marks the end of the curse and brings us to the closing episodes of the novel. Some time after the death of Mrs. Cosgrove, "the Linden with its creaking branches had bowed to the axe, and . . . great changes had been wrought inside the house as well as out" (193–194). The most defining change was that "Sir Clifford's portrait and its companions of both sexes, had been publicly exposed in the market and

knocked down to the highest bidder" (194). It is ironic that the curse of the
heartless slavemaster should finally end at public auction. In the arena that
slaves are bought and sold and stripped of their humanity, Sir Clifford and
his long line of plantation aristocrats are reduced to negotiated property. Like
the linden tree, the curse lives to fruition. With this resolution, the novel
quickly winds down with the final five chapters relating the story of Hannah's successful flight to freedom.

The overriding tale in *Bondwoman's Narrative* is the protagonist's journey from bondage to freedom; however, among the novel's numerous thematic layers is the tension between Africanity and western/white civilization.
Crafts's protagonist aligns herself with the latter, particularly as it is manifested in white religiosity, and she offers her Christian allegiance as evidence
of her tie to what she deems the culturally superior white world. Although
Crafts navigates the narrative through Anglo Christian discourse, she nevertheless evinces markers of Africanity that also surface in black women's
spiritual narratives. The curse of Lindendale that is so central to the novel's
course is predicated on the presumption that the spirit and carnal worlds are
interconnected and that there is a living spirit in all of God's creations. While
curses abound in biblical stories, God is master and maker of curses, and
from its beginnings, American Christianity has condemned those who would
presume to possess such a divine power. In countless African societies, however, the belief that certain humans under certain conditions can possess the
power to curse and remove curses is maintained. The curse that the dying,
persecuted slave metes out to the inheritors of Lindendale echoes an African
spiritual legacy that deems humans capable of dispensing God's will.

Traditional African notions regarding the nature of death, including the
belief that the living have a responsibility to the dead and the dying, also
surface in Crafts's novel. Not unlike African spiritual belief in the transformative human spirit, Crafts represents the human spirit as an entity that is not
bound by death or the physical world. Again, this is exemplified by Rose,
whose reach extends beyond the grave. For generations, her spirit is resurrected in the creaking linden tree, reminding all of Lindendale's horrific
legacy. Even the portraits of deceased Vincents suggest that the spirits are yet
alive. Hannah notes as she muses the long line of De Vincents that their
portraits seem to come to life, revealing the personalities behind the painted
faces (16). As she stands among the portraits for some time, Hannah becomes transformed herself: she recalls

> there surrounded by mysterious associations I seemed suddenly to have grown
> old, to have entered a new world of thoughts, and feelings and sentiments. I
> was not a slave with these pictured memorials of the past. They could not
> enforce drudgery, or condemn me on account of my color to a life of servitude.
> As their companion I could think and speculate. In their presence my mind

seemed to run riotous and exult in its freedom as a rational being, and one destined for something higher and better than this world can afford. (17)

Hannah's transformation is reminiscent of spiritual transformations that can occur between the living and the dead in such African-rooted rituals as ring dances and voodoo spirit conjurations.

Crafts represents a literary imagination that is not confined by rules of physics—the dead and the living are not disconnected entities. Death does not mark an end—only a transformation, and as in traditional African spirituality, the disposition of the dead and the relationship between the living and the dead have much to do with whether there was proper treatment of the spirit journeying from the carnal world. The importance of death vigils and burial ceremonies in African societies is no less evident in African American culture; hence, Hannah's grief over the absence of a proper burial for her mistress echoes this African spiritual sensibility. While her mistress has been freed from the torment of slavery, her death and burial do not signal a peaceful resolution. Given her mistress's sudden and traumatic death, Hannah notes that she could have been better reconciled to the tragedy had she known "the place of her burial" (112). She maintains that "[i]t would have been so comforting to associate the idea of her last resting place with some green spot overswept by soft shadows and adorned with wild flowers" (112). Hannah is left instead with the haunting memory of her mistress's sufferings in this world and her horrific entry into the next. In a similar experience, she again mourns the death of a fellow female fugitive whose death occurs without ceremony and community. Hannah's anguish illustrates Elizabeth D. Blum's argument that nineteenth-century black women maintained traditional African views about land and nature, particularly the belief that community extended beyond death (249). Gravesites were extensions of community, connecting the living to their history and their common ancestral bond. While Hannah dismisses much of slave ceremony as insincere, she nevertheless maintains that death marks "the hour which should be sacred to grief, and the highest and holiest emotions of the human race" (218). It is, then, a sacrilege that humans, innocent and decent, should be denied their most sacred moment in the material world.

The final two chapters of Crafts's narrative are prefaced with allusions to the Bible. Chapter 20, "Retribution," ties the death of the inhumane Mr. Trappe to the well-known biblical parable of sowing and reaping. Mr. Trappe's violent end cannot be easily mourned "[s]ince he that sows the wind, must reap the whirlwind" (236). The narrator implies that Mr. Trappe meets his deserved end through the workings of a divine system that ultimately metes out good to those who are good, and disaster to those who are not. William Andrews argues that in this respect, Crafts's narrative ultimately "confirm[s] that this heroine deserves all the wonderful, near miraculous, blessings that she receives at the end of the story" (16). As Andrews points out, Crafts's unrealistic happy-ever-after ending is not consistent with typical mid-nineteenth century slave narratives; however, the narrative is consistent with mainstream women's fiction of this period. The heroine, who has suffered and sacrificed for the well being of others throughout the tale, is rewarded as she has foreshadowed in the preface, because "the hand of Providence . . . giv[es] to the righteous the reward of their works." While the hand of providence plays out for the protagonist, this overriding theme fails so many other characters. The old slave woman hung by her master, Hannah's mistress who is hunted to her death by Mr. Trappe, the fugitive siblings Jacob and his sister who travel with Hannah but die before reaching freedom—these are self-sacrificing, innocent victims who find no just reward in this life. Perhaps, they meet their fatal ends because, unlike Hannah, they failed to accept Christianity and thus are not under the protection of providence. Hannah does not reveal the spiritual state of her mistress or of the persecuted slave, Rose; however, in the case of the runaway siblings that she joins for a short while during her escape, she emphasizes their rejection of Christianity. When Jacob expresses doubt that he will ever know freedom, Hannah asks does he not have faith in God and the heaven that follows this life. Jacob's lack of faith leaves Hannah saddened that "in his trials, and difficulties he was unaware of the greatest source of abiding comfort" (217). In a similar dialog with Jacob's dying sister, Hannah asks the young woman whether she has ever prayed. She explains to Hannah that as a child she prayed, but after recognizing the slavemaster's self-serving purpose in teaching slaves to pray, she refused to submit to such deceit. Hannah expresses her pity for "the poor benighted soul to whom the sweetest influences of religion had become gall and wormwood" (220).

Hannah's expression of regret for her dying, unenlightened companion seems both an illustration of her compassionate nature and a confirmation of Christianity's preeminence. She is grieved that her companion faces death without the promise of Christian salvation in the next world. But the primacy Hannah awards the blessing of the Christian hereafter is compromised by her account of the young woman's dying moment. Although the young woman dies unconverted, she meets death with a vision of a liberating hereafter. Though unconverted, she has not been damned to a hopeless eternity. Instead, death reunites her with her mother and others in the spiritual world. She tells Hannah, "I hear them calling me. . . . I think one of them is my mother. It's time for me to go to her. . . . She looks happy and blessed" (220). This dying woman does not have the comfort of a death vigil with loved ones watching over as she transitions into the spiritual world; however, she is beckoned to a happy eternity by her dead mother and other spirits. As she dies, she sees a light that Hannah describes as "the sun of righteousness" (220). Hannah's use of the word sun may be likened to a commonly employed Christian pun, sun/son, that collapses the image of Jesus son of God with that of the celestial sun, the seemingly eternal light of the cosmos. Hannah's employment of a pun that ties the woman's death to Christian experience seems inconsistent since she has described this woman as unconverted. If, as America's nineteenth-century Christians typically believed, salvation comes only through Christian conversion, Hannah's dying companion cannot know the comfort of the son—Jesus—who guarantees Christians salvation at death. However, the young woman's vision of a light that she equates to the sun rising is consistent with traditional African worship of the sun as a god or powerful spiritual entity. The final vision of this dying slave is not then a promising hereafter born out of Christian salvation, but rather the bright light of eternity and union with the ancestors rooted in traditional African spirituality.

The unwavering rejection of Christianity espoused by Hannah's dying companion echoes a similar rejection by a nineteenth-century black heroine. Frado, Harriet E. Wilson's persecuted heroine, cannot give herself over to Christianity because she cannot disassociate this religion from the earthly inequity often propagated in its name. Just as Hannah Crafts's young persecuted heroine cannot separate Christianity from the cruelties inflicted by those claiming to be Christians, Wilson's protagonist cannot resolve this paradox. *Our Nig* ends with Frado alive but destitute, and though she has struggled to accept Christianity she never gives herself over fully. In an earlier published article, "Reworking the Conversion Narrative: Race and Christianity in *Our Nig*," I discuss in detail Frado's inability to realize a full Christian conversion. Christianity fails Frado, offering her no spiritual solace:

> She has been taught that true Christians give over concerns of the mortal world to thoughts of the hereafter. But Frado is not certain that heaven receives black souls, and even if blacks do go to heaven, Frado finds it difficult to imagine that their lot in heaven would be less painful than their sufferings on earth. Frado's doubts, then, leave her unable to profess a faith in Christianity, which only promises her in the afterlife more of the pain she has known in her mortal life. (West 19)

In contrast to the unconverted heroine in *Bondwoman's Narrative*, Frado, finding no solace in Christianity, is left with a spiritual void. Frado has no link to ancestors, no spiritual legacy passed from mother or community: in the absence of Christianity as a viable spiritual resource, Frado has only the rewards of the material world as potential sources of comfort. Thus, the novel's commentary on nineteenth-century America's racial and gendered discriminatory labor practices is apparent. In the absence of community, both Mag and Frado are forced into a marketplace that exploits women workers (Short 10).

Frado is born to Mag, a white mother who has been ostracized by the white community for her out-of-wedlock relationship. Their immoral behavior results in Mag's pregnancy and the delivery of an infant that dies soon after birth. Mag's alienation is sealed when she marries a black man, Jim, later giving birth to two mulatto children—Frado and an unnamed sibling whose fate is not revealed in the narrative. Not long after Jim's death, Mag and her male companion desert the children. Frado is left at the doorstep of the Bellmonts, a white family that take her in as a live-in servant. While she wins over members of the family who take an interest in her religious development, Mrs. Bellmont, the matriarch of the household, is unrelenting in her effort to remind Frado that she is in no way an equal in the household. When the pious Bellmont members attempt to guide Frado to Christian conversion, Mrs. Bellmont undermines their efforts. Mrs. Bellmont will not permit Frado to attend church: she has determined that "[r]eligion was not meant for niggers" (68). Frado's stanch Bellmont allies, the sickly son, James, and the spinster, Aunt Abby, take Frado to prayer meetings and counsel her in making the journey to conversion. Upon his death, James encourages Frado to continue in the path of Christian enlightenment: "Frado, if you will be a good girl, and love and serve God, it will be but a short time before we are in a heavenly home together. There will never be any sickness or sorrow there" (95). James's dying words cannot sustain Frado in the cruel reality of her existence. In a moment that proves pivotal in the narrative, Frado finally forsakes any hope in Christian deliverance: "Frado pondered: her mistress was a professor of religion; was she going to heaven? Then she did not wish to go. If she should be near James, even, she could not be happy with those fiery eyes watching her ascending path. She resolved to give over all thought of the future world, and strove daily to put her anxiety far from her" (104).

Shortly after this revelation, Frado halts an attack by Mrs. Bellmont, threatening that she will work for Mrs. Bellmont no longer if she strikes her again (105). Frado is not saved from Mrs. Bellmont's wrath by a providential intervention: it is only after she abandons the dream of heavenly salvation and turns to a material and pragmatic assessment of her own leverage that she is able to check Mrs. Bellmont's rage. From this moment, Frado's narrative of spiritual introspection ends and shifts into a narrative of personal, economic struggle. When Frado's servitude to Mrs. Bellmont ends, she enters adulthood independent but poor, and her subsequent years are spent in constant struggles to meet her financial needs, and later, the needs of her child also. With her husband dead, Frado is left to care for herself and child. Frado's story concludes with the narrator's assertion that God has thus far watched over her and that Frado's struggles should certainly move readers to her aid (130). The narrative itself does not bear out the narrator's conclusion, however. Frado's long suffering and unending financial uncertainty do not translate into a narrative of providential deliverance. Frado's life of destitution begins early and by the novel's end, she still faces a future with little promise of betterment. Having spent her growing years with no meaningful contact with a black community and with a constant feeling that she is an outsider in the white world where she resides, Frado finds no spiritual center. Unlike black protagonists who find consolation in African-rooted spirituality, Frado, the product of a culturally and spiritually isolated world, finally rejects a Christianity that she finds rooted in racist repression. Frado's rejection of Christianity leaves her disconnected and alone: she has no memory of and no tie to a black spirituality. Although she finds confidants and supporters among white women, Frado "is never . . . comfortable with white New England's Christian religion because of her experiences of its pervasive hypocrisy" (Ellis 87). Frado is always the charity case, never finding herself a member of the white Christian female fold that lends her aid and never establishing a connection to a community of black women.

In striking contrast to the isolation that defines Frado's existence, Harriet Jacobs tells the story of her slavery-to-freedom experience that comes to fruition only through the cumulative efforts of a community that extended across racial and social boundaries. In contrast to Frado, Jacobs's literary alias, Linda Brent, is never without a community. It is after a white gentleman friend of her family reveals to Linda Dr. Flint's plan to condemn her children to plantation slavery that she makes the hasty decision to flee. When she flees, her early successful evasion of Dr. Flint results from the joint effort of a neighboring white mistress and her trusted servant, Betty. Likewise, her voyage to freedom in the north is made possible through the planning and sacrifice of her Uncle Phillip and Peter, a friend whose loyalty stemmed from the friendship Linda's father had once shown him. At every turn, Linda survives overwhelming adversity through the hand of friendship and community. Unlike Frado, she finds white sympathizers who take decisive action to protect her, and unlike Frado, Linda is never without the assurance of contact with and the aid of fellow blacks. While clearly a narrative of the protagonist's journey to freedom, *Incidents* also tells a story of community and family in African American survival. Jacobs reports a slave experience that is connected as strongly to white southern ruling class as it is to the slave population that she is considered a member. The genealogical account that opens the narrative ties her more clearly to white ancestry than the victimized black slaves whose plight is to be revealed through the example of her experience. Jacobs opens the story with the declaration that she was born a slave, but she quickly shifts to a discussion of her personal ancestry—specifically the white southern upperclass. She tells us that both her parents were mulattoes, and that her maternal grandmother was the product of a slave mother and a South Carolina planter (3). While she draws no connections between her family and their African ancestry, she proudly tells of her family's white legacy. All are some shade of near-white complexion and are bright, loyal servants, highly respected by whites in the community.

Jacobs's enthusiastic acceptance of her family's ties to whiteness may seem a paradox in a narrative emphasizing the horrors of slavery and those who enslave others. If we consider, however, the importance of community in this work, Jacobs's link to whiteness is not altogether confounding. Jacobs reveals in her narrative the complexities of slave society. In particular, she shows that lines were not so clearly drawn between white and black, or those free and those enslaved. The lives of blacks and whites were in many circumstances intricately intertwined, and as Jacobs shows, blacks in search of freedom often reached their destinations by the joint efforts of blacks and whites. Jacobs's narrative captures the cultural gray area where the lives of blacks and whites were not so easily divided. This transfixed area of black and white highlights the reality of cultural development in America—the dynamic of diverse ethnic and racial groups encountering, responding to, and sometimes aiding one another. For both blacks and whites, cultural intersections often present opportunities to borrow and reshape ideas and practices. Jacobs's narrative demonstrates again that for blacks in America, cultural encounters with whites too often require blacks to cloak themselves in whiteness. Jacobs's emphasis on her white ancestry has much to do with legitimating her humanity. The near-whiteness—in both complexion and ancestry—of Jacobs and her family members makes their suffering more troublesome. Jacobs emphasizes the similarity between her family and nineteenth-century middle class white America. Though slaves, her family comes from one of the fine families of the south. They are a family of skilled and industrious workers—none are the product of the grueling field slave class. Her father was a carpenter who was often sought out to consult on extraordinary projects, her grandmother was so intelligent that she became central to the running of her master's household, and her Uncle Benjamin was so intelligent that at age ten he drew a high price when sold (5–6). Blacks in the nineteenth-century south were not heralded for their expertise as tradesmen or their efficiency in household economy or their usefulness for their intelligence. These were qualities that signaled white middleclassness, and Jacobs's use of these images to describe her family highlights their humanity and their equal place among whites.

Community and family, both black and white, are central to Jacobs's cosmos. While she offers no account of her African lineage, Jacobs paints the picture of an African American community that is protective and self-sacrificing. This community extends beyond her southern home, for when she arrives north and meets with racism, she finds comfort and support among black northerners who offer aid to new arrivals like her. When she and her companion, Fanny, arrive in Philadelphia, they are directed to a black minister, who takes them home where he and his wife welcome them until they journey further northward (159–160). When Linda arrives a stranger in New York, she is not without friends. She immediately contacts a friend from the south who helps her arrange a meeting with her daughter, Ellen. She encounters others from her southern home, and she and her daughter share in a reunion that gives her courage in her new place: she reports, "there was quite a company of us, all from my grandmother's neighborhood. These friends gathered round me and questioned me eagerly. They laughed, they cried, and they shouted. They thanked God that I had got away from my persecutors and was safe on Long Island" (165). Similarly, Linda's reunion with her brother is a reminder of the enduring bonds between those who shared the horrors of slavery. She notes that upon seeing her brother after years of separation, she was pleased that there was no loss of affection: "His old feelings of affection for me and Ellen were as lively as ever. There are no bonds so strong as those which are formed by suffering together" (170). At the conclusion of the narrative Linda is working in the home of Mrs. Bruce, the kind employer who settled her dilemma by purchasing freedom for Linda and her two children. Mrs. Bruce has risked legal persecution to hide Linda from those who would return her to slavery under the decree of The Fugitive Slave Law. While she does not find herself in a home of her own at the story's end, Jacobs is content that this is God's will. She further submits that "[l]ove, duty, [and] gratitude keep her at the side of her faithful friend: she confesses, "[I]t is a privilege to serve her who pities my oppressed people, and who has bestowed the inestimable boon of freedom on me and my children" (201). Linda's role as servant to Mrs. Bruce and the newness of their friendship does not allow for the kind of relationship that she shares with her friends from her southern home. Linda does not engage in the kind of laughter, tears, and shouting with Mrs. Bruce that she describes in her reunion with her southern friends.

From the onset, Jacobs describes her protagonist as both in and apart from the larger slave community. Again, family lineage and class distinguish Linda from the larger population of unskilled, illiterate field slaves. Jacobs emphasizes this distinction throughout the narrative; however, the narrator's few but telling departures into African-rooted spirituality reveal her common cosmological roots with the larger slave community. In keeping with what had by the mid-1800s become an emerging tradition of an embedded spiritual narrative in black women's writings, Jacobs interjects a secondary narrative of spiritual enlightenment. As a child, Linda learns the tenets of Christianity through the teaching of her mistress and her grandmother. She recalls having to bite the bitter pill of Christian hypocrisy when she learned that her deceased mistress had bequeathed her to a family member: "My mistress had taught me the precepts of God's Word: 'Thou shalt love thy neighbor as thyself.' 'Whatsoever ye would that men should do unto you, do ye even unto them.' But I was her slave, and I suppose she did not recognize me as

her neighbor" (8). Linda found that even her grandmother, whom she ad-
mired as a determined and self-sufficient woman, had been deluded into the
presumption that slaves must accept their lot. She explains, "[m]ost earnestly
did she strive to make us [children and grandchildren] feel that it was the will
of God that He had seen fit to place us under such circumstances; and though
it seemed hard, we ought to pray for contentment" (17). But Linda will not
concede to her grandmother's request, and she repeatedly questions the
Christianity of slave masters who suppose themselves faithful Christians
while they exploit and terrorize blacks.

Linda cannot accept her grandmother's Christian obeisance. This difference between the two, along with Marthy's unrealistic demand for Linda's
chastity, signals a strain in their relationship. Critic Gloria T. Randle argues
that the tension is so severe that Marthy fails to function as a meaningful
mother figure for the orphaned Linda (46). While the seriousness of their
differences cannot be dismissed, Marthy is ultimately a central and powerful
influence in Linda's life. She is reminiscent of "the position elders held in
many African communities," and her "marked intelligence, sense of self, and
creative abilities afford her a central role in the community and in Linda's
life (Beardslee 39). Marthy is initially harsh with Linda when she learns that
Linda is pregnant out of wedlock; however, the two are reconciled and it is
with Marthy's sacrifice and protection that Linda successfully hides from Dr.
Flint and eventually makes her way to freedom. Although Marthy is reluctant
to have Linda escape to the North, it is her determination that her family be
free that influences her children and grandchildren to seek their freedom:
"although Marthy fails in her efforts to purchase her children's freedom, her
undaunted attempts to do so instill in Linda the African concern for the next
generation's ability to define themselves while keeping the ancestors'
dreams, visions, and overall culture alive" (Beardslee 39). Linda can both
reject her grandmother's blind Christian allegiance and see her as a maternal
role model: while Marthy "problematically upholds the slave system by
preaching passive Christian values . . . she empowers Linda with a living,
independent mothering example" (Blackford 323). In all matters central to
the survival and health of family and community, Marthy does not fail.

Throughout the narrative, Linda's grandmother is represented as mother
figure in the community and devout Christian, but the overall failure of
Christianity in the slave south is also underscored. Jacobs's narrator maintains a "doubt and ambivalence" that highlights "a critical ideological tension
between the experience of African Americans and those of whites within the
American Christian tradition (Carson 53). Jacobs shows the hypocrisy of
white Christians through their unChristian behavior, but it is through the
discourse of folk culture that she articulates divine retribution. Two episodes
in the narrative serve as explicit examples. The first is the case of a local
slaveholder who had been so cruel to his slaves that when he died, "his

shrieks and groans were so frightful that they appalled his own friends. His last words were, 'I am going to hell; bury my money with me'" (47). Jacobs explains further that

> [a]fter death his eyes remained open. To press the lids down, silver dollars were laid on them. These were buried with him. From this circumstance, a rumor went abroad that his coffin was filled with money. Three times his grave was opened, and his coffin taken out. The last time, his body was found on the ground, and a flock of buzzards were pecking at it. He was again interred, and a sentinel set over his grave. The perpetrators were never discovered. (47)

Jacobs's account of the slaveholder's death echoes a number of African American precepts about death. The horrifying death that he experiences is consistent with traditional African belief that the evil do not leave the world peacefully. In contrast to the death scene of Jacobs's poor, maltreated aunt who dies with the blessing of her mother standing vigil, the slaveholder's wealth cannot save him from the reckoning he faces at death's door. Although Aunt Nancy suffered in life, she died happy, and in the tradition of African burial, she was given "a mighty grand funeral" (145–146). The community has acknowledged Aunt Nancy's life in the material world and they have given her over to her journey in the spirit world. There is no presentiment of doom for Aunt Nancy at death; however, that the dead slaveholder must have his eyes forcibly shut is a dreadful omen. In African American folk culture to die with one's eyes open is an ominous sign. In this case it signals the miserable state under which the slaveholder will reside in death. The mutilation of his dead body symbolizes his eternal wretched state.

In another account of a slaveholder's death, Jacobs reveals a story of retribution that is again grounded in an African, rather than a Christian cosmological view. Through a chance encounter, Linda, on an errand for Mrs. Bruce, recognizes a young man, Luke, who has also escaped from her southern hometown to New York. Luke shares with Linda the story of his escape and explains how he came into the money that will carry him safely to Canada:

> I'd bin workin all my days fur dem cussed whites, an got no pay but kicks and cuffs. So I tought dis nigger had a right to money nuff to bring him to de Free States. Massa Henry he lib till ebery body vish him dead; an ven he did die, I knowed de debbil would hab him, an vouldn't vant him to bring his money 'long too. So I tuk some of his bills, and put 'em in de pocket of his ole trousers. An ven he was buried, dis nigger ask fur dem ole trousers, an dey gub 'em to me. . . . you see I didn't steal it; dey gub it to me. (193)

The masterful tricksterism on Luke's part is obvious, but what we may overlook is the message of spiritual reckoning. Despite his bedridden state,

Luke's master had been a tyrant: Jacobs recalls that when she fled for freedom, "poor Luke [was] still chained to the bedside of this cruel and disgust-
ing wretch" (192). Although his master had ruled him in life, in death his
master had been defeated. Luke's victory had not occurred by the hand of
providence, rather it was through Luke's own craftiness that his freedom was
secured. The blow that he deals his master in death is born out of a traditional
African view that one's character in death is merely a carryover from life.
Hence, this slaveowner, who had been a tyrant in life, would be no less so in
death. While alive, his cruelty had caused those around him to hope for his
death; therefore, in death, there is no community to honor him. For the cruel
slaveholder whose dead body was ravaged by vultures, and Luke's master,
whose ragged remains become Luke's passage to freedom, a deserved end is
realized. As Jacobs reveals in the account of Aunt Nancy's death, slave
communities found value in the meanest of existences. The community's
indifference at death, as in the case of the cruel slaveowners, signals a life
that has had no value and a soul that will go unremembered and unrespected
into the next world.

Just as treatment of the dead was central to the community in traditional
African society, slaves showed considerable regard for the dead. The contrast
between Jacobs's account of the death of the slavemasters and the death of
members of the slave community highlight this cultural carryover. Again, the
death of her Aunt Nancy is a tribute to the meager suffering slave, whose life,
in the eyes of the slave community, is no less important than that of the
wealthy, respected planter. This is especially evident in the case of Aunt
Nancy whose family refused the special offer of her mistress to bury her in
the master's family lot. Instead, Linda's grandmother insisted that her daughter be buried with her family, and Linda's Uncle Phillip sought permission to
pay for his sister's funeral (146). It was no small matter that Uncle Phillip, a
slave himself, felt so compelled to pay for his sister's funeral. Recalling the
importance of burial rites among diasporic Africans, it is clear that Uncle
Phillip's determination stems from a tradition that requires family and community to give their utmost efforts to the care of the dead. Such care is
imperative, for the dead look out for the living. This relationship is further
exemplified with Linda's visit to her parents' graves before she embarks
upon her escape. Given the importance awarded the dead in African diasporic communities, "Jacobs's decision to visit the burial site of her parents may
indicate an African sensibility of ancestor reverence" (Connor 52).

The dead are ever present and ever connected to the fortunes of the living.
Jacobs's visit thus confirms that she has made the right decision. Here, "at
the graves of [her] poor parents, in the burying-ground of the slaves," Jacobs
seals her vow to save her children from slavery (90). Jacobs leaves the
graveyard renewed in her conviction after being guided by the spirits that
reside there:

> I knelt down and kissed them [the graves of her parents], and poured forth a
> prayer to God for guidance and support in the perilous step I was about to take.
> As I passed the wreck of the old meeting house, where, before Nat Turner's
> time, the slaves had been allowed to meet for worship, I seemed to hear my
> father's voice come from it, bidding me not to tarry till I reached freedom or
> the grave. I rushed on with renovated hopes. My trust in God had been
> strengthened by that prayer among the graves. (90–91)

It is no small matter that facing an overwhelming decision for herself and her
children, Jacobs prays to God—the God of Christianity who she accepts as
supreme. Ironically, however, Jacobs seeks God out in "the burying ground
of the slaves," a sanctuary that connects her to the spirits of parents and
ancestors.

Though she avows herself a Christian and offers customary credits to
providence, no where does Christianity serve as the impetus for divine revelation or reckonings. The supernatural world of slave culture informs Jacobs's presumed Anglo-rooted cosmology, a fact made apparent by Jacobs's
recollection of a vision she experiences at the time her children are freed
from Mr. Flint. To free the children of Jacobs's master, the children's father,
Mr. Sands, arranges to have a speculator purchase them. Mr. Sands and the
speculator agree that he will then sell the children to Mr. Sands. It is a risky
scheme, for if the speculator decides not to sell, Mr. Sands has then turned
the children over for trading. Because Jacobs is in hiding, she cannot be
informed right away on the outcome. During the interval that Jacobs waits
without word, she has an experience that she is willing to share, but not
before warning readers that they might "think it illustrates the superstition of
slaves" (107). Hidden away in the home of a friend, Jacobs sits by a window
thinking of her children. She recalls,

> [a] band of serenaders were under the window, playing "Home, sweet, home."
> I listened till the sounds did not seem like music, but like the moaning of
> children. It seemed as if my heart would burst. I rose from my sitting posture,
> and knelt. A streak of moonlight was on the floor before me, and in the midst
> of it appeared the forms of my two children. They vanished; but I had seen
> them distinctly. Some will call it a dream, others a vision. (107–108)

Jacobs was shaken by the vision, misreading it as a sign that something
terrible had happened to her children. She is relieved to learn that the plan
was executed as designed, and her children were free of Mr. Flint. Though
Jacobs admits she knows not what to make of the vision, she admits that it
was a powerful experience. While she allows readers to dismiss the experience as mere slave superstition, Jacobs, will not herself draw that conclusion.
Perplexed, she can only admit that she has no explanation to offer. This
unsettling experience points at the incongruity between western and African

cosmologies. Having declared herself Christian and presuming herself free of ties to African spirituality, Jacobs cannot find words to frame her African experience for her western audience. On the surface, western religiosity prevails in this negotiation of experience and language: allowing readers to reduce her experience to superstition, Jacobs maintains nineteenth-century Anglo Christian presumptions of religious authority. Supernatural experience that cannot be explained through Christian discourse can only be read as superstition, which for Jacobs's contemporary readers meant the childlike beliefs of inferior/nonwhite peoples.

The overtures to Christianity that we find in Jacobs's narrative are reminiscent of Hannah Crafts's narrative, and Jacobs, like Crafts feels compelled to distinguish herself from the larger slave population. Jacobs and Crafts find validation in their internalized Anglo ideals; however, it is their deference to the dominant culture that renders their detours into African-rooted cultural experience the more striking. This is exemplified in the contrast between their outward professions of Christian faith and their inadvertent awe of superstition. It is further evident in their memory of African-rooted beliefs in the primacy of community and family and the mystical connection between the living and the dead. Notwithstanding these shows of Africanity, Jacobs and Crafts maintain Christianity as the defining spiritual voice of their narratives, a literary construct that by the end of the nineteenth century becomes a common denominator in black women's novels. Elizabeth Keckley's *Behind the Scenes* (1868), a post–Civil War memoir of her time in the Lincoln White House, exemplifies the continuation of this construct in the post-bellum narratives of black women.

Keckley's text can be examined for both its break with and continuation of anticipated trappings of the antebellum slave narrative. In keeping with its antebellum predecessor, Keckley's narrative gives the account of her slavery-to-freedom journey with the concurrent tale of her struggle for self-improvement. With its detailed account of Keckley's success as a respected dressmaker, the narrative has also been read as a commentary on gender and race in the American labor market.[5] Given Keckley's focus on the affairs of the Lincoln household and Mary Todd Lincoln's fall from grace after the president's death, the text seems to offer dual biographies. In this respect Keckley breaks from the tradition of black authors who indirectly gaze whiteness: her observations and judgments of her white mistress/boss are detailed, direct and candid. Keckley's depiction of Mrs. Lincoln is not restricted to that of one subordinated: emphasizing her independence and the paradoxical support that Mrs. Lincoln and other white friends have elicited from her, Keckley posits a gaze of authority. With respect to the narrative's treatment of Christianity, however, Keckley does not stray from tradition. Keckley's critiques of Christianity are framed in an indictment of the slave-

holder's Christianity while Christianity, in general, is represented as the religious foundation of the protagonist.

In the fashion of antebellum slave narratives, Keckley calls into question
the Christian convictions of those who hold her in bondage. Early in the
narrative, she highlights the hypocrisy of both her master and his wife, showing them to be less than models of Christian compassion: "Mr. Burwell, he
who preached the love of Heaven, who glorified the precepts and examples
of Christ, who expounded the Holy Scriptures Sabbath after Sabbath from
the pulpit, when Mr. Bingham refused to whip me any more, was urged by
his wife to punish me himself" (37). Mr. Burwell desires to break Keckley of
what he deems her misplaced pride; however, it is Keckley, who, in the end
breaks Burwell and his wife. Refusing to submit to their beatings, Keckley
endures until finally Mr. Burwell's "hard heart" is subdued and he asks her
forgiveness (37). Mr. Burwell's hard heart is not softened by a spiritual
revelation. On the contrary, the source of Keckley's victory is her own resolve. Whereas Keckley offers no evidence of a divine influence in her own
struggle, she paints a contrasting picture of the Civil War and emancipation.
Keckley's references to the war and President Lincoln's hand in emancipation are repeatedly cast in biblical discourse. She reflects on the horror of
war, but likens the objective of emancipation to the biblical Jews' search for
freedom: "as the people of my race watched the sanguinary struggle, the ebb
and flow of the tide of battle, they lifted their faces Zionward, as if they
hoped to catch a glimpse of the Promised Land beyond the sulphureous
clouds of smoke which shifted now and then but to reveal ghastly rows of
new-made graves" (117). Similarly, Keckley paints Lincoln, the leader of
this divine struggle, as a divine icon. She proclaims, "He has been a Jehovah
to my people—has lifted them out of bondage, and directed their footsteps
from darkness into light" (154). With Lincoln's assassination she expresses
her grief at the loss of one who she deems "the Moses of my people" (190).

It is perhaps Keckley's strong ties to the white southern community of her
early years that inform her interpretation of the war as divinely sanctioned.
Keckley describes herself as part of a southern community—black and
white—to which she will always be connected. This bond is evident in a
letter she writes to her mother after being taken by her master to their new
home in North Carolina. Keckley writes to her mother, expressing her loneliness and her desire to know how all are doing back home in Virginia. Near
the close of her letter, she directs her mother to "Give [her] love to all the
family, both white and black" (41). Though a free woman living in the north,
Keckley is sustained through the memories of her years in the south. She is
not dismissive of the hardships she suffered in slavery, but she is also unwilling to abandon the bonds of family and community that she believes are
everlasting. To her northern friends who find this peculiar, Keckley tries to

explain the intersection of memory and community that bind her to those in her past:

> "[Y]ou forget the past is dear to every one, for to the past belongs that golden period, the days of childhood. . . . To surrender it is to surrender the greatest part of my existence—early impressions, friends, and the graves of my father, my mother, and my son. These people are associated with everything that memory holds dear, and so long as memory proves faithful, it is but natural that I should sigh to see them once more. (241–242)

Keckley will not acquiesce to the expectations of northerners who would have her confirm their simplistic view of black/white relationships in the south. Like Jacobs and Crafts, Keckley constructs a narrative of community—echoing African belief that an individual's importance is inextricably tied to his or her relationship to the community. Hence, Keckley provides considerable detail about her contribution to those she finds herself bound. As a slave in the St. Louis household of Anne Garland, Keckley had been permitted to purchase her freedom for herself and son. Through the loan of a friend and patron, Keckley bought her freedom from the family that she had served and even supported financially for many years (45, 55). After the war Keckley visits the Garland family, now in Virginia. Theirs is an emotional reunion, five weeks of remembrances and confirmations of mutual affection.

Keckley's benevolence extends to blacks suffering during wartime. She spearheads a relief society, mobilizing blacks to raise money and provide aid to the many freed people left destitute during the war (113–115). The most prevailing example of her understanding of community is her loyalty to Mrs. Lincoln. Keckley, who has no financial support outside her own work, sacrifices her business and her reputation in schemes devised by Mrs. Lincoln to raise money after the president's death. Keckley's commitment to Mrs. Lincoln is the outgrowth of her gratitude to the deceased president. Therefore, upon Mrs. Lincoln's request, Keckley puts her business aside, travels to New York to help Mrs. Lincoln who, in the hopes of raising money to answer her debts, has been taken in by a scheme to auction off her Whitehouse wardrobe. Mrs Lincoln's white peers abandon her and leave her to her own fate. However, Keckley and other prominent blacks—Frederick Douglass among them—offer the financial aid of a black community that remembered Lincoln's deed. Mrs. Lincoln refuses their aid—the only semblance of community that is left her. In many ways, Keckley stands as the contrast to Mary Todd Lincoln. Keckley is self-sufficient, modest, giving, honest: Mrs. Lincoln is dependent and weak, materialistic, self-consumed and often dishonest. By the conclusion of the narrative, this contrast is especially evident in the difference between the alienated world to which Mrs. Lincoln has been cast and the world of memory and friendship that sustains Keckley.

Keckley's representation of memory echoes the place of memory in African American spirituality. Memory is what grounds the spiritual self—it is a definitive act with a definitive purpose. At the narrative's beginning, Keckley makes clear that memory is not simply a chance act, but rather a deliberately accessed avenue to the past. Through memory the past is brought back and experiences relived—this Keckley makes evident in the narrative's introductory lines. Keckley's words serve as the medium that transports her into the past: "as I sit alone in my room the brain is busy, and a rapidly moving panorama brings scene after scene before me, some pleasant and others sad; and when I thus greet old familiar faces, I often find myself wondering if I am not living the past over again. The visions are so terribly distinct that I almost imagine them to be real" (17–18). Much like revisiting the past under the influence of drugs or hypnosis, Keckley is not simply recalling and recording past incidents. Through memory, Keckley enters a state that lies outside past and present. When her narrative ends, she is brought back to the reality of her material surroundings—her "garret-like room" that she shares with a close friend. With satisfaction, Keckley reflects on the journey that she has traveled through memory, a journey that has included both "the shadows and the sunshine of the past" (330).

The narrative weave of memory and community that runs through Keckley's work illustrates the survival of an African-rooted cultural legacy captured in early black women writings. Despite the dominant cultural rhetoric of individuality that came to define Americanness by the late nineteenth century, African American women writers maintained a tradition that privileged community. The writings of Crafts, Jacobs and Keckley demonstrate that early black women novelists planted the seed for a tradition of black women fiction that would maintain at its narrative core the belief in community that had guided their African ancestors. While these writers would preserve this traditional African philosophy in the face of a dominant counter-cultural view, its African origins would go unacknowledged. Early black women's writings echoed the survival of Africana in black society; these works also echoed the absence of explicit acknowledgment of these survivals as African in origin. In the culture as well as in the literature, Christianity had emerged as a repository for many African beliefs and practices, and when Africanisms could not be transformed into Christian discourse, blacks often simply maintained a coexistence of cosmologies. Hence, many African-rooted practices and beliefs dismissed in Anglo Christian discourse as superstition, were nevertheless preserved in black communities.

The novelized autobiographies of early black women captured the Christian discourse that was crystalizing into the language of African American spirituality. In their narratives, Hannah Crafts, Harriet E. Wilson, Harriet Jacobs, and Elizabeth Keckley illustrate the negotiation of Christianity and Africanity in early black women's fiction. They foretell the solidification of a

Christian discourse that would inform the black female literary imagination for generations. Their works demonstrate a constant negotiation of African American spiritual survivals and accepted paradigms of spirituality in the dominant culture. The spiritual voice of Christianity in early black women's fiction would become commonplace in the late nineteenth-century novels of black women. In keeping with their predecessors, late nineteenth-century black women novelists would maintain Christianity as the moral and spiritual ideal to which America's rising generation of free blacks aspired. In these novels, the confirmation of blacks as deserving citizens was signaled by black Christian communities and protagonists who held deep Christian convictions. However, as demonstrated in mid-nineteenth century black women's narratives, the authors' failure to openly validate Africanity does not result in its complete eradication.

NOTES

1. William Kaufman's introduction to the 1997 Dover edition of Truth's *Narrative* and Carla Peterson's discussion of Truth in *Doers of the Word* (1998) illustrate emerging critical inquiry that considers the influence of Africanity in Truth's life and works.

2. See Henry Louis Gates's *A XanEdu Educational Companion: The Bondwoman's Narrative* (2002) for in-depth discussion on the nature of Crafts's narrative as autbiography or novel. William Andrews and Nina Baym make convincing arguments for the work as a novel.

3. A range of critical essays that consider the multiple plots and conflicts in Crafts's narrative acan be found in *In Search of Hannah Crafts: Critical Essays on the Bondwoman's Narrative*. Eds. Henry Louis Gates, Jr., and Hollis Robbins. NY: Basic Civitas Books, 2004.

4. While modern biblical scholars have suggested that Solomon is not the speaker and perhaps not the author of "Song of Solomon," Crafts likely presumes that Solomon is author and speaker as this was a widely accepted reading of the work among blacks.

5. For a detailed look at what Keckley's narrative suggests about black female labor in nineteenth-century America, see Xiomara Santamarina's "Behind the Scenes of Black Labor: Elizabeth Keckley and the Scandal of Publicity."

WORKS CITED

Andrews, William L. "Hannah Crafts's Sense of an Ending." *A XanEdu Educational Companion: The Bondwoman's Narrative By Hannah Crafts*. Ed. Henry Louis Gates, Jr. Ann Arbor, Michigan: XanEdu, 2002. 1–21.

Beardslee, Karen E. "Through Slave Culture's Lens Comes the Abundant Source: Harriet A. Jacobs's *Incidents in the Life of a Slave Girl*." *MELUS* 24.1 (Spring 1999): 37–58.

Blackford, Holly. "Figures of Orality: The Master, The Mistress, The Slave Mother in Harriet Jacobs's *Incidents in the Life of a Slave Girl: Written by Herself*." *PLL* 37.3 (Summer 2001): 314–336.

Blum, Elizabeth D. "Power, Danger, and Control: Slave Women's Perceptions of Wilderness in the Nineteenth Century." *Women's Studies* 31(2002): 247–265.

Brooks-De Vita, Alexis. *Mythatypes: Signature and Signs of African/Diaspora and Black Goddesses*. Westport: Greenwood Press, 2000.

———. "The Tree of Terror: *The Bondwoman's Narrative* as Witness of the Struggle." *Griot* 22.2 (2003): 1–13.

Carson, Sharon. "Dismantling the House of the Lord: Theology as Political Philosophy in *Incidents in the Life of a Slave Girl*." *Journal of Religious Thought* 51.1 (Summer/Fall): 53–66.

Connor, Kimberly Rae. "'Keep the White Folks from Meddling': Africanisms in Slave Narratives." *MultiCultural Review* 5.2 (June 1996): 44–54.

Crafts, Hannah. *The Bondwoman's Narrative*. Ed. Henry Louis Gates, Jr. New York: Warner Books, 2002.

Ellis, R. J. *Harriet Wilson's Our Nig: A Critical Biography of a "Two-Story" African American Novel*. New York: Rodopi, 2003.

Gates, Henry Louis Jr., ed. "Introduction." *The Bondwoman's Narrative*. New York: Warner Books, 2002.

Jacobs, Harriet A. *Incidents in the Life of a Slave Girl*. 1861. Ed. Jean Fagan Yellin. Cambridge, MA: Harvard University Press, 1987.

Kaufman, William, introd. *Narrative of Sojourner Truth*. 1850. Mineola, New York: Dover Publications, 1997.

Keckley, Elizabeth. *Behind the Scenes*. 1868. Introd. James Olney. New York: Oxford University Press, 1988.

Prince, Mary. *The History of Mary Prince, a West Indian Slave* (1831). Orig. Ed. Thomas Pringle. in *Six Women's Slave Narratives*. Introd. William L. Andrews. New York: Oxford University Press, 1988.

Randle, Gloria T. "Between the Rock and the Hard Place: Mediating Spaces in Harriet *Jacobs's Incidents in the Life of a Slave Girl*." *African American Review* 33.1 (1999): 43–56.

Short, Gretchen. "Harriet Wilson's *Our Nig* and the Labor of Citizenship." *Arizona Quarterly* 57.3 (Autumn 2001): 1–27.

Truth, Sojourner. *Narrative of Sojourner Truth*. 1850. Mineola, NY: Dover Publications, 1997.

West, Elizabeth J. "Reworking the Conversion Narrative: Race and Christianity in *Our Nig*." *MELUS* 24.2 (1999): 3–27.

Wilson, Harriet E. *Our Nig*. 1859. 2nd ed. Introd. Henry Louis Gates, Jr. New York: Vintage Books, 1983.

Chapter Five

Christianity and a Reawakening Africanity

Black Spirituality in the Post-Reconstruction Novels of Frances E. W. Harper and Pauline Hopkins

The juxtaposition of Frances E. W. Harper's 1888–1889 serialized novel *Trial and Triumph* and her 1892 novel *Iola Leroy* illustrates her shifting fictional treatment of black spirituality and Anglo Christianity. These two fictional works draw contrasting conclusions about African American religious practices that originated in slave culture. In part, this shift may be representative of what Farah Jasmine Griffin describes as Harper's transition from outsider to one "more in tune with the masses of Black Southerners" that she went south to serve after the Civil War (45). Without question, Harper's life among the freed people informed her increasingly sympathetic representation of them in her fiction, particularly her shifting judgment of slave religion. Perhaps *Trial and Triumph* and *Iola Leroy*'s contrasting commentaries on slave religion are born out of the duality of Harper's real-life upbringing—she was a free-born black in the slaveholding state of Maryland, living among a vast population of illiterate blacks while she was herself educated. Moreover, her Unitarian affiliation must have on occasion left her alienated from the greater numbers of blacks who elected more evangelical denominations, such as Methodists and Baptists. Harper held to the Unitarian conviction that while "religion should touch the heart . . . faith must be rationalized, assented to on the basis of intellectual reasoning" (Peterson 125). In *Trial and Triumph*, Harper reveals an antipathy for the commonplace emotionalism in black churches. In particular, she suggests that the shouting and moaning practices of slave religion lies outside mainstream

Christianity, and blacks must therefore abandon these practices as they emerge out of the ignorance and drudgery of slavery. *Trial and Triumph* privileges the more restrained and stoic worship of America's high churches—the Episcopal and Presbyterian Churches and Harper's own affiliation, the Unitarian Church.

Set in a northern black urban community, *Trial and Triumph* echoes a late nineteenth-century black bourgeois view of slave culture—including slave religion—as a way of life that former slaves and their descendants had to overcome. Slavery had wrought generations of blacks unlearned in the social, economic, religious, and educational institutions of dominant white society. The late nineteenth-century talented tenth, the elitist circle of racial uplift leaders, were in general agreement that the poor black masses had to be prepared in all these areas in readiness for full American citizenship. Harper focuses her writing and her social activism on this premise. She is convinced that through education and Christianity, blacks will become the morally up-standing and civic-minded people capable of raising themselves to influence and self-sufficiency. While she is quick to criticize the inhumanity and hy-pocrisy of white America's governmental and religious legacy, she neverthe-less awards primacy to western learning and religion as models of civiliza-tion. *Trial and Triumph* depicts educated and industrious blacks as the exam-ple of race leaders, but not without emphasizing that they are foremost model Christians.

Trial and Triumph is, in many ways, the classic sentimental text. Annette, the story's heroine, is a young girl orphaned at an early age. While scorned by the more privileged yet less moral members of the community, she pre-vails in the end. Replete with well-known trappings of sentimental fiction— chance meetings, clearly good and evil characters, Christian conversion ex-periences, the husband provider as reward for the heroine, the middle class as the model community, and tear-jerking deathbed scenes—*Trial and Triumph* is also decidedly political. Harper offers numerous dialogues and authorial commentaries that promote racial uplift, particularly through black enterprise and united efforts to secure voting rights and protection under the law. Harp-er's politics are tied to her choice of literary conventions. As sentimental fiction, the novel creates the portrait of black middleclassness and black civility, demonstrating the readiness of educated, Christian blacks for accep-tance into the greater society. Annette's narrative symbolizes this cultural transformation: emerging from less than respectable origins, through educa-tion and Christianity, Annette rises above her illegitimate birth. She then turns the benefit of her academic and religious training to the benefit of fellow blacks. She is the exemplum of Harper's belief in the necessity of black self-help. Annette's achievements do not simply serve Annette, but rather a larger community of blacks in need of intellectual and moral guid-ance.

As a child, Annette is sometimes mischievous and self-consumed, but she develops into the sentimental middle class heroine who sheds her aggressive and independent nature for the genre's iconic model of dependent, domestic, and virtuous woman. Although her illegitimate birth renders her a problematic sentimental protagonist, Annette does not otherwise steer wayward from the stock portrait of the pious heroine of sentimental fiction. Harper constructs Annette within the boundaries of middle class worthiness, and in kind, she constructs a black middle class community that is validated by its adoption of Anglo cultural paradigms. Harper's deference to western culture follows an established practice among early black writers and thinkers, and this includes the heavy-laden Christian subnarrative. Unusual in *Trial and Triumph*, however, is the broad brush with which Harper paints black Christianity. The folk worship and spiritual beliefs that survived throughout black communities is noticeably absent in Harper's fictional hybrid community of poor and middle class, educated and uneducated blacks. Unlike her mid-century contemporaries, Harper takes no notice of folk beliefs in visionaries and the supernatural. The narratives of Sojourner Truth, Hannah Crafts, and Harriet Jacobs include predictable ovations to Christianity; however, they also give accounts of a black spiritual culture originating outside the margins of Anglo Christianity. These recollections are generally offered in the guise of juxtaposing the protagonist's more cultured nature against that of the larger black/slave community. Harper's narrative differs from these works not in purpose but in design. These mid-century narratives dismiss pre-Christian black spirituality by openly acknowledging the existence of folk beliefs and practices but suggesting that Christianity represented a higher or more civilized religion. In *Trial and Triumph,* however, Harper dismisses black spirituality by rendering it nonexistent. She offers up conservative Christianity as if it is the only spiritual discourse that informs the emerging post-war black community.

Trial and Triumph acknowledges the class hybridity of black communities in post–Civil War America. Given the reality of segregated housing, economically privileged blacks could not readily isolate themselves from the larger population of poor and uneducated blacks. Therefore, in countless black communities, middle class and wealthy blacks found themselves in close proximity to the poor and the working class. Such is the case in Harper's fictional black community: at the center of the community is Mrs. Lasette, the icon of middle class womanhood. With a husband provider who is the source of economic comfort in their home, she is left to the womanly responsibilities of homemaker and community servant. Her place as the educated, devout Christian strikes a sharp contrast to the less genteel working-class women who also comprise this community. The narrative begins with the introduction of Annette and her grandmother, Mrs. Harcourt, a hard working midwife who is often called away from her own home to care for others. In an early conversation between Mrs. Harcourt and two women neighbors, Harper introduces a well-known class of working black women by the turn of the century. In their discussion about the hard life of their neighbor, Mrs. Johnson, these women highlight the lives of hardworking washerwomen who toil to provide for their families, oftentimes in the absence of a male co-provider (181).

In this diverse class strata, Mrs. Lasette stands out as the exemplum of middle class Christian charity, balancing the sometimes oppositional entities of wealth and caring. She becomes the surrogate mother who guides Annette along the path to both Christian and intellectual development. She exemplifies the refined and educated finished product that the young, unpolished, emotionally driven Annette will become. With her role as surrogate to the illegitimate and orphaned Annette, Mrs. Lasette also represents the complicated nature of black mothering (Toohey 212). Through Annette and Mrs. Lasette's relationship, Harper highlights the practice of community parenting that was integral to slave culture: in the absence of biological mothers, black children were cared for by others in the community. Thus, Annette is not fated for destitution and alienation. The contrast between the young Annette and the mature Mrs. Lasette reflects the contrast between the larger masses of uneducated blacks and the talented tenth who imagined themselves the model for the masses and the leadership destined to guide them.

Like many of her contemporaries, Harper considered religion an important signifier of black progress, and this belief plays out in the transformation of her fictional heroine, Annette. The pride and willfulness of Annette's preconverted youth unfold almost immediately in the narrative. She is introduced in a dialog with her grandmother who scolds and questions her about her naughtiness—particularly her most recent mischievous behavior towards Mrs. Larkins, the elderly neighbor who is always quick to share her criticisms of Annette. Showing no sign of introspection, Annette explains with a devil-may-care answer that she is not certain what drove her to pour oil on Mrs. Larkins's steps. She flippantly confesses to her grandmother, "I don't know . . . I specs I did it for the devil. The preacher said the devil makes people do bad things" (183). Annette's witty application of a well-used religious dictum points not only to her disingenuous religiosity, but also to the superficiality often found in the church. Annette is mischievous but bright, and her suggestion that the devil may have instigated ill conduct is a veiled critique of preachers and self-righteous churchgoers who sit in judgment of those they deem sinners.

Harper further critiques the church through the novel's assessment of the ritualistic emotional expression that is associated with African American religious worship. Rather than consider this cultural practice a conscious and worthwhile retention, Harper suggests that it represents the underdeveloped religion of uneducated blacks. This is exemplified in a conversation between

Mrs. Lasette and the recently unemployed educator Mr. Thomas. Mrs. La-sette encourages Mr. Thomas to consider the ministry as a profession. Through his recollection of a young black man who landed in the ministry ill suited for the profession, Mr. Thomas explains why he would not consider such an option. Regarding the Rev. Mr. Lamson, Mr. Thomas explains, "I have heard him preach to, as I thought, an honest, well meaning, but an ignorant congregation, and instead of lifting them to more rational forms of worship, he tried to imitate them and made a complete failure. He even tried to moan as they do in worship but it didn't come out natural" (187). Mr. Thomas appears impressed with the congregation's spiritual sincerity; how-ever, he clearly finds them in need of religious guidance—specifically in their worship ritual. Educated and therefore a seemingly fit candidate to lead this group of unlearned parishioners, Rev. Lamson fails them in his indul-gence of their religious emotionalism. Mr. Thomas argues that if they are to be "lifted" to the superior religion of the cultured and the educated, they must abandon what he regards as their misguided religious practices. Although it is not his intention, Mr. Thomas belittles the unrefined religion of the unedu-cated. While his prevailing criticism is directed to those who would condone these practices, Mr. Thomas clearly conveys his impatience with, and disre-gard for, folk religion.

Offering a more sympathetic analysis of the emotionalism of folk wor-ship, Mrs. Lasette explains that the moaning of these congregants comes out of the horrific experiences of slavery. She proposes that slaves, unable to openly express their suffering and sorrow, "learned to mourn out in prayers, thoughts and feelings wrung from their agonizing hearts" (187). While she does not disagree with Mr. Thomas's conclusion that blacks must abandon their excessive religious emotionalism, she will not overlook the need to understand the experience that has informed these rituals. Her analysis falls somewhat short, however, for she does not recognize the pre–Middle Passage origins of these practices. Furthermore, with her description of the moaning congregants as "dear old people," she implies that the emotionalism that Mr. Thomas finds so disturbing is limited to the older generation of freed blacks (187). With Mrs. Lasette's passing reference to these worshipers as old and her suggestion that their unfavorable religious practices are tied to an institu-tion that is now dead, the narrative anticipates a rising generation of blacks who will recognize and adopt the more restrained and presumably superior worship practices of high western Christianity. Harper exemplifies this point through Annette's first serious attempt at a conversion experience.

Much like the misguided Rev. Lamson, Annette attempts to emulate the emotional practices of fellow worshipers. Disappointed that after having gone down to the mourner's bench she does not rise with a new spirituality, Annette reports this confounding experience to her grandmother: "Why, I went down in the garden and prayed and I got up and shouted, but I didn't get any religion" (194). The narrator recounts Annette's failed conversion, but readers are provided no account of her later authentic conversion moment. The failure of Annette's initial anticipated conversion is tied to a presumption that religious emotionalism signals spiritual vacuity and disingenuousness; therefore, readers are left to presume that the real conversion entailed a quiet, restrained experience. This is further intimated in the narrator's description of Annette's changed demeanor toward her long-term nemesis, Mrs. Larkins. While she had long despised this spiteful, meddlesome woman, Annette "had become friendly in her manner and considerate in her behavior to Mrs. Larkins since she had entered the church" (240). Annette's conversion delivered her from the impulsiveness and emotionalism that had defined her youthful resentment of Mrs. Larkins. As the exemplum of Christian maturity and reflectiveness, Annette now tables her own reactions and impulses and becomes a beacon of Anglo Christian stoicism. Annette exemplifies the emerging generation of blacks who will shed their past and step into a new life.

Trial and Triumph seems to teeter on the question of how the past informs the future. In part, with its periodic references to the "dead past" that must be forgotten and left behind, the novel takes on a thriving nineteenth-century American rhetoric that extols the "self-made man" who breaks free of past barriers of birth and circumstances and creates himself through his own initiative and hard work. With the exception of Annette's triumphant graduation speech that traces the journey of blacks in Africa to their bondage and subsequent freedom in America, the novel suggests that the past is a detriment to the future. This idea is introduced in the opening chapter in a conversation between Annette's grandmother and some of her neighbors. Mrs. Harcourt explains that her devotion to Annette is born out of a promise she made to her dying daughter to provide for the child she bore out of wedlock. Although her neighbor acknowledges the sorrow and hardships of Annette's circumstances, she chides Mrs. Harcourt for staying so connected to the past. She advises Mrs. Harcourt that "we cannot recall the dead past. . . . [I]t is the living present with which we have to deal" (181). Mrs. Lassette employs a similar paradigm of the past and the future as she recalls the advise she offered Annette's mother after her fall from grace. She remembers telling Lucy, "[Y]ou can never recall the past, but you can try to redeem the future. Men may build over the wreck and ruin of their young lives a better and brighter future, why should not a woman? Let the dead past bury its dead and live in the future for the sake of your child" (259). Mrs. Lasette's advice to her wayward friend is in some ways revolutionary, for the fictionalized assertion that a woman can redeem herself after a fall from virtue (except through death) is not commonplace in late nineteenth-century American fiction. However, Mrs. Lasette's advice falls otherwise into the mainstream American discourse of the self-made success story.

Traditional African belief systems hold that not only can we recall/relive the past, but in the interest of our spiritual and communal health, we must return to the past. Although *Trial and Triumph* suggests otherwise, this belief still informed black communities in late nineteenth-century America. The novel's insistence that the past should not be revisited contrasts sharply with African-rooted spirituality that calls on the living to regularly and ritualistically revisit the past. The novel's emphatic criticism of those who maintained ties to the past hints at Harper's awareness that despite the black elite's insistence that the past linked blacks to an uncultured legacy, blacks were not readily abandoning these spiritual views. Outward expressions of emotions were welcomed and expected in the more popular Baptist, Methodist and Sanctified churches. Harper's narrative depiction of new generations of black congregants abandoning folk practices seems a reflection of Harper's own desire that folk religion be transformed beyond its slave origins and become the refined and rational religion of white and black bourgeois America.

Trial and Triumph's message of racial unity and uplift is predicated on a vision of the black racial self made over into the image of American middle-classness. That blacks must disconnect themselves from the past and particularly their emotion-centered religion is a view that Harper sustains throughout the novel. Christianity serves as a significant indicator of black social and spiritual maturity, and the height of that achievement is the absence of unrefined religious practices in the black church. Again, with the exception of Harper's explicit criticism of shouting and moaning in black worship, *Trial and Triumph* relies on silence to dismiss the reality of black folk religion. Harper constructs black religion as synonymous to the nonevangelical church community commonly depicted in white middle class fiction: she ignores the folk beliefs and practices that inform the Christianity of most blacks. Despite this dismissal, *Trial and Triumph* does capture the survival of a key manifestation of traditional African spirituality. The belief in the primacy of community, in particular, the greater importance of the group over the individual is a thread that Harper weaves throughout the novel. Harper illustrates this through her contrasting depictions of characters who are morally flawed against those who are community icons. With her attention to the fine points of keeping house and her presumptions about proper childrearing, Mrs. Larkins epitomizes the spiritually bankrupt who reside in the community but contribute little or nothing to its well being. The narrator explains that "[w]hat was missing from her life was the magnetism of love. She had become so absorbed in herself that she forgot everybody else and . . . thought more of her own rights than her duties" (199). She is clearly the contrasting image of the benevolent and kindspoken Mrs. Lasette: "The difference between Mrs. Lasette and Mrs. Larkins was this, that in passing through life one scattered sunshine and the other cast shadows over her path" (199). Whereas Mrs. Larkins can only find fault with the young, impulsive Annette,

Mrs. Lasette recognizes Annette's intellectual strength and guides Annette to use her education for the betterment of the less privileged of the race.

In *Trial and Triumph* as in her later novel, *Iola Leroy*, Harper's mulatto characters offer further commentary on the primacy of community through their willingness to place the needs of family and community above their own desires and opportunities. The dual racial constitution of mulattoes makes them especially useful models of black community and solidarity. For those mulattoes, like *Trial and Triumph's* entrepreneur Mr. Thomas, the choice to identify with the degraded and marginalized black race when one can alternately choose whiteness and social assimilation, represents a spiritual connection that is more powerful than the material gains that whiteness can offer. Mr. Thomas, the son of a Southern planter, confesses that though the greater part of his blood is tied to his father's race, his kinship ties lie with his mother's race (236). It is out of this personally inspired conviction that he advises the dejected Charley Cooper not to submit to the temptation of racial passing. Expelled from his employment after the shop owner learns that his mother is black, Charley, who had concealed this information from his employer, contemplates abandoning his black ties and living as a white man. Mr. Thomas dissuades him from this course, explaining that injurious consequences to self and race would follow: "No, Charley, don't go away. I know you could pass as a white man; but Charley, don't you know that to do so you must separate from your kindred and virtually ignore your mother?" (212).

Mr. Thomas further suggests that while whiteness might open the door to wealth and influence, the strength of character that comes with claiming and living among his fellow struggling and disadvantaged blacks is a greater reward. This intangible reward, which in traditional African religions might be tied to requirements of ancestral and communal obligations, is instead connected to Christianity in Harper's novel. Mr. Thomas instructs Charley that as a Christian it is his obligation to "clasp the hand of Christ through faith and try to make the world better" (212). His advice to Charley is consistent with his conviction that individuals must work and sacrifice for the good of the community. Mr. Thomas is not unlike his female counterpart, Mrs. Lasette, who also encourages fellow blacks to make successes of themselves and to use that success for the good of the community. Their activism echoes African belief systems that hold each individual accountable for the community's survival and well being. Given that late nineteenth-century black activists did not connect their racial pride and race advocacy to African origins, it is not astonishing that Harper's fictional icons of racial leadership identify Christianity as the spiritual force behind their activism. Mr. Thomas and Mrs. Lasette harbor a pride and love of race that names and defines black achievement—secular and spiritual—through Anglo discourse. Nowhere in the text are readers offered an explanation of black communal ties that acknowledges an African or non-Christian cultural origin.

The pervasive deference to Anglo Christianity that defines black spirituality in *Trial and Triumph* is tempered in Harper's subsequent novel, *Iola Leroy*. Published in 1892, four years after the first installments of *Trial and Triumph*, *Iola Leroy* is less critical of slave religion, perhaps because the increasingly dismal racial climate of the 1890s made the picture of a racially assimilated America seem unlikely. The end of Reconstruction that followed the Great Compromise of 1877 marked the beginning of a return to accepted practices of racial discrimination and a renewed anti-black sentiment that was pervasive by the century's end. The 1880s ushered in a period marked by the legal disenfranchisement of black voters throughout the south, a notable rise in the number of blacks lynched throughout the south, and the concomitant presence of the Ku Klux Klan, the white terrorists whose mission was to reestablish white dominance in America's south. Published in 1888, *Trial and Triumph* with its steadfast optimism about black progress, was cast against the reality of waning political and economic opportunities for blacks. Laws affirming the second-class citizenship of blacks were being passed and a public discourse of black inferiority was as prevalent as the black bashing of antebellum days. In 1888 many black leaders still believed that blacks could attain social and economic equity by demonstrating their cultural malleability—specifically their adaptability to western culture. Black writers would continue to depict black success in the image of a black middle class that reified the cultural mores that while often not lived by middle class whites, were nevertheless claimed as representative of that class.

The publication of *Iola Leroy* does not suggest that Harper had by 1892 abandoned the belief that racial equality would ensue as blacks demonstrated their ability and readiness to transform themselves into the image of western respectability. Harper's show of tolerance and recognition of slave culture, however, hints at a waning hope for racial harmony and a diminishing sense of investment in western culture. Harper was aware of the increasingly marginalized status of blacks—even those among the educated, middle class. The law that would incite the famous Plessy vs. Ferguson case had been enacted; Ida B. Wells had begun publishing accounts of barbaric lynchings of blacks across the United States; and the first wave of black migration to Northern cities was underway. Times were clearly not good for blacks, and Harper's genteel black society hardly represents the predominant rural and poor black population of late nineteenth-century America. But even against the backdrop of a struggling and marginalized black population, Harper persisted in her representation of a black bourgeois that would guide the black masses to social and economic acculturation. While Harper does not waver in her vision of a westernized black race, *Iola Leroy* is notable for Harper's distinct shift in treatment of slave culture. This contrasting representation may not be evident at first glance to readers of *Trial and Triumph* and *Iola Leroy*. In both works Harper remains silent on the folk practices and beliefs that blacks maintain concurrently with Christianity. However, in contrast to *Trial and Triumph's* intolerance for the spiritual expressions of slave religion, the narrator and characters in *Iola Leroy* celebrate the "old time religion" of the slaves, and this includes their moaning and shouting. While *Iola Leroy* is more accepting of slave religion, the work does not suggest that the slave's religion originates outside Christianity. Harper simply suggests that the Christianity of the slave people differs from that of the stoic and less heartfelt Christianity of white slaveholders. Christianity stands as the religious core of the fictional black communities in this work; however, in contrast to *Trial and Triumph's* picture of black slave religion as cultural primitivism, the old time religion in *Iola Leroy* is held sacred by both the uneducated slaves and their educated counterparts. Harper clearly distinguishes between African American Christianity and the Christianity-at-large that was the product of a hypocritical white society.

With the exception of Thomas Anderson who dies halfway into the novel, and the unmistakably black but educated Miss Delany and Rev. Carmicle, *Iola Leroy* is for the most part, the story of mulatto and near-white slaves who emerge as race leaders in the post–Civil War era. Harper highlights these characters as race leaders, and even as slaves their speech, their literacy and their Anglo heritage distinguish them from the larger slave population. These race leaders, however, differ from their counterparts in *Trial and Triumph*. In contrast to the shortcomings that Mr. Thomas and Mrs. Lasette find with "ignorant" and overly emotional black congregations, Iola and her uncle, Robert, both revere and participate in the religion of their less educated fellow slaves. Like their near-white counterparts in *Trial and Triumph*, Iola and Robert forego the opportunity to claim themselves white, thus binding themselves to the inevitable hardships that come with being black in America. Robert, who early in the novel joins the union forces, chooses to serve among the black military ranks. He explains to his white military superior that one chooses race for reasons that extend beyond mere physical appearance: "[W]hen a man's been colored all his life it comes a little hard for him to get white all at once. . . . [M]y place is where I am needed" (*Iola Leroy* 43). Similarly, Iola refuses a marriage proposal from a kind and affluent white physician she has worked with during the war. Even after he is made aware that Iola is black, Dr. Gresham remains determined to marry her. He does not understand why Iola, whose skin is as fair as his, has apprehensions about marriage to him. She understands, however, that marriage to Dr. Gresham would require that she forsake personal and community ties more valuable than the life of comfort and wealth that the doctor can provide (114–119). When Dr. Gresham finds Iola later in the post-war North, he hopes that she will respond positively to his second proposal of marriage. But

Iola is as determined in her convictions as she had been during war times. She has found her mother and brother and been united with other family members, and she casts her lot with those who need her. Once again Iola rejects the doctor's offer of marriage, explaining that she cannot forsake her race to whom she feels indebted (235). Iola and Robert's alliance with fellow struggling blacks again speaks to the value of community among African Americans, and they stand out as more integral participants in the community than their middle class counterparts in *Trial and Triumph*.

Robert and Iola participate in slave prayer meetings, and their mutually respectful and endearing relationship with fellow slaves further highlights their place among them. They demonstrate the deep spiritual bond that exists between educated, middle class blacks and their less privileged fellows when those who are privileged do not become isolated from the community. Iola and Robert are integral members of the black folk community that has nurtured them and provided them spiritual support: they are not outside observers offering a western gaze on slave beliefs and behaviors. That they teach white cultural conventions to fellow slaves, yet worship with them in their old time religion, suggests the need for balance. To define and maintain their identity and their own distinct way of life, slaves must balance those beliefs and practices that they adopt from white society and those from their own culture that they deem worthy of maintaining. Harper's prominent black characters in *Iola Leroy* hold community and the religion that binds them in high regard; however, while Harper clearly portrays black Christianity as distinct from white Christianity, she again will not assert a connection between black Christianity and Africanity. She highlights distinct characteristics of slave or what the novel deems old-time religion, and then simply suggests—without regard to questions of origin—that these peculiarities define slave Christianity.

The religion of the slaves—the old-time religion—becomes the slave's Christianity rather than the portrait of isolated superstition or pre-Christian peculiarities so often depicted in early written accounts of slave life. Black writers often couched African-rooted beliefs in Christian religiosity when the two belief systems were in accord; however, when faced with inconsistencies, they either ignored the contradictions or they dismissed black spiritual practices as peculiarities yet to be shed by blacks. Throughout *Iola Leroy* Harper maintains a reverence for the Christianity of the slaves, praising them for their deep rooted and heartfelt spirituality, and contrasting their religious sincerity against the hypocrisy of white Christianity. While the novel offers no explicit acknowledgment of or deference for African-rooted religion, Harper casually incorporates the seemingly innocuous account of an African born slave whose rejection of Christianity leads him to extract an extraordinary promise from his master. It is a story that is told by Tom Anderson, who remembers the old African with apparent reverence. Explaining to Aunt Linda his preference for "de good ole time religion" of fellow slaves to that of the written/biblical religion of white folks, Tom veers off to tell the story of a slave, a "real Guinea man," who like him was reluctant to submit to the religion of the master (22). Tom remembers this remarkable man who informed his master that he had no need for a heaven that included his master. Compelled on his deathbed to be free of his earthly bondage and the possibility of an afterlife in his master's heaven, this African native secured his freedom from his master. Free at the time of death, he could then return to Africa a free man and join his ancestors. Tom does not explicitly validate the religion that guides the Guinea slave to his spiritual journey home. However, holding up this native African to further explain his skepticism of white Christianity, Tom inadvertently reveals the awareness and tolerance of non-Christian spiritual experiences among the slaves. Tom's "ole time religion" is the Christianity of the slaves, but this religious affinity does not prevent him from revering the religious conviction of this native African.

The story of the Guinea slave highlights the novel's foremost image of black spirituality as a cultural experience that springs from deeply held spiritual convictions. Black spiritual resolve is not born out of white influence, but rather has remained in spite of the contrasting superficial and hypocritical Christianity imposed on the slaves. Through repeated dichotomies of slave and white Christianity, Harper highlights the superior spirituality of her fictional black community. Throughout the novel, Harper's black characters express a general skepticism of white Christianity, and they nor the narrator presume that white Christianity represents the religious model for the unlearned and uncultured slave masses. In fact, this sentiment is unveiled early in the novel by the leading male mulatto character, Robert Johnson. As the war progresses with black regiments forming in Southern territories under siege by union forces, slaves find that they have the opportunity to participate in their own liberation. Robert Johnson and fellow slave Tom Anderson are eager to meet the challenge, and they are staggered by ole Uncle Daniel, who out of loyalty to his master, chooses to stay. Uncle Daniel explains that, upon her deathbed, his mistress asked him to take care of her young son who was about to become parentless. Uncle Daniel thought of his mistress as a "saint in glory" and considered her request a divine obligation. Robert dismisses Uncle Daniel's loyalty, expressing his doubt about the merits of "white folks' religion" (21). Robert's rejection is striking, for he belongs to that class of educated mulatto slaves who, based on any number of claims—one of which was their acceptance of white Christianity, often distinguished themselves from their less fortunate fellows. Robert, whose physical appearance is more akin to his white ancestors, stands out for his repeated affirmations of black Christianity. Older slaves and the darker, alienated masses were often depicted as favoring folk religious practices, but in general, mulatto characters, in both black and white authored nineteenth-century texts, were represented as the example of black acculturation to western ways. Robert Johnson and his niece, Iola, defy these expectations. At every turn, they reaffirm the superior Christianity of the slaves, and along with their less-privileged fellows, they demonstrate that the threat of impending white influence is what in fact threatens the sacredness of slave Christianity.

Iola's reverence for slave Christianity echoes that of her mother who before being separated from Iola, imparts to her the foundation of her spiritual strength. Iola, painfully aware after the death of her father that she and her mother will be cast among the lot of slaves, questions the Christianity of whites that allows their inhumane treatment of blacks. Marie asks Iola to place her faith not in the Christianity of those whites, but "from the foot of the cross and from the book [Bible]" (107). She tells Iola that the religious faith and trust of the slaves has served as a model: "Some of the most beautiful lessons of faith and trust I have ever learned were from among our lowly people in their humble cabins" (107). Marie's reference to the slaves as "our lowly people" is significant, for even though she has lived the privileged life of a planter wife, she feels a kinship with those in the slave community. It is no insignificant matter that in a prayer led by Mammy Liza, Marie's servant and friend, Marie is brought out of her hysteria over her husband's death. Mammy Liza both comforts and counsels Marie at this crossroad. She tells Marie that she must put her faith in God and persevere, and after she has kneeled by Marie and "breathed out a prayer full of tenderness, hope, and trust," Marie emerges with the strength to face her hardships (94).

Iola has lived her early years presuming that she is white; however, upon discovering that she is black, she finds no difficulty taking up the Christianity of the slaves. Iola learns that faith and community are integral, and that the most genuine level of living Christian faith can be found among the slaves and in the post-war black community. Once delivered to the harsh world of slavery, Iola finds that despite the horrors, blacks have maintained a religious conviction that has secured their humanity in the midst of a horrific and inhumane system. She attends the religious meetings held by blacks in the woods and finds them spiritually moving, and she also learns that these meetings are central to the sharing of experiences and information. It is in one such meeting that she witnesses Robert Johnson's discovery of the mother who had been torn from him in his youth. As Robert and his mother stand before members of the congregation offering testimonies of their sad separation from family, they soon realize that their stories of separation tell the same tale, and that they are mother and son (182). Out of this reunion Robert becomes more convinced that his mother is Iola's grandmother, who had also been separated from Marie, Iola's mother. In a later but similar religious meeting, Iola is reunited with her brother, Harry, who, after finding their mother, had been attending religious meetings throughout the south in search of Iola.

The tragic story of Iola's family is shared with the community, and in turn, the community is the medium through which their family is restored. Black religion is thus restorative, not simply in a metaphysical sense, but its power is also evident in the material world. Through the power of communal worship, black slave families like the Leroys were reunited and returned to the community. For the Leroy family, the return to community comes with the obligation to serve the community, and in this regard Harper maintains the African-informed philosophy of individual/community reciprocity. The Leroys's choice to cast their lot with fellow blacks and their belief in the Christianity of their black community further highlights Harper's dichotomy of black and white Christianity. That the Leroys, educated and white by all impressions of the human eye, find greatest consolation in the black community speaks to the spiritual deficiency in white Christianity. The less privileged, uneducated blacks see Christianity as a black/white dichotomy, but they do not assume that whiteness stands as the model of Christianity. This is made especially clear in the convictions of the older slaves who turn down the opportunity to learn the religion of whites. When Robert Johnson attempts to convince his old slave friend, Aunt Linda, that reading the Bible might bring her comfort should she find herself sick and shut in, Aunt Linda declines his suggestion that she learn to read, even for that presumed benefit. She does not imagine that she would encounter such a predicament, for she lives in a community that diligently brings religion to all its members. Her answer to Robert is a reminder of the oral and communal nature of black folk religion: "Oh, I could hab prayin' and singin'. Dese people is mighty good 'bout prayin' by de sick" (156). Aunt Linda has no need for the written religion of whites. Her spiritual needs have always been met by the black community that she has worshipped with since her days in slavery. Her fear, born out of the post-war climate, is that the spirit of the slaves in their pre-war meetings in the woods had been diminished and that now in the aftermath of slavery, "folks is took up wid makin' money an' politics" (162).

Robert receives a similar answer after he extends another well-meaning offer to another old slave friend. Remembering that Uncle Daniel was a preacher during their days in slavery, Robert suggests that he might want to study theology with the northerners who were teaching young men how to preach. To Robert's misguided presumption that whites could offer meaningful spiritual counsel, Uncle Daniel responds, "Look a yere, boy, I'se been a preachin' dese thirty years, an' you come yere a tellin' me 'bout studying yore 'ologies. I larn'd my 'ology at the foot ob de cross. You bin dar?" (168). Uncle Daniel's answer highlights the time honored respect for experience that is integral to black spirituality—pre– and post–Middle Passage. Blacks in America have maintained communal rituals and practices that bring spiritual experience to life, much like the dance and song rituals of their ancestors that rendered religion an experience-based phenomenon. Religion is felt by experiencing the presence of the spirit. Uncle Daniel needs no instructions from the books of whites: he has learned about God in the way that is most personal and most enduring, and as a preacher among fellow slaves, he brings the knowledge of his experience to their communal religious gatherings. Uncle Daniel and Aunt Linda's rejection of the written religion of whites speaks to the centralness of experiencing religion—religion is not a study. When individuals bring their experience to the community, the power of the spirit can be realized. Uncle Daniel emphasizes that his place as preacher in the community is the result of encounters with, rather than speculations about the divine.

Black Christianity is the reigning voice of black religiosity in *Iola Leroy*. In this respect, Harper's work follows a tradition of religious discourse in early black women's writings. Unlike her predecessors, however, Harper speaks of black Christianity as if it has no spiritual antecedents, as if slaves had always been Christians and as if no outside spiritual influences were being negotiated in slave society. The supernatural world of the slaves that is commonly depicted in black women writers' accounts of black folk culture (free and enslaved)—particularly folk concepts of visions and visionaries, of the transitory bounds between corporeal and spiritual worlds, and of nature's roles in the manifestation of the spiritual—is for the most part disregarded by Harper. Even though *Iola Leroy* offers a more sympathetic look at slave religion than *Trial and Triumph,* Harper is careful not to validate the world of the slaves that subsisted at the fringes of Christianity. Therefore, while Harper legitimates the emotion-filled worship of slave religion, she does so presuming that they are integral Christian practices—she will not consider that this spiritual emotionalism has meaning outside a Christian context.

Similarly, Harper offers only cursory acknowledgement of the slave's predilection to trust spiritual revelations as central to human affairs. She includes only scant accounts of visions experienced by her black characters, and the insignificance of these spiritual revelations is evident by her failure to connect them in any substantive way to the plot. Therefore, Aunt Linda's proclamation early in the novel that the coming emancipation has been revealed to her in a vision seems an empty prophecy. While the emancipation of the slaves certainly occurs, that event is in no way connected to Aunt Linda's sketchy vision. Offering no detailed account, Aunt Linda simply tells Robert that according to her vision they will all be free (13). The lack of consequential agency leaves Aunt Linda's vision sounding more like a hunch than a spiritual revelation. Visions generally reveal the unknown, oftentimes allowing the seer or the recipient(s) of the message to act on what is foretold. Aunt Linda shares the prophecy of her vision at a time when the slaves are well aware that the war is not looking good for the Southerners and that the North's likely victory will result in the emancipation of the slaves.

Aunt Linda's vision lacks the detailed description and the purposefulness of those visionary accounts in the earlier autobiographical works of Rebecca Cox Jackson and Jarena Lee and Hannah Crafts's autobiofictional narrative. In these earlier writings visionary experiences prompt these women to act or to inform others to act, and oftentimes these visions are the means to knowledge that helps the visionary better understand her condition. In a more descriptive vision by Uncle Daniel, Harper comes closer to representing the vision as a revelatory experience. Speaking of his former master, who had been a cruel man, Uncle Daniel suggests that his sudden death was fitting. Struck and killed by a tree, the cruel master had been delivered up to the devil, and according to Uncle Daniel, "ef eber de debil got his own he got him" (20). The confirmation that his master had succumbed to evil was delivered in a vision Uncle Daniel experiences after the master's death. Uncle Daniel describes seeing his master "hangin' up in a pit, sayin' 'Oh! Oh!' wid no close on" (20). Uncle Daniel's vision serves as a parable of retribution: those who are evil will meet their due.

In *Iola Leroy*, a pre-Christian ethos cannot inform African American Christianity; however, African American Christianity can serve the rising freed population in the post-war era, and it can serve as the model of spiritual balance that white Christianity fails to deliver. Iola reiterates this point throughout the novel as she repeatedly speaks to the humanity and genuineness of black religion. Much like Wheatley in her admonishment of the young white male scholars whose education obscures their spiritual vision ("To the University of Cambridge in New England"), Harper critiques white presumptions of superiority through charges of white spiritual deficiency. This message especially resonates in one of the novel's final discursive moments on white and black civilization. In one of many gatherings of leading blacks in the community, the respected Rev. Carmicle argues that white civilization does not stand alone as the model of human achievement because it is, in fact, a world lacking in vital signs of humanness. He suggests that the model for blacks emerging out of their long slave past is a synthesis of the wealth and learning of whites and a "religion with life and glowing with love" (260). Of course, one of Harper's compelling messages in the novel is that black Christianity represents such a religion.

In her turn-of-the-century novel, *Contending Forces* (1900), Pauline Hopkins connects black humanity and progress to a similar synthesis of black Christianity and white materialism. While Hopkins represents Christianity as the monolithic religious institution in African American society, the centrality of the black church to black religious and social life does not negate the influence of African-rooted spirituality that had been preserved in slave culture and that coexisted with black Christianity. Hopkins recognizes a spiritual ethos that lies outside Christianity, one that oftentimes shapes the fortunes of blacks in more powerful ways than Christianity. In her subsequent serialized novels, *Hagar's Daughter, a Story of Southern Caste* (1901), *Winoma, a Tale of Negro Life in the South and Southeast* (1902), and *Of One Blood, or, the Hidden Self* (1902/03), she more explicitly constructs African mysticism as central to plot development. However, *Contending Forces* represents Hopkins's groundbreaking full-length fictional exploration and validation of African spirituality in African American life. It is therefore the focus novel for this study of Hopkins's importance to the shifting spiritual discourse in black women's fiction at the dawn of the twentieth century. Hopkins's serialized novels highlight her deliberate fictional representation of her race theory, but these works are not so much a challenge to Christian hegemony but an assertion of Africa as the spiritual and biological origin of humankind.[1] While Claudia Tate insightfully points out that *Of One Blood* is important because the heroine, Candace, "marks a very early appearance of the 'brown' heroine in Afro-American fiction" (64),[2] the novel's focus lies outside America and beyond the African American community. Again, Hopkins's race theory informs this novel, as its conclusion affirms Ethiopia/Africa as the seat of humankind's spiritual and civilized self.

The supernatural practices and experiences that are silenced in Frances Harper's novels are at the forefront of the fictional black world in Hopkins's *Contending Forces*. Hopkins gives voice and agency to African American folk belief in the power of visionaries or seers and in the connections and communications between earthly and otherworldly beings. The spirit of the deceased Grace Montfort is the novel's first account of black folks' unquestioning assumption of the presence of the supernatural. The slaves report that Mrs. Montfort, who was led to suicide at the hands of Anson Pollock, can be found "weeping and wringing her hands, night after night about the plantation" (71). Pollock does not corroborate the slaves' account of Mrs. Montfort's ghostly wanderings; however, instead of the satisfaction he had anticipated at having Grace Montfort at his mercy, Pollock is left haunted by her death. Unable to enjoy his triumph, "he grew morose and unsociable . . .[and] [h]e seemed to have a superstitious fear of the children" (71). Grace Montfort's spirit walks about the plantation haunting the diabolical Pollock, leaving him to a lonely and miserable existence. Alternatively, Mrs. Montfort appears to her young son, Jesse, giving him strength. Jesse is left under the control of Pollock who treats him severely; however, it is after a brutal flogging from Pollock that Jesse experiences a visitation from his deceased parents. He cannot see them, but he feels their presence and is made aware that they will always be with him (75). After this visitation, Jesse finds that he has the resolve to endure, and he is further strengthened throughout his childhood by recurring visits from his deceased mother.

Hopkins clearly suggests a link between the spiritual practices of continental Africans and their descendants in America; she locates Africa as the origin of the supernatural beliefs and practices maintained by slaves. In this respect she differs from Harper, who again, either ignores African survivals in black culture or speaks of them as manifestations of black Christianity with no apparent tie to a pre-Christian ethos. *Contending Forces* exposes the cracks in the black Christian stoicism that defined much of late nineteenth-century black bourgeois discourse on race uplift. Hopkins discounts constructs of black virtue and civilization that are anchored in white middle class religiousity. The virtue of her black characters is not compromised by the dual Christian and pre-Christian (African) ethos that defines their world. On the contrary, this Afro-Christian mergence echoes Hopkins's ongoing call for "the inclusion of folk knowledge in the world's epistemological base" (Allen 23). Hopkins is careful not to give over completely to the non-Christian ethos that informed black life, however, even though the racial climate in 1900 was a continuum of political, economic, and social losses for blacks, race leaders did not fully abandon the expectation that through their show of cultural assimilation, blacks would gain acceptance into the larger society.

Contending Forces resonates with the theme of racial uplift that pervades Harper's novels, and as with Harper, Hopkins constructs a black community that is being led in great part, by its mulatto population. This has prompted much critical disfavor from some readers who suggest that Hopkins reifies white standards of beauty and superiority.[3] While this criticism of Hopkins's fiction persists, many contemporary scholars argue that Hopkins engages in a complicated, yet determined subversion of white hegemonic discourses on race. In her landmark study, *Domestic Allegories of Political Desire* (1992), Claudia Tate opened up the possibility of reading early black domestic fictions as works that used a seemingly repressive form, that is, sentimental fiction, as a means to assert black female agency. Since Tate's publication, a new wave of scholarship on Hopkins has surfaced. Scholars are exploring Hopkins's challenges to dominant white discourses of race and gender. In keeping with Tate's exploration of late nineteenth-century's black women's fiction as assertions of political agency, Gloria T. Randle argues that contrary to readings of *Contending Forces* as a submission to dominant racialized paradigms, the text was a maverick work:

> To empower a maligned people and a subjugated gender, Hopkins stolidly advocates self-determination, equality in society and in marriage, liberating friendships, romantic relationships and parenting that encourages children to explore their full potential. Many of the feminist views that she advances are commonplace to today's reader but were virtually revolutionary at the turn of the century. (194)

Thomas Cassidy argues that Hopkins manipulates late nineteenth-century constructs of race and gender to dupe her white readers: according to Cassidy, "*Contending Forces* complicates the issue of race essentialism and then uses class as a marker of social worth to make the rise of a black middle class palatable to a white audience" (670–671). Jennifer Putzi argues that Hopkins's narrative design implicates whites in the historical stigma or degradation that has been the legacy of blacks and slavery. She argues that Hopkins recalls the stigma of slavery not to simply free blacks from this history, but rather to identify the white community's responsibility in this shameful legacy (2). These contemporary explorations of Hopkins's fiction do not dismiss her ultimate reliance on European features as models of physical beauty; however, these scholars do not allow this contradiction to overshadow Hopkins's clear assertions of black empowerment, achievement, and potential.

While Hopkins's leading characters are for the most part blacks whose phenotypes suggest that they are not black, they are more profoundly black by matters of community and family that inform their black self-identification. In *Contending Forces*, blacks who forego the alternative to pass into the white world, remain with their fellow blacks and dedicate themselves to the improvement of the race. The exception is the young Charles Monfort, who after his parents' death, is rescued and sent to England. Charles is raised as white while his sibling, Jesse, who spends his boyhood in slavery, casts his lot with his downtrodden black fellows. These disparate conditions are the result of speculation by the Montfort's North Carolina neighbors that Mrs. Montfort is of African ancestry. While she is for all outward appearances, white, the skepticism raised renders the orphaned boys susceptible candidates for slavery. Hopkins's narrator never confirms the racial identity of the Montfort parents. Instead, she points out that the possibility of African ancestry in the lines of both was not unlikely. The narrator reminds readers of the history of the early Spanish in Bermuda, the home of the Montforts. These white planters intermingled with the slave population, resulting in some instances in colored offspring who became planters themselves. These colored planters often married into the Spanish population, and their descendants reassimilated into the white population. Readers are told that both Charles and Grace Montfort may have been descendants of such interracial mingling (23). This is the extent to which the narrator will speculate; however, readers are never certain of the Montfort's racial heritage. In contrast to his older brother who is rescued into the white population, Jesse removes to Boston after he flees the south. He marries a mulatto, and they and their offspring live as blacks. The Smith family's Ma Smith is one of the children of this union, and she inherits her father's commitment to the race. Even with the death of her husband, Ma Smith manages to raise their children and become a central figure in the race and religious activism of her community. Their children, Will and Dora, grow in the likeness of their parents, both active in race work and community uplift.

Like Harper's *Iola Leroy*, *Contending Forces* begins on the prewar plantation, allowing readers to follow the main characters' transitions from slavery to freedom. The novel opens on the Montfort plantation in Bermuda.

Here in Bermuda the world of the slaves is brought to life through their music and dance. The narrator introduces the slaves not through individual dialog or description, but rather through their collective pleasure-making on a Sunday afternoon. In contrast to the Montforts who have settled into a quiet afternoon after attending Anglican services, the slaves have gathered to enjoy themselves in noisy merrymaking: "In the direction of the square a crowd of slaves were enjoying the time of idleness. Men were dancing with men, and women with women, to the strange monotonous music of drums without tune, relics of the tom-tom in the wild African life which haunted them in dreamland" (26). Although the slaves' music represents a connection to a crude cultural legacy, "there was [still] pleasure for even a cultivated musical ear in the peculiar variation of the rhythm" (26). The peculiar music of the slaves in Bermuda parallels that of the slaves working away at the North Carolina harbor where the Montforts arrive after leaving their island home: these slaves "sang in a musical monotone, and kept time to the music of their songs as they unloaded a barge that had just arrived" (32). Again, the narrator finds a beauty in this music that is generally dismissed as simplistic and unremarkable. The "rich and plaintive voices" of the slaves are said to have "blended together in sweet cadences" that the narrator compares to the biblical children of Israel who sang similarly in their captivity (33–34). This juxtaposition of the black slaves and the biblical enslaved Israelites antici-pates the African-Christian dialectic that runs throughout the novel.[4] Hop-kins weaves a narrative that ultimately unveils African-Christian tensions in African American culture but also demonstrates the delicate coexistence of the two seemingly antithetical systems.

Recalling the early scene with the dancing and jubilant slaves in Bermu-da, the novel seems to corroborate white constructs of black inferiority. The idle slaves who can think of nothing more serious than dancing and music making on their day off—and a holy day at that—are contrasted against the solemn Montforts and their fellow white islanders. The laboring songs of the North Carolina slaves paint a more serious and suffering people, but what remains is the supposition that these are nevertheless the musical conventions of an uncultured people. As the narrative winds its way to the house of the Smiths in post-war Boston, the show of mainstream conventions of middle-classness confirms the Smiths and their community as exemplums of racial progress. In the black middle class home of the Smiths, young people gather for socializing that often leads to singing and dancing. At the first of such gatherings described in the novel, the narrator paints a picture that markedly contrasts the African-rooted music and inclinations of the slaves. In this post-war illustration of black middle class refinement and learning, these upstand-ing young blacks of the community meet on a Sunday and engage in art forms that signal an association with western/high culture and religiosity. Their art is solemn and restrained: "Dora played . . . a medley of Moody and

Sankey hymns; Will sang 'Palm Branches' in a musical baritone voice; John contributed a poem, and two young friends gave the duet from 'Il Trovatore'" (108).

This scene is at once undermined, however, with Sappho Clark's subsequent dramatic narration from *Ben Hur* and the southern born, uneducated Mrs. Davis's rendition of Suwanee River. Sappho's presentation was so reminiscent of an actual stage performance "that the Rev. Tommy James, the young theologian, felt that possibly he might have made a mistake in going into such hilarious company on the Sabbath" (108). The group joins together in singing popular songs and acting out parts from popular dramas, behavior that even when not on the Sabbath, was generally frowned upon in middle class settings. Popular culture was looked upon by many in the black middle class, particularly the clergy, as bordering on the immoral. It is thus noteworthy that as the gathering progresses, the group seems more lighthearted, and despite himself, "even the divinity student [Rev. Tommy] was drawn into the magic circle" (111). The "magic" of this group of model young blacks is not far removed from that of the slaves in Bermuda who spend their Sundays engaging in lighthearted song and dance. This less-than-somber picture on the Sabbath underscores an African-Christian tension that undermines affirmations of Christian rightness found at the surface of the novel. Hopkins does not sustain this subversion of social and religious protocol for long, however. This Sabbath merrymaking concludes with the singing of a well-known hymn, "Praise God, from Whom All Blessings Flow," and these young people ostensibly return to their middle class, Christian solemnity.

In another social gathering at the Smith home, Hopkins again explores the tension between black middle class Christianity and African predispositions. Although Hopkins does not explicitly connect the slaves' song and dance tradition to the social frolics of the young black Bostonians, her recurrent juxtaposition of the youthful song and dance gatherings and the stoic and restrained conventions of the church suggests a tension between the two legacies that informs this community. This is once again exemplified at the conclusion of a woman's meeting sponsored by Mrs. Smith. While Mrs. Smith's more august guests depart for the evening, the young people pour into the Smith home. Sam Washington, "a young fellow who was the life of all social functions," suggests that a dance in the Smith's parlor would provide the opportunity for Ma Smith to sell off four gallons of ice cream that had been bought to raise funds for the upcoming church fair (158). Ma Smith responds with an immediate and emphatic rejection of this plan, explaining to Will, "Oh . . . I've been a church member over thirty years, a consistent Christian, and I never was up before the board for behavior unbecoming a professor [of Christian faith]. Think of the disgrace on me if the church took it up" (158–59). Will prevails, nonetheless, as he convinces his mother that she will be absolved of any wrong doing should the matter come under public scrutiny: "[W]e'll have the dance, and it shall be my dance for my company. No one shall trouble you; you will have nothing to do with it" (160).

Young Rev. Tommy James finds himself once again in the midst of a questionable gathering, but caught up in the moment, he proceeds to escort the widow, Mrs. Davis, onto the dance floor, "forgetful of the fact that he was within a few months of his ordination" (162). The dance begins with the more conservative waltz, but concludes with the "'Virginy' reel," a popular folk dance that dates back to Colonial America. This dance seems to inspire dancers to do away with all pretensions of solemnity:

> All reserve was broken down the instant the familiar strains of the Virginia reel were heard. The dance was seen in full swing—an up-and-down, dead-in-earnest seeking for a good time. . . . It was a vehement rhythmic thump, thump, thumpity thump, with a great stamping of the feet and cutting of the pigeon wing. Sam had provided himself with the lovely Jinny for a partner, and was cutting grotesque juba figures in the pauses of the music, to the delight of the company. (164)

The narrator's description of the music's rhythmic thumping sounds is reminiscent of the early account of the rhythm of the slave music on the Montfort's Bermuda plantation. The humorous juba images contrived by Will and Jinny draw clear connection to African dance and the dance of the young partygoers at the Smith's house.[5] The dance ends with the Rev. Tommy declaring that "he hadn't enjoyed himself so much since he came up North" (164). That this merriment kindles fond memories of Rev. Tommy's life in the south, suggests again the survival of Africanity in black America. Despite Ma Smith's reservations, the affair incited no commentary from the community. That this wild dancing and merry making goes uncriticized hints at the ambiguous place of Africanity in this black middle class Christian community.

The thread of African-Christian tension is further woven in two extraordinary members of this black Boston community. Dr. Abraham Peters and Madame Frances are southerners who migrate to the north after emancipation. While neither is among the influential members of the community, both nevertheless elicit a respect that is born out of their supernatural gifts. Dr. Abraham Peters, the janitor at a prominent black church, does not come by his title of doctor through formal education. Peters is a former slave, who having never had the advantage of a formal education, is well regarded by whites as well as fellow blacks in his own community. His medical talent, referred to in the North as magnetics, was called "hoodoo" in his native southern community. One of the many ironies in his life is the simultaneous occurrence of his Christian conversion and his awakening to his supernatural powers. Peters is a man of the church, but he is also a practitioner in the art of the occult. The convergence of the two worlds can make for ironic and humorous moments, as evinced in the story Peters tells of a revelation that changed his life. He recalls working as a ship's cook when the ongoing trial of supporting a large family is suddenly magnified with the death of a child that he and his wife cannot afford to bury. While working in the steamboat kitchen, Peters is astonished at hearing the voice of God speak to him: "Git up, Abraham Peters, an' go out an' hoodoo the fust man you meet" (136). This is a paradoxical moment: Peters is ordered by God, the Christian divine, to engage in the sacrilegious act of hoodoo. With this charge, Peters leaves his post, not knowing what the command has meant in practical terms, but trusting that God will make things clear.

In this state of confusion, Peters comes across the ship's captain and in the following exchange, he learns how it is that he will meet with financial security:

> I says, not thinkin' what wurds I was goin' ter utter: "Mornin', Cap'n; how's yer corporosity seem to segashiate?" Cap'n he roared; you could a heard him holler up to Boston. He slapped me on the back, an' says he: "Abe Peters, that's the gol darndest thing I ever heard." With that he hauled out a five-dollar bill an' gave me, an' walked off laughin' fit to kill hisself. By night I had twenty dollars in my pocket, an' everybody on the boat was a callin' me "corporosity segashiate." I've used that hoodoo ever since, an' I ain't found nary white gempleman can seem to git 'way from it without showing the color of his money. (137)

Shortly after this revelation on the ship, Peters lands a job on shore as a janitor in the building of a Christian Science congregation. Through his association with this group, Peters learns to "make an hones' dollar" with his gift of healing. Under the influence of the Christian Scientists he "determined to adop' magnifyin' as a perfeshun" and for nearly ten years he had survived well in this capacity (139). In the winding and humorous tale that Abraham Peters narrates, Africanity meets Christianity and the result is not that one consumes or overrides the other, but rather that a fusion and a renaming occur. Hoodoo is still hoodoo for Peters—he does not change his art. He simply changes the name from hoodoo to magnetism, thereby rendering his art acceptable in the middle class north where he resides. Not insignificant is the access to money that his accommodation allows him as well.

Like Abraham Peters, Madame Frances is a practitioner of the supernatural arts. She enters the novel in yet another ironic encounter between Christianity and the occult—she has set up a booth at the church fair. Also worth noting is the location of Madame Frances's home: she dwells in the historic section of black Boston where we also find "the first church the colored people owned in Massachusetts" (275). After introducing Madame Frances as "spiritualistic soothsayer and marvellous mind-reader," the narrator intrudes with an elucidation on the ineptness of the supernatural in the white world. According to the narrator, as with the East Indian and the Egyptian, the supernatural powers of blacks is neutralized when transported from their native shores: "We hear much of spells and charms being put upon unpleasant neighbors. . . . But if we notice, these wonderful and terrorizing acts were never perpetrated against the inhuman master or mistress of the isolated plantation, never upon enemies wearing a white skin, but always upon the humble associate and brother in bondage" (199). It appears that the same is to be presumed about Madame Frances who "was supposed to be skilled in the occult acts which were once the glory of the freshly imported African" (199).

Hopkins's narrator deems African spirituality powerless in the face of white authority; however, the narrative unfolds in such a way that the contrary is the case. It is from the prophecies of Madame Frances, the black seer, that the plot unfolds.[6] Madame Frances accurately foretells the fall and the death of the villain, John Langley. Although he is engaged to Dora, Langley has designs for Sappho. He pursues Sappho, despite knowing that his good friend and would-be brother-in-law, Will, hopes to marry her. His deceitfulness carries over to his business transactions, and this includes his betrayal of those in his community as he seeks wealth. In her first prophecy to Langley, Madame Frances warns him to do away with his deviousness else face the costly consequences. In a later meeting, she predicts that his schemes will fail and that he will not enjoy his wealth. She leaves him with a despairing vision of himself in "a field of ice and snow, vast and unbroken— terrible in its dreary isolation" (285). This scene proves to be the vast cold wilderness that Langley finds instead of the promised wealth that he seeks out west. As Madame Frances foretells, Langley does not live to enjoy his wealth—his fortune is left to his surviving family in Bermuda, including his mother who had conceived him out of her forced relationship years earlier with Anson Pollock, the father he had never known. At the moment of his death, "the field of ice and snow which had been shown to him stretched before him in dreary, unbroken silence," and Langley acknowledges that the old fortune teller had been right in her prediction (400).

In like fashion, Madame Frances's other predictions come to fruition. Dora discovers Langley's unfaithfulness and his dishonorable intentions for her good friend, Sappho. As Madame Frances has predicted, however, Dora finds a truer mate. Sappho meets with the improved fortune that Madame Frances has prophesied—Will finds her and they marry. At the novel's end the narrator's earlier contention of the ineffectiveness of black spiritual powers in the white world seems baseless. Returning to the image of the haunted Anson Pollock after he has brought about the death of the Montfort parents, black spiritual power ultimately prevails. Pollock lives a miserable existence after his heinous act: he is unable to enjoy his wealth, and like him, his son, John Langley is also cursed. The descendants of the ill-treated Montforts triumph in the end, and they use their wealth and privileges for the good of their community. Throughout their trials these upstanding middle class blacks maintain their commitment to community and church. But church, that is, Christianity, has not been the spiritual force behind their fortunes. From the slaves' ominous reports of the spirit of Mrs. Montfort walking about the plantation to the final manifestation of Madame Frances's prophecies, it is the spiritual force of their black ancestors that has steered these post-emancipation blacks to optimistic expectations.

In *Contending Forces,* the African-rooted priority for community prevails over American individualism, and this is especially evident in the character John Langley. Langley stands out as an evil presence in the community, in great part because he represents unchecked self-interest. Langley's fall can be tied to W.E.B. DuBois's warning of the ills of "moneygetting," that is, the reckless pursuit of wealth that leads individuals to sacrifice their integrity and the interest of the race for individual gain (Nerad 359). The implications of Langley's fall, however, are not so much his failure to "understand the complex connections among material gain, education, social equality, and political representation" (359), but rather his spiritual void. Langley willingly delivers his friends and his community to the destructive intentions of white politicians. While he harbors no particular dislike for his fellow blacks, he feels no special commitment to them either. His preoccupation with his own interests contrasts those of the Smiths and Dr. Lewis, and even the bourgeois "400" who step beyond their elitism to offer their services to the community.

Among the numerous recitations on the importance of race unity in the novel, Luke Sawyer's address to fellow members of the American Colored League stands out. Sawyer is not a major character; however, his words to this group of black activists, speak to the novel's theme. He reminds fellow blacks that it is submission to a system that promotes greed and selfishness that threatens the future of blacks. Sawyer argues that black progress depends in large part, on the commitment of blacks to one another:

> lack of brotherly affiliation, lack of energy for the right and the power of the almighty dollar which deadens men's hearts to the sufferings of their brothers, and makes them feel that if only they can rise to the top of the ladder may God help the hindmost man. . . . These are the contending forces that are dooming this race to despair. (256)

Ironically, John Langley listens to Sawyer, but is unmoved by his words. Instead, Langley is interested in the story Sawyer tells of a young quadroon girl in Louisiana raped by her white uncle. Recognizing that the victim is in fact, the mysterious, Sappho Clark, Langley then attempts to manipulate Sappho with the threat of revealing her secret. John Langley is the embodiment of evil and individualism—he is spiritually bankrupt—and his fall represents a triumph of community and those dedicated to the common good. A pawn under the control of white usurpers, Langley embodies the white political and economic exploitation of blacks in late nineteenth-century America. His death then also symbolizes a victory for blacks over the "contending forces" of greed and ruthlessness that Luke Sawyer finds infiltrating the souls of blacks.

Luke Sawyer's rejection of the corrupt materialism of the white world underscores the more critical gaze that late nineteenth-century blacks cast on the presumed portrait of a superior white society. As black leaders became more aware of their growing marginality in mainstream America, their isolation awarded them the position and opportunity to reflect more critically on the matter of black assimilation. The anticipated gains from constructing blackness through the discourse of white middle-classness proved unattainable. Blacks would not be welcomed into the American citizenry by simply shedding their ties to their African past and appropriating the sensibilities of western culture. This alienation opened the doors for black authors to rethink Africanity and to explore more favorably their connections to Africa.

The fiction of Harper and Hopkins marks a period during which black authors attempted to counter America's bleak turn-of-the-century treatment and representation of blacks. It was an era also marked by the dawn of western modernism, inviting more radical thinking about Christianity than perhaps any prior moment in American history. Intellectuals and artists began to explore biblical and spiritual questions that destabilized the image of Christianity as the religious center of western civilization and history. European artists, in particular, had begun to explore connections of eastern mysticism and Christianity, and to consider the "exotic/African" side of all human kind. The unconscious was becoming a new literary playing field and substituting images and symbols for narrative was an emerging method of storytelling. More than a decade before the celebrated era of American modernism, Alice Dunbar-Nelson's writings illustrated a mind experimenting with these hallmarks of twentieth century thinking. Ironically, scholarship on Dunbar-Nelson's fiction has typically focused on her work as regional or local color fiction.[7] Her use of New Orleans as a recurring setting and her recurring cast of near-white and white protagonists has contributed to this limited reading of her work. While Dunbar-Nelson clearly appropriates the local color of New Orleans in her early fiction, these sketches nevertheless offer striking reflections on the convergence of modernity and religiosity that unfastens Christianity's hold in the author's creative mind.

Although she publishes short fiction, Dunbar-Nelson warrants mention here because her writings highlight the transforming imagination of black women writers at the close of the nineteenth century into the celebrated, post-WWI era of African American Renaissance writing. Her sketches anticipate the lengthier Christian skepticism that is explored in the Harlem Renaissance novels of Nella Larsen and Zora Neale Hurston. Dunbar-Nelson's 1895 montage of fictional and essay sketches and poems, *Violets and Other Tales,* as well as her 1899 short story collection, *The Goodness of St Rocque and Other Stories* represent the junction between the cautiously constructed Christian/African negotiation of Harper and Hopkins and the more open critiques of the spiritual in the works of Hurston and Larsen. Both racial alienation and rising modernism would contribute to more daring explorations of spirituality in black women's fiction. While Harper and Hopkins's novels construct a fictional world of Christian/African spiritual coexistence, their twentieth-century successors would challenge Christianity in more radical ways. Dunbar-Nelson's late nineteenth-century publications bridge these differing literary negotiations of the spiritual: she moves beyond the construct of a conciliatory discourse of African-Christian mutuality to explore the failure of Christianity, particularly its failure in the lives of women. In this respect, she anticipates the spiritual struggles of Larsen and Hurston's protagonists.

In the introduction to *Violets and Other Tales,* Dunbar-Nelson, then Alice Ruth Moore, claims a lighthearted intention to her readers. She announces that this work "seeks to do nothing more than amuse." This innocent claim, however, becomes apparently misleading in the opening short story, "Violets." The story of a young woman who dies of a broken heart, "Violets" is marked in time by two successive Easter Sundays and framed by an unconventional use of Easter images and symbols. The story opens on Easter evening with a young woman retiring from an Easter day full of promise and happiness. In a letter written by the young woman to her lover, we learn that she has sent him violets as a reminder of her love. The violets are also symbolic of Christ whose greatness is remembered during the Easter season by the color purple—most commonly expressed by the purple colored robe that is draped over the cross during this season. The young woman's request to her lover to "keep them [the violets] in remembrance of me" (15), echoes Christ's command to his disciples to reenact their communion in remembrance of him. Just as Christ is betrayed by his disciple, Judas, the young woman is betrayed by her lover. On the next Easter the betrayed victim lies in a casket, prepared for burial on the day of Christ's resurrection. While the narrator proclaims that "she kneels at the throne of heaven" (16), her death does not echo the death and the glorious resurrection of Christ. Unlike Christ who is remembered, and whose sacrifice is celebrated each Easter, this sufferer is condemned to eternal obscurity. Her eternal fate is represented by the faded violets thrown into the fire by her lover who seems unable to recall who had given him these flowers. Dunbar-Nelson's inversion of Christian images ultimately suggests the failure of Christianity. The young suffering woman is not redeemed to a glorious hereafter; instead, she is remitted to the most horrible of fates—the realm of the forgotten. To have suffered and been remembered offers opportunity for eternity; however, to die and to be forgotten negates one's life.

In similar tales of betrayal such as "Little Miss Sophie," (found in both collections, *Violets* and *The Goodness of St. Rocque*) and "Tony's Wife" (in *Goodness of St. Roque*), Dunbar-Nelson again explores the victimization of women through the backdrop of Christianity. These stories tell the suffering of women, who betrayed by men, look to the church for guidance and solace but find neither. Like the young woman in "Violets," they are left alone and destitute by their presumed lovers, and the church offers them no earthly solace. Little Miss Sophie works herself to death to restore to her lover of long ago his pawned ring. She has sacrificed life and money for a man who has long since forgotten her. She prays ritually to the Virgin Mary, but her life remains despairing and toilsome. Similarly, in "Tony's Wife," Dunbar-Nelson's protagonist is the portrait of hopelessness. While she does not die at the story's end, Tony's in-name-only wife has been left with nothing after his death. Tony has refused to marry her, thereby denying her the financial and social benefits of widowhood. Though the priest at Tony's deathbed might have the power to influence him to legitimate his common-law wife, he refuses to intervene. Tony, who has been unkind and abusive in life, is awarded the Catholic rites of the dead. Ironically, his meek and victimized mistress finds herself desolate and marginalized. She was not his legal wife; she thus remains obscure and unvalidated.

Dunbar-Nelson broadens her critique of Christianity in such works as "In Unconsciousness" and "The Unknown Life of Jesus Christ." Published in the *Violets* collection, both sketches offer unconventional interpretations of Christianity and demonstrate her early modernist musings. "In Unconsciousness" traces the narrator's mythical explorations while under the influence of anesthesia in the dentist's office. In this drug-induced state the narrator experiences time and eternity, and she borrows from biblical, East Indian, and western classical images to tell the story of her spiritual travels. Similarly, in "The Unknown Life of Jesus Christ," the narrator challenges western notions of the mutual exclusivity of western and eastern spirituality. Dunbar-Nelson's deconstruction of the biblical story of Christ is particularly noteworthy: she entertains the legend that Christ traveled and studied with mystics in India during the period of his life unaccounted for in the Bible. She criticizes western thinking that does not permit inquiries beyond the perimeters of its own belief systems: "We are so steeped in tradition, and so conservative on any subject that touches our religious beliefs that it is somewhat difficult to reconcile ourselves to another addition to our Scriptures" (120). Despite this outward resistance in American thinking, Dunbar-Nelson suggests that the reality of spiritual multiplicities lies not too far beneath the surface. This she illustrates in the short story "The Goodness of St. Rocque," from the collection of the same name.

"The Goodness of St. Rocque" is the story of Manuela, a young woman, who, through the employment of an occultist, manages to thwart her lover's attempt at unfaithfulness. Manuela goes to a soothsayer, "a little wizened yellow woman," to counter the designs of her female rival, the "blonde and petite" Claralie (8, 5). Dunbar-Nelson's identification of the soothsayer as a yellow woman is not insignificant: her colored skin is immediately cast against the white Creoles who are the subjects of this story. The Wizened One prescribes an anecdote that calls on supernatural and Catholic rituals. She instructs Manuela as follows: "I give you one lil' charm fo' to ween him back, yaas. You wear h'it 'roun' you' wais', an' he come back. Den you mek prayer at St. Rocque an' burn can'le" (9). Manuela wins back her beloved Theophile after she has followed, to the letter, the instructions of the Wizened One. The story ends with the unanswered speculation as to whether Christianity or conjuration should be credited for Manuela's happy ending. The Wizened One symbolizes the spiritual world that is the legacy of Africa. While her mastery in the mysticism of Christianity as well as African rooted spirituality speaks to a merging of the two forces, she negotiates the two worlds much like Hopkins's mystics, Abraham Peters and Madame Frances. Like Peters and Frances, the Wizened One provides supernatural influence that promises success in the event that Christianity's powers should fail.[8]

The late nineteenth-century novels of Harper and Hopkins signal a loosening of Christianity's grip on the literary imaginations of black women writers. The period is clearly marked by the prevailing influence of Christianity in black women's writings, but as Frances Harper and Pauline Hopkins demonstrate in their novels, black Christianity clearly differs from its white counterpart. Harper and Hopkins open the door to the conception and representation of folk/African-rooted spirituality as integral to African American Christianity. They pave the way to literary explorations of Africanity that do away with apology and negations and the positioning of Africa as other. Many scholars have looked at the novels of Harper and Hopkins as works purporting African American worthiness through sentimental constructions of a black middle class; however, little regard has been given to their groundbreaking contributions to a revival of the African spirit in the black literary imagination. This failure to read works such as Harper's and Hopkins's beyond the prism of dominant gender and racial discourses "stems from embarrassment occasioned by inadequate understanding of African American cultural history. Many of us underestimate or misinterpret the texts themselves because we are not aware of the variety of sources for and the resources of their writers" (Foster 51). Harper and Hopkins demonstrate that black women writers were not far removed from knowledge of the black spiritual world that was conscious of and tied to a pre-Christian legacy. Furthermore, their works demonstrate that the centralness of Africanity in the works of celebrated modern writers such as Toni Morrison, Alice Walker, and Gloria Naylor comes out of a literary tradition. Harper and Hopkins demonstrate that black women writers have been influenced by an African presence, one that lay silenced and ridiculed for generations until the conditions were right for regeneration.

NOTES

1. In her essay "Pauline Hopkins and the Occult: African-American Revisions of Nineteenth-Century Sciences" (*American Literary History* 8.1 [Spring 1996]: 57–82), Susan Gillman recalls Hopkins's deep interest in the theory of race and her rejection of the leading white racist theories of her time. She argues that *Of One Blood* advances Hopkins's Ethiopianism and that "[t]he Meroe section of the novel brings us to the heart of Hopkins's Africa and the center of her strategy of using archaeological data to refute the claims of ethnological science (66).

2. Although Tate argues that Hopkins's choice of the name Candace for her fictional Ethiopian queen is inappropriate, on the contrary the name is a fitting choice given Hopkins's objective. Hopkins likely chose the name Candace from her knowledge of the biblical Queen Candace from Ethiopia (Acts 8: 27).

3. Gwendolyn Brooks is often cited for her criticism of *Contending Forces* in her afterword to the 1978 edition of the text. Brooks argues that the novel is little more than a continuum of slavery's self-effacing effects on blacks. In "Worldview and the Use of the Near-White Heroine in Pauline Hopkins's *Contending Forces*," (*Journal of Black Studies* 28.5 [May 1998]: 616–627), an essay twenty years after Brooks's criticism, Vashti Crutcher Lewis still finds fault with Hopkins for her failure to offer dark-skinned black heroines.

4. This recurring juxtaposition of Christianity and African spirituality in *Contending Forces* also represents Pauline Hopkins's interest in black Africa's place in and contribution to biblical and ancient history. It is an interest that blossoms in her serialized novel *Of One Blood*. In her essay "Not Black and/or White: Reading Racial Difference in Heliodoras's *Ethiopica* and Pauline Hopkins's *Of One Blood*" (*African American Review* 35.3 [2001]: 375–390), Marla Harris explains that "since one of Hopkins's aims in the novel is to 'prove' (through Reuel's Fictional expedition) that both Greek and Egyptian cultures actually derived from Ethiopian civilization, she means to critique the grounds on which white Americans base their claims to cultural superiority" (384).

5. Juba is a dance of African origin with a history that includes connections to American minstrelsy. See Donald M. Morales's essay "The Pervasive Force of Music in African, Caribbean, and African American Drama," for a similar discussion on August Wilson's use of juba to highlight African-Christian tensions in his play *Joe Turner's Come and Gone*. For a more detailed discussion of juba, see Marian Hannah Winter's essay "Juba and American Minstrelsy."

6. As visionary and seer, Madame Frances's fictional successor emerges in Hopkins's 1902–1903 serialized novel *Of One Blood, or, the Hidden Self*. In this tale, Aunt Hannah, the protagonist's grandmother, is the hoodoo practitioner who holds family and ancestral knowledge that lies at the center of the narrative.

7. For the most part Dunbar-Nelson's contemporaries considered *Violets* and *Goodness of St. Roque* stories of New Orleans Creole life. Today, critics have acknowledged Dunbar-Nelson's interrogation of paradigms and practices of race and gender in turn-of-the-century New Orleans. Current scholarship on Dunbar-Nelson has moved beyond the early presumptions of her work as simply a nexus to the Creole fiction of her white predecessors. For more detailed readings on race and gender in Dunbar-Nelson's works, see Jordan Stouck's "Identities in Crisis: Alice Dunbar-Nelson's New Orleans Fiction" (*Canadian Review of American Studies* 34.3 [2004]: 269–289); Pamela Glenn Menke's "Behind the 'White Veil': Alice Dunbar-Nelson, Creole Color, and *The Goodness of St. Rocque*" in *Songs of Reconstructing South: Building Literary Louisiana, 1865–1945*. Westport, CN: Greenwood Publishers, 2002; and Kristina Brooks's "Alice Dunbar-Nelson's Local Colors of Ethnicity, Class, and Place," (*MELUS* 23.2 [Summer 1998]: 3–26)

8. For a more detailed discussion of Alice Dunbar-Nelson's manipulations of Christian and African religiosity, see Elizabeth J. West's "Religion, Race, and Gender in the 'Raceless' Fiction of Alice Dunbar-Nelson," in *Black Magnolias* 3.1 (March–May 2009): 5–19.

WORKS CITED

Allen, Carol. "One Blood: Nationality and Domesticity in the Work of Pauline Hopkins." *Black Women Intellectuals: Strategies of Nation, Family, and Neighborhood in the Works of Pauline Hopkins, Jessie Fauset, and Marita Bonner*. New York: Garland Publishing, 1998.

Cassidy, Thomas. "Contending Contexts: Pauline E. Hopkins's *Contending Forces*." African American Review 32.4 (1998): 661–672.

Dunbar-Nelson, Alice. *The Works of Alice Dunbar-Nelson*. Ed. Gloria T. Hull. New York: Oxford University Press, 1988.

Foster, Frances Smith. "Gender, Genre and Vulgar Secularism: The Case of Frances Ellen Watkins Harper and the AME Press." *Tennessee Studies in Literature* 38 (1997): 46–59.

Griffin, Farah Jasmine. "Frances Ellen Watkins Harper in the Reconstruction South." *Sage* (1988): 45–47.

Harper, Frances E. W. *Iola Leroy*. 1893. 2nd ed. Introd. Frances Smith Foster. New York: Oxford University Press, 1988.

———. *Minnie's Sacrifice*. Ed. Frances Smith Foster. Boston: Beacon Press, 1994.

———. *Sowing and Reaping*. Ed. Frances Smith Foster. Boston: Beacon Press, 1994.

———. *Trial and Triumph*. Ed. Frances Smith Foster. Boston: Beacon Press, 1994.

Hopkins, Pauline E. *Contending Forces*. 1900. Introd. Richard Yarborough. New York: Oxford University Press, 1988.

Nerad, Julie Cary. "'So Strangely Interwoven': The Property of Inheritance, Race, and Sexual Morality in Pauline E. Hopkins's *Contending Forces*." *African American Review* 35.3 (2001): 357–373.

Peterson, Carla L. *"Doers of the Word": African-American Women Speakers & Writers in the North (1830–1880)*. New Brunswick, NJ: Rutgers University Press, 1998.

Putzi, Jennifer. "'Raising the Stigma': Black Womanhood and the Marked Body in Pauline E. Hopkins's *Contending Forces*." *College Literature* (Spring 2004): 1–21.

Randle, Gloria T. "Mates, Marriage, and Motherhood: Feminist Visions in Pauline Hopkins's *Contending Forces*." *Tulsa Studies in Women's Literature* 18.2 (Autumn 1999): 193–214.

Tate, Claudia. "Pauline Hopkins: Our Literary Foremother." *Conjuring: Black Women, Fiction, and Literary Tradition*. Eds. Marjorie Pryse and Hortense Spillers. Bloomington: Indiana University Press, 1985. 53–66.

Toohey, Michelle Campbell. "'A Deeper Purpose' in the Serialized Novels of Frances Ellen Watkins Harper." *The Only Efficient Instrument: American Women Writers and the Periodical, 1837–1916*. Eds. Susan Alves and Aleta Feinsold Cane. Iowa City: University of Iowa Press, 2001.

Chapter Six

Rethinking Religiosity in the Wake of Modernity

Transformations of Christian Idealisms in the Novels of Jessie Redmon Fauset

Since its 1923 publication, Jean Toomer's *Cane* has been hailed a landmark work of African American modernism. While Alice Dunbar-Nelson preceded Toomer by more than two decades in publishing a montage of short pieces that are arguably modernist in theme and style, Toomer and his celebrated black male contemporaries continue to be recognized as the founders of the Harlem Renaissance and black modernism. Though Toomer's contemporary and the author of four novels, Jessie Redmon Fauset would also be unacknowledged as a figure of import in the black Renaissance era. As Deborah McDowell reminds us in her introduction to the 1990 edition of Jessie Fauset's *Plum Bun*, it was Langston Hughes who deemed Fauset's role in the New Negro Movement of the 1920s as that of midwife (ix). By designating Fauset midwife to the movement, Hughes excludes her from the community of noteworthy black artists. Her role as editor for the NAACP's magazine, the *Crisis*, during the early years of the Harlem Renaissance earned Fauset the midwife accolade. As editor of the *Crisis*, she played a key role in publishing the works of many rising and would-be artists of this period. But of her own novels, her black male contemporaries offered nominal praise, and until the recent era of close and more informed readings of black women's writings, Fauset was repeatedly dismissed as a writer whose works collapsed black experience into middle class sentimental discourse. Among her contemporaries, Fauset's novels were viewed from the range of unremarkable to exceptional.[1] Whether critical or complimentary of Fauset's artistry, most reviewers acknowledged her work for its optimistic representation of an educated and thriving black middle class.

Until recently, scholars did not recognize Fauset's novels as illustrative of the modernist form and content identified in the fiction of her more celebrated male contemporaries. Jean Toomer's *Cane* (1923), Claude McKay's *Home to Harlem* (1928), and Langston Hughes's *Not Without Laughter* (1930) have been considered more artistically complex than the presumed simplistic novels by Fauset. In these works one could find techniques and themes that became markers of modernist writing: among these three works are found such recognizable techniques as stream of consciousness, imagism, symbolism, the nonlinear and the psychological plot. The plots in these works have been discussed for their complexity, for their nonconcentric depiction of God and humanity, for their challenge to conventional notions of rationality, and particularly in the case of Toomer and McKay's works, for their exploration of primitivism and innocence—further, with their association of primitiveness with blackness.

In critical works that have for the most part given more thorough examination and commendation to black male writers for their expressions of modernistic genius, Fauset's novels have been conspicuously reviled or disregarded. Fauset, of course, has not been singled out in this regard, for only in recent decades has the scholarship of Fauset's female contemporaries, Nella Larsen and Zora Neale Hurston, been awarded more favorable readings. Hurston and Larsen were also overlooked as serious artists of the New Negro Movement, and like Fauset, they would not live to see their works awarded the critical acclaim of their black male contemporaries. Today, Nella Larsen's *Quicksand* and *Passing* are recognized as works that demonstrate an exceptional technical and thematic talent, and Hurston's works are now explored in cross disciplinary contexts that reveal her insight as an anthropologist, folklorist, dramatist, and fiction writer. Perhaps the resurrection of Zora Neale Hurston to the reading public would have occurred without Alice Walker's central role. However, with Walker's search for Hurston's unmarked grave and her subsequent essay describing this search and the revelation of Hurston's importance, the Hurston revival was fueled large scale into the academy. Hurston has emerged as one of the most studied artists of the Harlem Renaissance. Today, she is acclaimed not only for her innovative and artistic use of black folk tradition, but also her manipulation of modernist sensibilities and artistic conventions.

While Nella Larsen and Zora Neale Hurston have emerged as celebrated artists of the modernist tradition, substantially less critical acclaim has been awarded Jessie Fauset. Fauset published four novels; however, the focus here will be her first three and more studied works: *There Is Confusion* (1924), *Plum Bun* (1928), and *The Chinaberry Tree* (1931). With its self-defining aim at the humorous, Fauset's last novel, *Comedy, American Style* (1933), diverges from the serious tone of her first three. By its very title, *Comedy, American Style* overtly promises to scrutinize and subvert, and in this sense it is a different work than its three predecessors. It is a text that deserves a different analysis than that of this study. While the novel plays to sentimentalism, it does so without pretense of commitment to its form or themes. In form, Fauset's first three novels are more reminiscent of sentimental fiction: in general, she maintains a linear plot structure, characters seem to be constructed in conventional good/evil dichotomies, plots unravel through chance meetings and deathbed confessions, plots end in happy marriage for the female protagonist, and main characters are seemingly models of middle class gentility, who in the end, reaffirm the rightness of this social order.

Fauset's lesser acclaim than Hurston and Larsen may have much to do with her more veiled use of modernist conventions in her novels. Her subversion of sentimentalism has only recently become the focus of scholarship on her fiction. Studies of Fauset's fiction are shifting from the more obvious sentimental dimension in her work to the subversive and modernist queries beneath the surface. Current favorable criticisms of her works do not, however, call on readers to ignore Fauset's sometimes glaring acquiescence to dominant class and gender paradigms. For example, Deborah E. McDowell hails Fauset for her keen insight into the gender-race struggle of black women: "The protagonists of all her novels are black women, and she makes clear in each novel that social conventions have not sided well with them but, rather, have been antagonistic" ("Neglected Dimension . . ." 87). McDowell is, however, equally candid about the shortfall of reading Fauset's novels as feminist tracts: "On the one hand, she appeals for women's right to challenge socially sanctioned modes of feminine behavior, but on the other, she frequently retreats to the safety of traditional attitudes about women in traditional roles" (88). McDowell's cautious recognition of feminist assertions in Fauset's fiction illustrates why black writers like Fauset and Hurston represent a "literary legacy [that] resists classification" (155). Early criticism of Hurston was limited to reading her works out of a black folk tradition, while Fauset's works were relegated to discussions of their connection to a white bourgeois informed tradition. In her study of race, class, and gender in the works of Hurston, Fauset, and Dorothy West, Sharon L. Jones explores the more complex nature of the fiction of these black women. In the case of Fauset, she emphasizes Fauset's interrogation of conventional gender constructs and thus aligns her with more recent feminist criticism on the writings of her contemporaries, Larsen and Hurston. Although her female protagonists marry at the close of the novels, Fauset develops them as autonomous in their thoughts and actions. Her heroines are aware of their own individual worth before they finally enter the world of matrimony.

Fauset's interrogation of sex and gender, particularly in *Plum Bun* with her heroine's challenge of and final disregard for dominant social conventions on female sexuality, situates her work in a modernist context. Her novels are further unacknowledged for their challenge to conventional notions of Christianity. Twentieth century religious deconstruction that scholars often associate with modernist introspection has much earlier origins for black thinkers. Early African American women's writings that revealed the coexistence of African-Christian spiritual dichotomies presaged twentieth-century black women's fiction that depicts Anglo Christianity as a failed spiritual option in black life. Recalling the focus of the previous chapter—the late nineteenth-century fiction of Frances Harper and Pauline Hopkins, we are reminded that prior to the twentieth century black women writers were critiquing western civilization's threat to the humanity and spirituality of black people as well as humanity in general. Additionally, in Alice Dunbar-Nelson's early writings we find the nexus to Harper and Hopkins's works. Dunbar-Nelson is a conduit between nineteenth- and twentieth-century black women's fiction: her religious and spiritual musings anticipate twentieth-century black women's fiction that subverts Christianity and western ontological ideals. She demonstrates that presumed markers of modernism in black women's fiction may in fact be traced to a pre-modernist black worldview.

Throughout their history, African American writers have been influenced by western literary traditions. However, their literary black predecessors as well as oral and performative traditions in black culture have equally informed black writers. This is particularly true in black literary representations of the spiritual. Because black spirituality has been shaped by both western and African influences, only through recognition of both cultural influences can we more fully appreciate the place of the spiritual in black writings. As in most studies of people of color in western society, those redeemable elements of nonwhite culture that can be linked to presumed markers of white cultural superiority are assumed to originate in white society—whether those people may have had a tradition that preceded contact with whites is generally overlooked. Therefore, one can readily find scholarship that explores Christianity's influence among blacks in the United States, but only in recent decades have scholars begun to look seriously and with depth at the influence of a pre–Middle Passage African cosmology among New World blacks. A significant body of research can be found on Christianity and black modernism, but much is yet needed in the area of Africanity and black modernism. Through the fictional works of Fauset, Larsen, and Hurston we can ascertain much about Africanity and modernism in the imagination of black women writers in early twentieth-century America. The fiction of these better-known Harlem Renaissance women writers reveals transformation of a veiled Africanist tradition to a more open and affirming declaration of Africanity. The validation of Africanity that emerges in Hurston's *Their Eyes Were Watching God* can be read as an outgrowth of the

Christian apathy in Fauset's novels and the spiritual despair in Larsen's *Quicksand*. The decades that mark the publication of Fauset, Larsen, and Hurston's fiction represent the decline of Christianity's persisting period in black women's fiction. This transformative period is highlighted by the authors' challenge to Christianity's presence and authority in black life.

A comparison of Fauset and her nineteenth-century predecessors, Harper and Hopkins, reveals her diversion from a black female literary tradition of the spiritual. The inhabitants of Fauset's northern, middle class black communities have become the spiritually empty, post-war money worshipers who threaten the "ole time religion" in Harper's *Iola Leroy* and the mirror image of those who forsake the community in Hopkins's *Contending Forces*. On the surface, Fauset's novels seem to mimic sentimental fiction, especially with predictable ovations to Christianity. Fauset maintains Christianity as the religious center in her fictional black communities, but it is a hallow core. With a black middle class that regards church as a social obligation, Christianity in Fauset's novels is marked by a spiritual void given form only through social genuflection.

With the portrait of Christianity as little more than window dressing in black middle class life, Fauset does not maintain Christianity as central to community ties. Fauset's novels maintain a discourse on community and individuality, repeatedly highlighting the inherent conflict between the pursuit of individual desires and the individual's obligation to community. This emphasis is most evident in her first novel, *There Is Confusion* (1924), which at its core explores the legacy of race obligation in two middle class black families. The history of the Marshalls and the Byes dates back to their enslaved ancestors, and it is their inherited sense of race duty that separates them from the larger, northern black community to which they belong. These two families highlight "Fauset's model family [which] differs significantly from the traditional, nuclear family. According to her, the family is a group of people who link their labor, form a common pool, and work for the unit's benefit. Any individual not working for the family's well-being is not a member, even though he or she might have biological ties to others in the group" (Allen 52). Although Carol Allen does not tie this reading of family in Fauset's novels to an African spiritual origin, she highlights an African-centered philosophy of family and community that as this study has shown, can be traced to some of the earliest writings by African American women. It is a philosophy that resonates in Fauset's fiction.

Joel Marshall, the patriarch of the Marshall family, is a self-made man whose successful catering business leads him to New York from his native Richmond, Virginia. Joel imparts to his children the history of black struggles, and he tells them of great blacks who dedicated their lives to the freedom and betterment of the race. Of his four children, Philip and Joanna most deeply internalize their father's call to serve and to become an example for those less fortunate. As a child Joanna enjoys her father's stories and is especially inspired by his accounts of leaders such as Frederick Douglass, Denmark Vessey, Nat Turner, Harriet Tubman, Phillis Wheatley, and Sojourner Truth. Joel explains to Joanna that like these greats she too must be prepared to serve: "So everyone of us has something to do for the race. Never forget that, little girl" (20). Sylvia and Alex are not so driven by the call to serve, but Philip and Joanna harken to their father's call. Joanna commits herself to breaking the race barrier in professional dancing, and Philip dedicates his life to working for blacks who are most in need. Even though they have experienced a privileged upbringing, Joanna and Philip understand the historical and cultural ties that bind blacks from all walks of life. Joel Marshall has successfully instilled in them a sense of duty and belonging to others of their race. They are distinct from the northern blacks in their community whose sense of identity and purpose has not been informed by a legacy of duty and history. It is, in fact, this legacy of duty and history that the Marshalls share with the Byes—the other black family of distinction in this fictional community.

Through Joanna's influence, the young Peter Bye, Joanna's classmate who eventually becomes her fiancé, comes to understand the legacy of race pride, history, and duty that defines his destiny. Orphaned as a child, Peter does not experience the ongoing reinforcement that the Marshall children get through their father's constant reminders and his living example of race uplift philosophy. Peter's legacy is not etched in oral lessons handed down from a living parent: the mystery of Peter's calling is unveiled through the brief inscription in the family Bible that has been passed down to him. Peter's grandfather, Isaiah, inscribed in the Bible his own adaptation of the biblical verse, Matthew 7: 20 that states, "by their fruits ye shall know them." This verse had been inscribed and signed by Aaron and Dinah Bye, the white Byes who gave the Bible as a gift to Joshua and Belle Bye who had once been their property. Responding to the white Bye's appropriation of this scripture, Joshua's son, Isaiah, revises the scripture to foretell the new legacy of the black Byes.

When Isaiah has a son, he transforms the inscription of the white Byes which he interprets as a proclamation of their dominance, into a proclamation of his own triumph:

> Isaiah and Miriam Sayres Bye had one son. "Meriwether," Isaiah wrote in Aaron and Dinah Bye's old gift, and under it in a script as fine and characteristic as that of the original inscription: "By *his* fruits shall ye know—*me*." It was a strange but not unnatural bit of pride, the same pride which had made him name this squirming bundle of potentialities, "Meriwether,—Meriwether Bye," a boy with the same name which old white Aaron Bye's son had borne and with as good chances. (29)

Thus, Isaiah issues in a new era: Isaiah negates the white Byes's assertion of authority and declares his own. The focus for Isaiah is not "their fruits" (the white Byes), but rather his own future generations. His son, the black Meriwether Bye, will mark a new beginning for the black Byes. Through the black Meriwether, the white Byes will come to know Isaiah and the legacy of the black Byes. Isaiah's inscription marks a rare moment in the text where narrative resolution is connected to a visionary; in contrast to nineteenth-century black women's fiction that is replete with visions and prophesies that shape the plot, *There Is Confusion* is not.

By the novel's end, Peter Bye overcomes the fall of the Bye family that is precipitated by his father's failures. He comes to understand the greatness of his grandfather, Isaiah, a free black man who provided economically well for his family but who also faithfully and diligently served his community. Isaiah Bye opened the first school for black children in his Philadelphia community, and because of his service, his name lived on long after him. Isaiah Bye's inscription in the family Bible is central to Peter's discovery of his past and his destiny, but Isaiah's words are also important because they signal the beginning of the black Bye's control of their identity and their future. When Isaiah rewrites the biblical verse that had been inscribed by the white Byes, he makes it his own, thus redefining the black Byes and reshaping their future. Like the biblical Isaiah, Isaiah Bye is patriarch and prophet; his vision foretells the future triumph of the black Byes. His reinscription further signals the black Byes neutralizing the historically denigrating influence of white Christianity on black self-worth and identity. His transformation exemplifies the kind of metamorphosis necessary for blacks to reclaim themselves, to take their futures and their fortunes into their own hands. It is ironic that through the Bible given them by the white Byes—a text that symbolizes their dominance—the black Byes find a voice of defiance and a physical manifestation of not only their connection to their white kin and enslavers, but more importantly, an object that functions as a kind of amulet. Two generations after Isaiah Bye's inscription in the family Bible, the adult Peter Bye discovers that his grandfather's words, preserved in a book that meant little to Peter in his youth, had been cast to connect newer generations of Byes to their past and to direct them, should they lose sight of their destiny. Although Peter was not the least bit religious, the inscription held within the Bible, passed down from his enslaved fore parents, would prove the key to unlock the mystery of his past (36). When Peter's family history is wholly revealed to him, he finds a spiritual peace, and he accepts the legacy of leadership and service into which he was born. It is not Peter's connection to a white familial line that defines him and shapes his fortunes: on the contrary, Peter's success highlights the difference between black and white inferred in Fauset's text. In keeping with the novel's overriding assertion that "African-American art, history, and people [are] the masked and heretofore

muted center of American culture (Kuenz 90), Peter Bye's triumph over the
white Bye's influence symbolizes the triumph of black culture and life over
white.

Peter's young years of restlessness and self-interest are reminiscent of the
fictional hero Milkman, the disoriented and spiritually lost son in Toni Morrison's *Song of Solomon* (1977). Through his search and discovery of his
family history, Milkman, like Peter Bye, is freed from the unexplained despair that has plagued him. *There Is Confusion* precedes *Song of Solomon* by
several decades, but the two heroes face similar spiritual journeys. Peter and
Milkman are born from exceptional ancestral lines. Both, however, wander
through their early years indifferent and unattached to community and family. Peter Bye's journey to self-revelation is connected to a central male
ancestral figure, presaging Milkman's journey more than a half century later.
Peter's emergence into self results from his connection to his grandfather,
Isaiah. Similarly, only after Milkman unravels the mystery of his mythical
forefather, Solomon, does he arrive at a complete understanding of himself.
For each man, the journey to self-revelation occurs through the counsel of a
black woman who sees his struggle and his destiny before he even knows he
is troubled. Milkman will counsel with and be led to the past of self-revelation by his aunt, Pilate. For Peter Bye, the guide is Joanna, the woman who is
also his romantic interest.

Joanna is the spiritual voice and guide for Peter, but Joanna along with
her brother Philip, also serve as fictional mediums through which Fauset
explores the tensions between race duty and self-interest. Like her nineteenth-century predecessors, Fauset overlays the story of the dutiful race
worker onto her sentimental narrative. However, whereas race work fits in
rather naturally with the middle class lives of Harper's and Hopkins's protagonists, race duty threatens Joanna and Philip with a paradoxical spiritual
emptiness that can occur when one is excessively duty bound. Joanna and
Philip, who feel most deeply their call to race work, nearly meet with spiritual ruin by their unrelenting and misplaced sense of mission. They both imagine that with Joanna as dancer and Philip as intellectual they will open doors
for other blacks to follow, and that their lives will serve as examples of black
excellence. Joanna finds success as a dancer, although it is a limited notoriety. She learns the bitter reality that black artists are confined to roles that
white producers deem appropriate—a black performer, no matter how talented, cannot be imagined by whites as a symbol of beauty or universal
Americanness. More disturbing for Joanna, however, is the realization that
her stage triumph has isolated her from the human connections that are most
important: "For the first time in her life she saw the importance of human
relationships. What did a knowledge of singing, dancing, of any of the arts
amount to without people, without parents, brothers, sisters, lovers to share
one's failure, one's triumphs?" (176–177). Joanna begins to reconsider her

ambitions, and she finally questions whether dancing is really the means through which she is to live out her father's great expectations. Dancing, as it turns out, is not the manifestation of greatness that Joel Marshall had envisioned for his daughter, and as the two acknowledge that her talents could be employed in worthier pursuits, Joanna begins her journey back to family and community (236).

Joanna's venture into public life symbolizes the ongoing experience of blacks who must step outside their communities into an unwelcoming white world to make their living. Her struggles highlight the tension between the community and the outside world. Joanna's journey is not so different from Toomer's black southerners who come north seeking their fortunes only to become stripped of their souls and their humanity in the materialism of the urban north. Unlike Toomer's spiritually castrated blacks in the north, however, Joanna has access to a return passage. She is not left destitute in the meaninglessness of white materialism; she returns home where she can rediscover self and place. Although she had believed that her determination to succeed as a dancer was part of her ambition for the race, Joanna finally realizes that her ambition originated in self-interest. She gives up stardom for marriage and finds in that the greatness of serving and belonging. Of course, it is this kind of change in her protagonists' ambitions that elicits charges that Fauset ultimately reaffirms white middle class gender constructs. However, a comparison of Joanna's arrival at her destiny with that of her father suggests that gender is not the defining factor in Joanna's choice. Unlike her father, who out of the greater need of his family settled into a profession not of his choosing, Joanna, in the name of the race, chose a profession that would bring her personal notoriety. Joel Marshall sacrificed personal ambition; he resigned himself to the profession of chef instead of pursuing his youthful and loftier dream of a higher education and a career as a minister. His heroism is exemplified in his sacrifice for his family, his commitment to his community, and in the ingenuity he shows with building a business out of the very profession that had consumed his dreams.

After his mother is stricken ill, young Joel Marshall takes his college savings and purchases a house that serves the dual purpose of restaurant and personal residence. Joel's purchase of a house and his decision to care for his ill parent is arguably a gender switch. He confines himself to domestic space and becomes a caretaker—a typically feminine designation. Out of this humble beginning he builds a highly successful catering business. In the end, he finds success and relative notoriety, but not out of self-ambition. Out of his selfless act to provide for his mother, Joel found his way to what proved to be his calling. It is initially in service to his mother, and later throughout his life his service to his family and community, that Joel Marshall becomes a well-known, well-respected, and well-liked member of his black community. He has instilled in Joanna the desire to achieve greatness—to explore the pos-

sibilities that eluded him. In the end, however, Joanna learns through experience the lesson that could have been learned through a more shrewd observation of her father's life: "Joanna, having come to understand the nothingness
of that inordinate craving for sheer success, surprised herself by the pleasure
which came to her out of what she had always considered the ordinary things
of life" (290). Having ventured out into the world of materialism and individualism, and learning first-hand the spiritual emptiness that is to be found
there, she better understands the legacy of duty and history that she will pass
on to her children. Joanna has walked the thin line that separates desire born
of self-interest and desire born of selfless responsibility. Her near fall into
self-indulgence and isolation is a reminder that a single-minded will to better
the race must be tempered by an ongoing connectedness to family and community. Joanna was so taken by the idea of herself as race hero that she lost
sight of the need to be part of the community. She finds that one cannot uplift
the race while standing apart from the community.

Philip Marshall will not be as fortunate as his younger sister; he discovers
the balance between duty to self and duty to community only as he faces
imminent death. With his health failing at the war's end, Phillip is reunited
with Maggie, his early love. Under Maggie's care, Phillip returns home
where he spends his last days with his family. He shares with Maggie his
understanding of his shortcoming, and his reflection serves as a warning
about the danger of neglecting the spiritual self. Philip tells Maggie he failed
to think of his personal needs (267). He understands too late the importance
of balancing duty to others and self, and thus spends much of his adult years
lonely. When he is reconciled with Maggie, he has only a short time to share
his life with her. Philip dies an early and a sad death, but his is not the
revered fictional role of heroic martyr. Fauset does not hold Philip up as a
model of Christian sacrifice, but rather challenges that model by suggesting
that Philips's fall is the result of his self-imposed martyrdom. His fall suggests that martyrdom is not a natural or healthy condition, particularly when
the martyr is disconnected from the very people he purports to serve.

Fauset's critique of martyrdom exemplifies the novel's prevailing tone of
indifference to Christianity. *There Is Confusion* can be read as a sentimental
work; however, the central place of church and Christian conversion in Harper and Hopkins's novels are absent here. The middle class black family at the
center of the novel constitutes a churchgoing household, but their affiliation
with Christianity is not grounded in a core Christian belief. Fauset depicts
church worship as mere social ritual and middle class black Christians as
lacking a central spiritual core. This is evident early in the novel as the
narrator reveals the church-going motives of the Marshall family:

> Rather remarkably the whole family still went to church, Mr. and Mrs. Mar-
> shall from years of long habit, Sylvia because she rather liked to please her

mother and because it amused her to have Brian Spencer, whom church-going bored to the point of agony, obey her wish that he should go. Sandy, now in the real estate business, thought it gave him standing in the community. (73)

The narrator explains further that Philip attends church because he enjoys gatherings of black people, and that Joanna attends because singing in the choir provides her another stage outlet. This spiritless engagement with church and Christianity remains the overwhelming air of religiosity in the novel. Even when Joanna faces her lowest moment—when she fears that her relationship with Peter has ended—she only self-interestedly turns to Christianity. Only out of despair does Joanna reduce herself to the emotionalism she has heretofore associated with religion: before this crisis "[s]he had never been religious. . . . Rather she somewhat despised any emphatically emotional display" (173). While this crisis will lead her to the Bible where she finds consolation in Psalms, this religious moment is just that—momentary. Psalms help to soothe Joanna's pain during her crisis, but Christianity and the church remain at the periphery of the narrative even after this crisis. Christianity is not the authoritative spiritual center in *There Is Confusion,* and Fauset does not even offer lip service to this time honored sentimental construct. Unlike Harper and Hopkins, Fauset does not offer racially contrasting depictions of Christianity. She does not suggest that black Christianity represents a purer, more genuine picture of Christianity than its white counterpart.

Christianity holds no meaningful authority in the black middle-class world of *There Is Confusion.* however, just as her nineteenth-century predecessors, Fauset draws no deliberate connection between blacks and an African ancestry. While neither Christianity nor Africanity maintains a spiritual stronghold in the novel's discourse, from the novel's opening chapters, Fauset presages the significance of memory and remembering to this story. With Joel Marshall's determination to convey to his children the stories of his past and that of great black leaders, readers become aware early of the intricate connections between memory, community, and duty. Joel's early call to Joanna hints at the novel's focus: he tells her "everyone of us has something to do for the race. Never forget that" (20). That Fauset follows Joel's storytelling in chapter 1 with his call to race duty in chapter 2 is not incidental: memory, community, and duty are themes that define the protagonists' struggles throughout the text. Out of their father's commitment to remember and pass on the names and deeds of past blacks, the Marshall children emerge into adulthood with a sense of historical grounding that binds them to their family and their community. The Marshalls are among the wealthy in the black community, but Mr. Marshall emphasizes the obligation of those who have to those who have not. He represents the racial uplift sentiments espoused in late nineteenth-century black writings and oratory. Joel's is not an isolated sentiment; he represents that order of "colored men . . . obsessed with the idea of a progressing younger generation" (68).

In this regard, Isaiah Bye offers the connection to the generational legacy of this sentiment. The grandfather of Peter Bye, Isaiah is a figure that Peter knows primarily through the inscription in the family Bible and the community's collective remembrance of Isaiah's contribution. Although Peter's father, Meriwether Bye, failed to live up to Isaiah's expectations, Isaiah would not live to know this. In spite of Meriwether's failure, the family's name is maintained by virtue of Isaiah's legacy as the pre-Emancipation founder of a school for black children. Moreover, through his inscription, Isaiah insures the survival of his legacy. Isaiah's inscription will spawn Peter's quest for self-discovery, leading Peter to people and places that string together memories of his family history. Peter's self-exploration is completed with the white Meriwether Bye descendant who confirms the familial bonds of black and white Byes. Peter is now free of the haunted self that had lived disconnected from the past and the community. While the novel concludes with a description of the new Peter as a "self-reliant man" (292), Peter is not the Emersonian individualist. Peter's self-reliance is not born out of an isolated search and emergence into self, but rather results from the reciprocal relationship of support from and duty to community. At the novel's end Peter is finally reconciled with his past and is secure in his understanding of self. His self-revelation and self-assuredness are informed by a commitment to family and community reminiscent of his ancestral guide, Isaiah Bye.

In *Plum Bun* and *The Chinaberry Tree*, the two novels by Fauset that followed *There Is Confusion*, Fauset does not offer a hero whose destiny has been presaged by a forefather. These subsequent novels begin with the portrait of a fictional black community framed by the church. *Plum Bun* and *The Chinaberry Tree* introduce the protagonists by establishing their relationship to the church. Just as the narrator reveals early the Marshalls' regimented but spiritually indifferent church attendance in *There Is Confusion,* the narrator in *Plum Bun* paints an early picture of the Murrays' church going practices. The Murrays' regular Sunday church attendance defined the world of young Virginia (Jinny) Murray. The younger daughter of Junius and Mattie Murray, Virginia thought their churchgoing ritual was "the core of happiness" from which "all other satisfactions must radiate" (22). Virginia's deeply sacred impression of church ritual is not shared by her older sister, Angela, who finds the long communion service especially boring (23). And when the Murrays return home to sing hymns after Sunday church service, Angela is alone in her indifference to this family ritual. While Angela's aloofness goes unnoticed by her parents, this disturbs her young sister. As a young child, Virginia finds Angela's separation from the family's Sunday hymnal singing a disturbing omen of future separation. Virginia suspects that Angela's disconnect signals her desire to leave her family. As the narrative unfolds, we find Virginia's premonition actualized as Angela passes for white, severing open ties to her younger sister, despite their parents' deaths. Angela will return to the black community with a sense of race duty; however, her racial connectedness is not tied to a Christian revelation or experience. In fact, in Angela's darkest hour her thoughts turn to religion, but with no conciliatory outcome. When she realizes that her relationship with Anthony cannot be mended, Angela finds herself feeling hopeless and alone. At this low point, she "found herself envying people possessed of a blind religious faith, of the people who could bow their heads submissively and whisper: 'Thy will be done'" (309).

In *The Chinaberry Tree,* Fauset again positions church as the point of entry into the black community. This is apparent with the arrival of Melissa Paul, the young cousin of the novel's protagonist, Laurentine Strange. New to town and knowing only her cousin Laurentine and her Aunt Sal, Melissa elects to attend church on the first Sunday after her relocation to Red Brook (24). While her cousin and aunt only attend church occasionally, Melissa is determined to immerse herself into her new community, and she understands that church is the doorway to this social world. Within two months, Melissa catapults herself into Red Brook's black society. Church has opened the door to respectable society for this girl of modest origins. Melissa and her mother, Judy, have not known the comforts and privilege of home that Sal and Laurentine have been provided: "She [Melissa] was poor, her father was dead, her mother a seamstress, not even a dressmaker" (14). While many in the community express contempt for Sal, her affair with Colonel Halloway, a prominent white man, resulted in material comfort for her and her daughter. Colonel Halloway has provided his mistress and daughter a fine home and after his death, Laurentine's white half sisters (Halloway's legal offspring) present her with a dowry that secures her financial future. In contrast to Melissa, Laurentine has the material and social capital for membership in Red Brook society. Melissa's poverty and her common background require a deliberate strategy for one like Melissa with desires of social mobility. Church is Melissa's initial point of entry into Red Brook society, and she determines later that marriage to Malory Forten will seal her social and economic transformation. She desires marriage to Malory foremost because he comes from a well-known and respected family in the community.

Melissa is not one who gives herself over to frequent introspection. However, in a rare moment, she considers her relationship with Malory and asks God whether there can be anything wrong with her pursuit of him. Because Melissa was "not much given to praying," she has no frame of reference for this attempt at spiritual introspection. She therefore answers her own question, drawing the self-satisfying conclusion that there is no wrong in her desire for Malory. Melissa never comes to appreciate churchgoing or religion as anything more than an instrument of social negotiation. When Malory recites verses from the Bible as poetry, Melissa is unaware that the Bible, the definitive text of Christianity, is his source (240). As for Malory, he likes the Bible; however, his interest in the Bible does not stem from a religious predilection. "Having read a great deal of it in company with Aunt Viny who took it quite literally," Malory insulated himself from his aunt's zealousness and the Bible's spiritual message by simply considering its "literary and poetical beauty" (267). For Malory, the Bible is little more than an artifact in a museum. It has no relevance to the living other than to serve as an object that stimulates human desire for the beautiful—in this case, the beauty of language.

The Chinaberry Tree depicts Christianity and the church as clearly present in black life, but ultimately it is a presence that offers little meaningful influence in this fictional community. The text concludes with individuals reconciling past and self with community. This has been the defining quest for Laurentine Strange who, for the sins of her parents, was alienated by the community. Laurentine's place in the community is confirmed not by spiritual connection, but rather through her economic self-sufficiency and validation through a socially sanctioned relationship. Laurentine's courtship with Mr. Denleigh frees her from the alienation that resulted from her mother's longstanding and publicly known affair. Like her cousin, Laurentine, Melissa is regarded with suspicion by those in the community. Both are considered examples of the Bible's adage about "the sins of the fathers,—and the mothers too" (58–59). The elders in the community remember Judy Strange, her flamboyant personality and her reckless affair with Mr. Forten, her friend's husband. They also remember Aunt Sal's affair with the Colonel, one of Red Brook's highly affluent and respected white citizens. As the offspring of two of the town's most ignominious females, Laurentine and Melissa are regarded as the inheritors of a tainted legacy.

In spite of a curse awarded biblical proportion and a community determined to marginalize them, the Strange family find eventual acceptance. The convoluted tensions are resolved at the novel's end. Laurentine and Mr. Denleigh are reconciled after a near devastating misunderstanding. Melissa is restored to her first love, Asshur, after the crushing discovery that Malory is in fact her half brother. These reversals occur not through divine influence but perhaps because the Strange family is able to transcend social convention. It is a change of fortune anticipated in Mr. Denleigh's answer to Laurentine's reflection on being both illegitimate and biracial: "Biology transcends society! . . . the facts of life, birth and death are more important than the rules of living, marriage, law, the sanction of the church or of man" (121). Denleigh's words highlight a challenge to social conventions that Fauset interjects in all three novels. Fauset's representations of Christianity in African American culture scrutinize dominant rules of engagement between the sexes and seem less concerned with counter-Christian alternatives in black life. This is especially the case in *The Chinaberry Tree* and *Plum Bun*.

Again, in *The Chinaberry Tree,* the church is simply a fixture in the social landscape. The spirit of the community has been relinquished to the social dictates of the larger society. The triumph of the Strange family is not then a spiritual one, but rather a victory over social hegemony and intolerance. Mixed-race unions in the turn-of-the-century United States were no less taboo (or illegal, in many jurisdictions) than they had been during the antebellum era. Sal and the Colonel are victims of the racialized social order of their time, but Sal refuses to allow these rules to discount the genuine affection that she and the Colonel shared. Sal rejects social dictum that would have her engage in self-denigration, and Fauset subverts any expectation that Laurentine will prove the stock tragic mulatto. With the dowry from her half-sisters and her marriage to Dr. Denleigh, Laurentine enters the realm of wealth and legitimacy. Dr. Denleigh rejects social discourses of legitimacy and identity, finding no need to justify Laurentine or Sal. Ironically, however, his marriage to Laurentine signals to the community her rightful place among them.

Fauset's novels maintain an indifference to Christianity and a concomitant silence on Africanity; however, despite the novels' absence of open acknowledgement of African influences, these works resonate with African-rooted principles of memory and community. In her study of aestheticism in Fauset's novels, Margaret D. Stetz argues that *The Chinaberry Tree* is "in part a celebration of the beauty of rootedness—both as a figurative and a literal concept—through the image of the connection between Laurentine and the chinaberry tree growing on the land where she was born" (265). Although she refers to *The Chinaberry Tree,* Stetz's argument could readily apply to *There Is Confusion* and *Plum Bun.* Stetz does not suggest that rootedness has spiritual connotations; however, reading rootedness as a spiritual component of African American culture, one could argue that the three novels make the case for the beauty of rootedness. Rootedness signals the confirmation of place and being, and it is secured through memory and community. Through memories that bind them to place and people, Fauset's protagonists discover where they belong and how they are to conduct their lives.

While the chinaberry tree marks the connectedness of Laurentine to family and community, the Marshall and the Murray households symbolize the collective memory and experience of the communities in *There Is Confusion* and *Plum Bun.* In *Plum Bun,* Mattie and Junius Murray tell the story of their courtship and marriage often to their daughters (33). Jinny listens eagerly each time her parents recount their early life and struggles. She will internalize her parents' convictions about family, community, and duty, symbolizing a black social ethic that significantly contrasts that of the white, commercialized ethic of her sibling, Angela. With her parents' sacrifices as her model, the young Jinny understands the importance of family and community bonds.

It is not coincidental that after the death of their parents, Jinny remains the anchored one, and Angela drifts in search of material gain and social freedom. This becomes apparent during a Sunday gathering of friends shortly after both parents have died. While Jinny is engaged with the groups' musings on race duty and progress, Angela finds herself once again uninterested and "cramped and confined" by these recurring conversations about race (67). Jinny, on the other hand, passionately expresses her conviction that blacks of means and accomplishments must lend their resources to the betterment of the race. She pleads this case particularly to a member of the gathering who suggests that he might escape to South America in search of a better life. She explains why he must not submit to this impulse: "We've all of us got to make up our minds to the sacrifice of something. . . .There are some things which an individual might want, but which he'd just have to give up forever for the sake of the more important whole" (69).

Angela Murray does not share her younger sister's deeply felt sense of race belonging and duty. Instead, Angela, who can pass for white, desires the freedom and material gain that she presumes whiteness brings. Early in the narrative she asserts that "the good things of life are unevenly distributed; merit is not always rewarded, [and] hard labor does not necessarily entail adequate recompense" (12). With this deconstruction of the Puritan work ethic, Angela readily justifies passing and engaging in an affair that her deceased parents would certainly have frowned upon. At the novel's end, Angela publicly reclaims her black identity but there is no similar reclamation of the Christian mores that had defined her childhood. Hence, the novel's subtitle, "A Novel Without a Moral," seems quite fitting.

Angela explains to Jinny that there are "a lot of things which are in the world for everybody really but which only white people . . . get their hands on" (78). At this point, Angela harbors no deep sense of race duty or belonging; she is motivated by the desire for material gain and social mobility. Passing for white, however, Angela discovers that while whiteness opens the door to material and social opportunity, this privilege comes at the heavy price of self-denial and removal from kin and community. It is only through her separation from the black world that Angela discovers the importance of belonging. She enters the world of whites, but not without Jinny in the shadows as a beacon reminding her of the way back to family and community.[2] Angela learns that the self-interestedness that marks white society also marks a world of disassociated beings. She begins to understand the fulfillment that comes with a sense of duty to others, and thus transforms her hopes for material wealth into a desire to aid blacks whose talents are sidelined by racism. Angela further discovers that whiteness alone does not bring wealth: social status and gender also inform opportunities for wealth. The loneliness and the void that come with passing are too great a price to pay: realizing that "companionship was her chief demand," Angela returns to her middle class black world (252). On the road back to self, Angela, who had never thought her parents words worth consideration, is reminded of and comforted by words her mother had spoken to her years earlier. As she recalls her mother's adage that "Life is more important than colour," she determines that the memory of these words signal her mother's presence (266). In death, her mother watches over her, and the realization brings a feeling of security and relief. It is a moment that sends Angela to her knees in prayerful tears (266). This is a definitive spiritual moment: the memory of her mother's words leads her to a spiritual experience that years in church had never offered. Angela now understands the source of Jinny's strength and stability. The memory of those departed shapes the experiences of those who live on.

In a similar manner, memory and community lead to self-realization for the two protagonists in *The Chinaberry Tree*. Memory brings pain before it brings resolution, however. Laurentine Strange and her cousin, Melissa Paul, are the living reminders of their parents' sins, and the community remembers. With the memory of the illegitimate affairs of Sal Strange and Colonel Halloway and that of Judy Strange and Mr. Forten, the black community in Red Brook alienates the offspring of these relationships. There are those, particularly the young, in the community who feel that the past hinders the future for those unable to break free of it. Young Kitty Brown explains to her mother that she rejects the myth of the cursed Strange family: "I'm sick of hearing about these Stranges and Colonel Halloway. What's it all about? You'd think a white man had never looked at a colored woman before in these United States?" (97). Similarly, Malory Forten explains to Melissa his impatience with those who feel compelled to revisit the past: "I lived with an old great-aunt who lived way back in the past. Certainly she wasn't unhappy but she was old and spent her whole life recalling memories of Isaac this one who was the first student at the Institute for Colored Youth. Oh I'm fed up with oldness and memories and grief" (115). In this regard the novel seems to confirm Carol Allen's argument that "Fauset viewed history as fragmented, floating back to the present only to be restructured and offered as contemporary narratives that centered the cohesive past's demise" (60). The young have an intolerance for the past, for remembering, but the question of memory's importance rests somewhere between the compulsion of the old to remember and the desire of the young to escape the past. The oldest inhabitants refuse to free the Strange daughters from the weight of their parents' transgressions. In part these old timers are moved by an innate human intolerance for those who refuse to submit to the rules and conventions of the group. Their steadfast intolerance, however, is also informed by a sixth sense or spiritual presumption of restitution. Wrongs have to be made right: sins do not go unanswered.

The old inhabitants did not know that Melissa Paul was born out of the illicit affair between Judy Strange and her friend's husband, making the young would-be lovers, Melissa Paul and Malory Forten, siblings. Their lack of this precise information did not, however, cloud their collective sense of a lurking sin that must be resolved:

> Some deep-lying natural sense of decency within them reared up to consider itself outraged at the thought of young Malory's marrying the daughter of the woman who had caused his mother such an agony of wounded pride and humiliation. . . . Such a matter, they felt, called for a direct visitation from God and they were rather waiting, half hopeful, half fearful, to see in what shape the wrath would come. (336–337)

The wrath came—a horror that Melissa herself had known was imminent. At the onset of her relationship with Malory, Melissa is plagued with dream visions that foretell the terrifying encounter that awaits them. When Malory fails to meet her at their appointed meeting place for their elopement departure, Melissa suspects where she can find him, "[a]nd the instant she set foot on the Road she knew that it was the road of her dream," and that what had been presaged would now come to fruition (329–330). Malory, who has dismissed memory and the past as inconsequential to the events of the present and the future, is crushed by what memory reveals. Through the remembrances of others in the community, the past is revisited and relived, and the truth is resurrected—the familial bond between Malory and Melissa is unearthed. While Laurentine sees Melissa and Malory's tragedy as God's curse, she and Melissa are reconciled through the experience. The community desire for truth and retribution is satisfied, and Melissa and Laurentine are now free to move forward.

Fauset's fictional treatment of community and truth in *The Chinaberry Tree* anticipates a similar connection drawn decades later by Toni Morrison in her celebrated novel, *Beloved*. A narrative of shifting points of view, *Beloved* captures the account of a slave woman's killing of her child. Through the memories of those in the community, the reader arrives at a panoramic picture of Sethe's act. Sethe and her surviving daughter are alienated from the community, but when the ghost of the dead child arrives and wreaks havoc, women of the community step in to free Sethe of the ghost and of the past. Like Sal and Laurentine, Sethe is proud and the community judges her harshly. However, in both fictional communities there lies a reverence for order and rightness. Just as Fauset's fictional black community anticipated that the wrongs of the Stranges would have to be reconciled, Morrison's fictional black community awaits the day of reckoning for Sethe's sin. That day arrives when women in the community, in particular the soothsayer, Ella, realize that the ghost has overstepped the boundaries between the living and the dead. Ella finds the ghost an example of the past intruding on the present. She accepts the presence of ghosts, in fact "[s]he didn't mind a little communication between the two worlds, but this was an invasion" (257). While the ghost's arrival has facilitated a collective remembering that is purgative, her presence has also proven degenerative. As she thrives, Sethe deteriorates. She thus represents a spiritual entity whose destructive influence must be quelled because she threatens the health and safety of those in the material world. Through the praying women who come to restore spiritual order, the ghost of Beloved is expelled, and the painful rememberings of the past no longer hold a destructive power. Sethe is free of Beloved and the ills of the past; she is spiritually healed and restored to the community.

Similarly, as *The Chinaberry Tree* draws to a close, the Stranges are no longer prisoners in a world of hidden and unresolved memories. Under the chinaberry tree that years ago Colonel Halloway had ordered from Alabama for Aunt Sal, Melissa and Laurentine feel "everywhere about them the immanence of God" (341). The chinaberry tree, which had been for Aunt Sal, the only living testament to and validation of her relationship with Colonel Halloway, was now a temple (341). The Strange family had survived: Laurentine and Melissa would not be condemned to eternal alienation, and Aunt Sal could have the tree and the memories of Colonel Halloway without feeling that their love had brought damnation on their child.

Fauset's novels paint an emerging twentieth-century black world in which Christianity's stronghold of black life is unloosening. In both her fictional small town and her urban sophisticated settings, blacks are co-opting mainstream America's world of materialism and self-interest. In Fauset's fictional world there is no old time religion connecting blacks to a unifying and shared legacy. Moreover, there is no alternative spiritual dimension to anchor the emerging urban, middle-class generation. With the exception of extraordinary black families such as the Byes, the Marshalls, and the Murrays, Fauset's fictional black communities have given themselves over to the pursuit of economic and social gain. Despite their growing spiritual emptiness, however, black communities thrive in Fauset's fiction, and her works do not conclude with black protagonists or communities in despair or anxiety. Fauset's novels suggest that blacks no longer find Christianity central to their survival, and no spiritual system promises to take its place. While the stellar black families in Fauset's novels symbolize a rootedness born out of memory and tradition, they seem rather the exception than the rule. In general, the Byes, the Marshalls, and the Murrays represent the models of family and community that sustained blacks through slavery; however, it is not clear that they are the model of black family and community that will thrive in the twentieth century.

Fauset does not identify a spiritual idealism that will ground blacks in modernity, and she hints at no tension between African and Christian that must be resolved. Again, Fauset's novels suggest that Christianity has no meaningful influence in modern black communities, but Christianity's ineptness does not lead blacks to engage an African-rooted alternative. As the final chapter in this study demonstrates, in this regard Fauset's works differ from those of her contemporaries, Nella Larsen and Zora Neale Hurston. In their novels, Larsen and Hurston explore Christianity's failure as a liberating force in black life; however, their works diverge from Fauset's silence on Africanity. Each author recognizes an African influence in black life, and each offers contrasting messages about the viability of Africanity as an answer to Christianity's failure. Larsen's *Quicksand* suggests that Africanity offers no greater promise than Christianity. Contrastingly, Hurston's *Their Eyes Were Watching God* signals African spirituality as the path to peace and the means to understanding and knowing self. If we consider the novels of Fauset, Larsen, and Hurston as a progression to Janie (*Their Eyes Were Watching God*), the fictional black heroine who emerges into self through an African-centered spiritual journey, Fauset's novels symbolize the opening moment to this transformative era in black women's spiritual imaginations. Fauset's novels represent the initiation of Christianity's displacement in black women's fiction. Larsen and Hurston expand on Fauset's representation of this budding spiritual transformation that ends with Janie's relinquishment of Christianity's hold and her emergence into a spiritual self shaped out of her journey into Africanity. While Fauset does not explicitly take on African-Christian tensions in her novels, she highlights the precursor to these tensions—that is, the acknowledgment of Christianity's failure and its meaninglessness in black life.

NOTES

1. See *Book Review Digest* (1924, 1929, 1932, 1933) for early reviews of *There Is Confusion, Plum Bun*, and *The Chinaberry Tree*.
2. See Eva Rueschmann's essay, "Sister Bonds: Intersections of Family and Race in Jessie Redmon Fauset's *Plum Bun* and Dorothy West's *The Living is Easy*" for a more thorough look at Fauset's use of siblings to develop her protagonist's struggle with racial identity.

WORKS CITED

Allen, Carol. "Migration Through Mirrors and Memories: The Family, Home, and Creativity in the Works of Jessie Redmon Fauset." *Black Women Intellectuals: Strategies of Nation, Family, and Neighborhood in the Works of Pauline Hopkins, Jessie Fauset, and Marita Bonner*. New York: Garland Publishing, 1998. 47–76.
Fauset, Jessie Redmon. *The Chinaberry Tree & Selected Writings*. 1931. Boston: Northeastern University Press, 1995.
———. *Plum Bun*. 1928. Boston: Beacon Press, 1990.
———. *There Is Confusion*. 1924. Boston: Northeastern University Press, 1989.
Jones, Sharon L. "Reclaiming a Legacy: The Dialectic of Race, Class, and Gender in Jessie Fauset, Zora Neale Hurston, and Dorothy West." *Hecate* 24.1 (1998): 155–164.
Kuenz, Jane. "The Face of America: Performing Race and Nation in Jessie Fauset's *There Is Confusion*." *Yale Journal of Criticism* 12.1 (1999): 89–111.

McDowell, Deborah E. "The Neglected Dimension of Jessie Redmon Fauset." *Conjuring: Black Women, Fiction, and Literary Tradition*. Eds. Marjorie Pryse and Hortense Spillers. Bloomington: Indiana University Press, 1985. 86–104.

———. Introduction. *Plum Bun*. Boston: Beacon Press, 1990.

Morrison, Toni. *Beloved*. 1987. New York: Penguin Books, 1988.

———. *Song of Solomon*. 1977. New York: Penguin Books, 1987.

Stetz, Margaret D. "Jessie Fauset's Fiction: Reconsidering Race and Revising Aestheticism." *Literature and Racial Ambiguity*. Eds. Teresa Hubel and Neil Brooks. Amsterdam, Netherlands: Rodopi, 2002. 253–270.

Chapter Seven

Transformed Religiosities

Africanity and Christianity in Nella Larsen's
Quicksand *and Zora Neale Hurston's* Jonah's Gourd
Vine *and* Their Eyes Were Watching God

Note: In this chapter, all quotes from *Jonah's Gourd Vine* are taken with permission from HarperCollins Publishers for their 1990 edition of Hurston's text. All quotes from *Their Eyes Were Watching God* are taken with permission from HarperCollins Publishers for their 1990 edition of Hurston's text.

Jessie Fauset's novels illustrate the shifting discourse of Christianity in the imagination of black women writers. Fauset abandons the practice of her late nineteenth-century predecessors who maintained Christianity as the spiritual life force of the black community. Christianity remains an institution in Fauset's fictional black communities, but only as a mere fixture in the social landscape. Blacks do not turn to the church for spiritual sustenance; instead, they meet on Sundays to participate in a ritual that has little spiritual depth. In her 1928 novel, *Quicksand*, Nella Larsen, like Jessie Fauset, defines the church as an inept institution. However, while Fauset paints the black church as an institution anchored in mere social performance, Larsen suggests that while blacks still seek spiritual enlightenment and deliverance in the church, the church cannot answer their needs because it is little more than a tool of white exploitation. This is explicitly illustrated when in a moment of dejection and despair, Larsen's heroine, Helga Crane, surrenders to the promise of Christian redemption and salvation in Rev. Mr. Pleasant Green's emotionally charged sermon. Helga quickly discovers, however, that her conversion is little more than delusion: she has "embrace[d] a Christianity that depends heavily on scapegoating rather than on true soul-searching or social harmony" (Chandler 45). By coming into the fold of the church, she has simply entered a world where blacks, especially women, meet with ongoing suffering and only the promise of recompense in the afterlife. Helga's rejection leads her into an existence of ubiquitous despair. Christianity is the spiritual weapon of whites, and Helga finds no spiritual resource that originates in black experience or that serves the needs of blacks.

Though Helga is biracial, she finds the world inextricably divided along the color line—black and white. Her racial anxiety stems from the reality that phenotypical expressions of black/white unions are not consistent with the western construct of polarized racial identities. With the black/white dichotomy that grounds western discourse on race, the products of racial mixing complicate the simplistic notion of a distinct division between black and white. Helga knows first-hand that mixed-race unions exemplify the need for a more representative language on race. Offspring of black/white unions, who like Helga have an appearance that is not altogether black or white, generally identify themselves as black. Those whose physical appearance suggests that they are white can claim either blackness or whiteness. Those who reject this racial polarization find themselves absent a racial identity because American black/white dichotomous discourse prevails.

On the surface, Helga symbolizes the struggle with identity and belonging faced by those born of mixed race unions. Beyond this more obvious question of racial identity, however, Helga's struggles highlight the cultural and spiritual struggles of blacks who must give themselves over to dominant white paradigms of civilization. This is evident in one of Helga's opening reflections on Naxos. Helga recalls with disdain a particular lunch period that had been shortened, with children and teachers hurriedly devouring their food to be rushed into the chapel and forced to listen to "the insulting remarks of one of the renowned white preachers of the state" (2). Naxos, the fictional portrait of Booker T. Washington's Tuskegee, was founded to uplift the uneducated and socially unrefined blacks in the rural south. Helga finds that the uplift of these rural blacks comes at a great expense and that the school is ironically draining blacks of their will and creativity: "[t]his great community was no longer a school. It had grown into a machine. It was now a show place in the black belt, exemplification of the white man's magnanimity, refutation of the black man's inefficiency. Life had died out of it" (4).

Larsen's reflection on Helga's biraciality is then more than a look at Helga's individual struggle. Again, Helga's splintered self is symbolic of the splintered African American self that pervades *Quicksand*. Helga's revolving door of identities highlights her inability to reconcile the selves that reside within her, and in general her struggle demonstrates the uncertainty of an authentic black or white identity (Jenkins 133). Helga experiences alternating moments of racial desire and need: she tires of being black; she tires of life among whites; she embraces opportunities to live among blacks; and at other moments she longs to escape blackness and live among whites. She is unable to find a lasting sense of identity and place. Though readers might conclude that Helga's sinking world at the novel's end simply speaks to her individual experience, Helga's despair mirrors the sinking souls of blacks in a white world with a religion that uses and negates them. In the end, Helga concludes that religion is an illusion, but she understands that she had turned to it because even in its ineptness religion could numb the senses and obscure reality. For Helga, this delusional power was only temporary. Fully awakened from the intoxicating influence of her religious conversion several years and several children earlier, Helga decides that blacks have been deceived by "this fatuous belief in the white man's God, this childlike trust in full compensation for all woes and privations in 'kingdom come'" (133).

Blacks have no meaningful community or family ties in *Quicksand*. Larsen signals this disconnect with the introduction of Naxos as a place mired in an atmosphere of mendacity. Helga finds that the administrators are cruel to each other, and more alarming is the cruelty they mete out to the very ones they claim to serve. This is especially illustrated with the harsh words of the dormitory matron, Miss MacGooden. A black woman of notable social standing, she distinguishes herself from her uneducated, ill-bred charges. Miss MacGooden finds her young charges less like ladies and more like "savages from the backwoods" (12). She feels no community or spiritual connection to the children at Naxos. she lives among them, but she is not of them. Though Helga despises Miss MacGooden's air of superiority, the two are ironically similar in their disconnect with the community they serve. Miss MacGooden considers herself a better class than the poor black children at Naxos, and Helga too thinks herself better. Helga's disconnect is more far reaching and isolating, however, because she extends her notion of separateness to her colleagues. Helga pities the children who are made to feel that the demonstration of their civility lies in their ability to emulate whites. She presumes herself free from such self-denigration and thus she observes the children's humiliation as outsiders. She finds the administrators at Naxos contemptible yet pitiable. Their paradoxical proclamations of race pride and self-loathing highlight their unanswered longing for acceptance in a world that marginalizes them. Helga is particularly annoyed by their suppression of the "most delightful manifestations" of the race—"love of color, joy of rhythmic motion, naïve, spontaneous laughter" (18). Away from Naxos, Helga finds blacks similarly afflicted in Harlem. When her brief period of contentment in Harlem fades, Helga grows impatient with Harlem's blacks. It is an impatience that rings similar to that of her Naxos experience. Even her good friend, Anne, becomes an object of her resentment. Helga observes that despite Anne's deep hatred for whites, just as the acquiescing blacks of Naxos, Anne also "aped their [white's] clothes, their manners, and their gracious ways of living" (48).

Helga's criticism of black elites is, again, ironic, in light of her own love-hate sentiments regarding blackness. On the brink of her voyage to Copenhagen, Helga again reflects on the disconnect she feels with blacks: "She didn't, in spite of her racial markings, belong to these dark segregated people. She was different. She felt it. It wasn't merely a matter of color. It was something broader, deeper that made folk kin" (55). Not unlike Miss Mac-Gooden at Naxos, Helga assumes herself superior to most blacks. This air of superiority is threatened when Helga returns from Copenhagen and finds herself momentarily transformed in a Harlem nightclub. The uncontrollable impulses provoked by the music in the club drives Helga to fear that she has unleashed her "jungle" instincts. She found herself "drugged, lifted, sustained, by the extraordinary music. . . . The essence of life seemed bodily motion. And when suddenly the music died, she dragged herself back to the present with a conscious effort; and a shameful certainty that not only had she been in the jungle, but that she had enjoyed it" (59). Helga has been momentarily swept into the uninhibited world of black music. She experiences freedom from the stifling and constraining world of whiteness, but she cannot free herself from the white gaze that judges this world. Helga buys into white racial discourse that connects the music and dance of blacks to their presumed primitiveness: "Like the black female body, made to signify sexual excess and pathology, the sensual movement of the body in time to music calls attention to the physicality of the body, and is therefore positioned as opposing the civilizing refinement of white rational thought" (Defalco 28). Like the blacks she accuses of "apeing" whites, Helga fears and hates what she deems her black self. Paradoxically, she too recognizes the stifling influence of whiteness in the lives of blacks; however, it is whiteness that informs her notions of culture and class.

Helga has little love or patience for either blacks or whites, and she is unable to find a meaningful or lasting sense of community and belonging. She has been emotionally and physically abandoned by black and white family members. She has no memories to draw from, or a past with which she can connect: she is alone with no spiritual force to offer her solace. Christianity has proven a tool for white exploitation and blacks have no spiritual resource—Christianity or other—to unite and strengthen them. The depth of this despairing and prophetic vision is evinced in the closing chapter. Helga, barely hanging on to life after another debilitating pregnancy, faces the cruel, vacuous existence of her life and the lives of blacks in general:

> With the obscuring curtain of religion rent, she was able to look about her and
> see with shocked eyes this thing that she had done to herself. She couldn't, she
> thought ironically, even blame God for it, now that she knew that He didn't
> exist. . . . The white man's God. And His great love for all people regardless of

race! What idiotic nonsense she had allowed herself to believe. How could she, how could anyone, have been so deluded? How could ten million black folk credit it when daily before their eyes was enacted its contradictions? (130)

Quicksand is a narrative of despair—for the individual and the community. Larsen's narrative of Christian skepticism leaves her protagonist spiritually void, sentenced to a desolate end. The multitude who are unlike Helga are no better off—unable to see the hopelessness, they simply live their despair in blindness.

Larsen's interrogation of Christianity is echoed in Zora Neale Hurston's 1937 novel, *Their Eyes Were Watching God*, however, to a notably different end for the protagonist. Just as with Faucet's Helga Crane, Christianity cannot offer Hurston's heroine, Janie, a path to self-realization. Unlike Helga who finds no alternative to Christianity's suffocating legacy, Janie frees herself. Africanity emerges as the spiritual foundation of her journey and transformation. While Janie is Hurston's most celebrated protagonist, *Their Eyes* is not Hurston's first full-length fictional exploration of Africanity. Three years before the publication of *Their Eyes*, Hurston offered a resounding affirmation of African-rooted spirituality and life in her 1934 novel, *Jonah's Gourd Vine*. Hurston's main character in this text significantly contrasts Janie. John Pearson is more like Janie's stifling husband, Joe Starks, than Janie. John is the center of the Eatonville community; he is a big voice, and he is financially successful. The novel's female protagonist, John's wife, Lucy, is forced to live in the shadow of his grandness. Readers might argue that neither John nor Lucy triumph in this tale of disappointing love; however, through their narratives Hurston unveils a world of black life that is superficially anchored in the church but guided more profoundly by the subtle influences of African spirituality and practices.

The title, *Jonah's Gourd Vine*, immediately suggests the novel's connection to a biblical figure and story. God calls on the biblical Jonah to deliver a message of repentance to the wicked inhabitants of Nineveh. Jonah rejects God's call and flees, but he cannot escape. After he faces God at sea and is delivered from the belly of the whale, Jonah accepts and fulfills his mission. Jonah, however, is outraged at the sinfulness of the inhabitants of Nineveh and becomes angry with God for offering them redemption. As Jonah sits in anguish and grief, God provides a gourd to protect him. The next day God releases a worm that causes the gourd to wither and die, and Jonah faints from the heat of the sun. God explains to Jonah that he is not unlike the people of Nineveh who depend on God's good will. Why, then, should God offer any less grace to them than to Jonah? Like Jonah, John Pearson answers God's call, and like Jonah, John is stripped of God's protective gourd vine when he presumes himself as powerful as God. John fails to heed Lucy's warnings and her attempts to steer him down a humble and God-fearing path.

Lucy dies and the gourd vine soon withers: John is eventually forced to step down as pastor, and he faces alienation and dejection in the community that had once raised him to god-like status.

Given John's Jonah-like fall from grace, one might argue that the thematic core of the work rests in biblical allegory. However, the shortfall of this reading becomes apparent with closer examination of the hero and the culture Hurston constructs in *Jonah's Gourd Vine*. John Pearson's arrogance before God links him to the ancient prototype, Jonah, but John's character and his fate are more ubiquitously connected to the heroic tradition in African American folklore. John emerges as a larger-than-life figure just as many biblical heroes—through a divine call. He is called to preach, and while readers might connect this calling to Christian tradition, John is the product of a black Baptist preacher tradition. His highly emotional, poetic, call-and-response style represents a sermonic legacy that survives to date in black churches but has its roots in African oral tradition. John preaches from the authoritative text of Christianity, but Hurston makes clear that John's words emerge out of his African soul. When he came before his congregation, "[h]e rolled his African drum up to the altar, and called his Congo Gods by Christian names" (89).

John is the product of a spiritual tradition and community, and this is evident early in the novel with his return to his place of birth. John has been made to feel like an outcast by his stepfather, but when he returns to his birthplace, John comes to know a sense of family and place. He meets his grandmother unknowingly until her inquiry reveals that he is her daughter's son. When John identifies his mother as Amy Crittenden, Pheemy rejoices in the discovery and shares details of his birth that give him familial and community roots: "Hush yo' mouf, you yallar rascal, you! Ah knowed, Ah seed reckerlection in yo' face. . . . Well, Lawd a'mussy boy! Ahm yo' granny! Yo' nable string is buried under dat air chanyberry tree. 'Member so well de very day you cried. (first cry at birth)" (19). Through Pheemy, John is connected to family, ancestors, and tradition. Her significance to John goes back to his birth. She delivered him and took special care to follow birth practices that would ensure his future health and fortune. With the placement of the umbilical cord under the chinaberry tree, Pheemy anchored John to the place of his birth and secured his future. Later, when John becomes a father, Pheemy will perform similar rituals for his newborns.

John is a big voice; he is divinely inspired. While he does not realize his gift until he reaches manhood, his almost mystical return to his homeland hints at the destiny that awaits him. Not long after John's arrival, he battles a fearsome snake that lurks along a path frequently traveled by Lucy and others in the community. John's encounter with the serpent that strikes fear in the community portends his spiritual greatness. Lucy describes the snake as cunning and frightening. She tells John, "He got uh hole back under the bank where you kin see 'im, but you can't git 'im 'thought you wuz down in de branch. He lay all 'round dere on de ground and even on de foot-log, but when he see somebody comin' he go in his hole, all ready for yuh and lay dere and dare yuh tuh bother 'im" (34). When John kills this dreaded creature, Lucy is ecstatic: "Ooh John, Ahm so glad you kilt dat ole devil. He been right dere skeerin' folks since befo' Ah wuz borned" (34). The demon has been destroyed and all in the community can now safely cross this path. The paradoxical fear and reverence that the snake incites among these locals represent a cultural legacy that survived the Middle Passage and was maintained among the descendants of Africans throughout the Americas.

Among continental and New World Africans, the snake is viewed as a being with a spiritual essence, endowed with supernatural power. In African tradition the snake is a reverential creature, who because its body structure allows it to "connect itself in a circle, [is] the symbol of the unending cycle of life . . . [representing] the ancestors, who, though dead, continue the circle of life" (Montgomery 97). In western cosmology, particularly as it is informed by Anglo Christianity, the snake is seen as symbolic of evil. Lucy's paradoxical awe and fear of the snake symbolizes its dual legacy in African American culture. Her awe of the snake reminds us of its place of reverence in traditional African societies. Her view of the snake as demonic represents the influence of Christianity's representation of the snake in the Garden of Eden. With its transformed image as demon in African American culture, the human who has power over the snake is then considered one who holds supernatural ability. John's triumph over the snake seems to suggest that he is divinely empowered, but if we consider Lucy's description of the snake perhaps John's conquest is more accurately read as the signal of his ultimate doom. While Lucy tells John that the snake strikes fear in all of the community, she reports that he retreats when others approach, daring them to disturb his ground. According to Lucy, the snake predates her: he is legendary. Though she reports that the snake is threatening, she does not indicate that the snake has ever harmed anyone. The community has lived in a longstanding truce with the snake: they fear and revere it, but they accept its place among them. The snake comes among them, but they know that they are not allowed in the snake's refuge. John disturbs this balance with his aggressive pursuit and slaying of the creature. He has broken the cycle, and while Lucy celebrates his momentary victory, John ultimately cannot find peace or balance in his life.

When John answers the call to preach, this seems a confirmation of his spiritual or supernatural pre-eminence. Eight years into his pastorship in the black town of Eatonville, John must deliver a sermon to quell the criticisms of his detractors; his sermon both reveals his mastery of words and the source of his power. John's womanizing has become a matter of grave concern for some in his congregation, and there are rumblings about deposing him. When

Lucy becomes aware of the seriousness of the matter, she advises John to go before his congregants and address his transgressions, and she warns him to avoid lying. John responds by delivering a powerful sermon in which he humbles himself before his listeners. He takes heed to Lucy's warning and does not deny the charges against him. Instead, John reminds his audience that he is only a man, distinct from them only by the divine word that he is elected to deliver in the pulpit. He tells his congregation, "When Ah speak tuh yuh from dis pulpit, dat ain't me talkin', dat's de voice uh God speakin thru me. When de voice is thew, Ah jus' uhnother one uh God's crumblin' clods" (122). John's sermon frees him from the expectation that he, a man of God, must be an example of righteousness. He grants himself a two-fold place in the community—he is one among them, and he is one above them.

While John's words clearly serve his own self-interest, he alternatively captures the nature of spirit possession and divination in African and African American spirituality. In the spiritual practices of slaves, just as with their African foreparents, supernatural entities were called on through the collective effort of the community. Gathering members in song and dance, the living secured the presence of spirits who then channeled their messages through the chosen among the living. As John suggests in his sermon, he has been divinely chosen to deliver the word of God. While some in the community may deplore him for his human frailty, they cannot challenge his sanctioned role as messenger of God's word.

As Christian preacher and folk hero, John personifies the delicate coexistence of Christianity and African-rooted spirituality among blacks. While he is arguably a biblical type—in particular the likeness of the fallen prophet, Jonah—John's funeral confirms his greater connection to an African-informed legacy. Hurston describes John's funeral not in the tradition of Christian ritual, but rather with the sound and imagery of African ceremonial practices:

> the hearers wailed with the feeling of terrible loss. They beat upon the O-go-doe, the ancient drum. O-go-doe, O-go-doe, O-go-doe! Their hearts turned to fire and their shinbones leaped unknowing to the drum. Not Kata-Kumba, the drum of triumph, that speaks of great ancestors and glorious wars. Not the little drum of kidskin, for that is to dance with joy and to call to mind birth and creation, but O-go-doe, the voice of Death—that promises nothing, that speaks with tears only, and of the past. (202)

Through recurrent dichotomies of African and Christian spiritualities, Hurston further confirms Africanity as the central influence in her black fictional world. One of the first of these contrasting images is John's return across the creek to visit his mother and siblings. After John is welcomed back with a great homecoming celebration, the community awakens the next morning from their drum and dance celebration to the desolation of their laboring existence in the white world. After they have clapped and danced well into the night, "[t]he fire died. The moon died. The shores of Africa receded. They went to sleep and woke up next day and looked out on dead and dying cotton stalks and ripening possum persimmons" (31–32). This scene seems to suggest the triumph of white authority over blacks. However, Hurston offers subsequent moments that subvert white hegemonic discourse that discounts the authority and merit of black life. This black/white tension is humorously explored in the account of Mehaley and Pomp's wedding. Mehaley informs Pomp that she wants "tuh be married real" (82). Pomp graciously agrees, and they plan a wedding that will be officiated by a church preacher. On the day of the wedding, however, a quarrel ensues as Mehaley's father insists that he, Woody Grant, not the church preacher, will perform the ceremony. The contrasting images of Woody, the self-appointed authority and Elder Wheeler, the church sanctioned preacher, capture the legacy of the tension between the church (as a white institution) and the folk (black spirituality). In this case, the authority of folk-sanctioned religion wins out as "Mehaley Grant stood up to marry Pomp Lamar and her father Woody Grant, who had committed the marriage ceremony to memory anyway, grabbed an almanac off the wall and held it open pompously before him as he recited the questions to give the lie to the several contentions that he could not read" (83).

In another comical twist, Hurston again juxtaposes Christianity and Africanity and seats Africanity at the forefront of black spiritual experience. With Lucy dead and Hattie now married to John, Hattie is disappointed that her seemingly well laid-plan has gone awry. As she conveys to Harris her dissatisfaction with John, Harris suggests that the aid of a conjurer might help her get John under control. A standing member of the church, Harris explains that hoodoo is not outside Christian practice and that, in fact, one of the most revered biblical figures employed hoodoo:

> Look at Moses. He's de greatest hoodoo man dat God ever made. He went 'way from Pharoah's palace and stayed in de desert nigh on to forty years and learnt how tuh call God by all his secret names and dat's how he got all dat power. . . . And then agin his wife wuz Ethiopian. Ah bet she learnt 'im whut he knowed. Ya, indeed, Sister Pearson. De Bible is de best conjure book in de world. (147)

Similarly, when John's rival, the ostentatious Rev. Cozy, preaches his sermon to upseat John, he focuses on blacks in biblical antiquity. His reading of biblical history is as humorous as that of Harris's historical account of hoodoo. Rev. Cozy, who identifies himself as a race man, aims to educate the congregation on the presence of blacks throughout biblical history. Among his many assertions, Rev. Cozy proclaims that

Je-sus, Christ, wuz uh colored man hisself. . . . When he lived it wuz hot lak
summer time, all de time, wid de sun beamin' down and scorchin' hot—how
could he be uh white man in all dat hot sun? (159)

He further asserts that

Adam musta been uh colored man 'cause de Bible says God made 'im out de
dust uh de earth, and where is anybody ever seen any white dust? (159)

Though humorous, Harris and Rev. Cozy's explications on blacks in biblical
antiquity are informed by a longstanding and serious discourse among black
leaders. Prince Hall's highly anthologized *A Charge, Delivered to the
African Lodge* (1797) illustrates an early black leader's assertion that the
whitened version of biblical history and people did not accurately represent
the stories in the text. Prince Hall addresses fellow Masons, charging them to
take on the struggles of their brethren in bondage. In this address, however,
Hall reminds his listeners of prominent black figures in the Bible: he highlights the important role of Moses's Ethiopian father-in-law; he reminds
listeners that the wise and revered Solomon welcomed the Queen of Sheba to
his court; and he recalls the apostle Philip, who counseled with an Ethiopian
Eunuch from the court of Queen Candace. Through black activists like Hall,
in churches and meeting places, blacks have been reminded that their ancestors can be traced throughout biblical history. While readers may find Harris
and Rev. Cozy comical, their references to legendary black biblical figures
would certainly have struck a chord with black readers of Hurston's time.

 While *Jonah's Gourd Vine* affirms the place of Africanity in black culture, it does not represent Africanity as a transformative power for its central
characters, John and Lucy. With her immediate sense of home upon their
arrival to Florida, the narrator leads the reader to anticipate a transformative
experience for Lucy. In Alabama on Mr. Pearson's plantation, John and Lucy
began their married life, but John quickly proves unfaithful in love and
unreliable as a provider. When Lucy arrives in Florida to begin again with
John, however, she is struck with the feeling that life has begun anew, and it
is a feeling precipitated from sensory perceptions that recall an ancient homeland. Lucy's promotion of education and financial success can be read as a
sign of her connection to modernity (Wilson 68). However, with Lucy's first
view of Florida, a chord of unconscious remembering is struck. Lucy does
not connect the images to Africa, but she has responded to Florida's hot and
colorful scenes as if she had happened upon images from a mythical past:
"She seemed to herself to be coming home. This was where she was meant to
be. The warmth, the foliage, the fruits all seemed right and as God meant her
to be surrounded. The smell of ripe guavas was new and alluring but some-
how did not seem strange" (109).

Lucy's contentment is short-lived, however. John answers the call to preach, and he becomes a reliable provider for his family. Despite their financial stability, however, Lucy becomes aware of an ever-increasing feeling of coldness and uneasiness when she attends church services. She soon identifies the source as Hattie, a woman who is engaging in an affair with John. Although Lucy's move to Florida seemed a homecoming, home has not been liberating. In Florida, she faces death with a husband who fears her dying spirit. John avoids Lucy in her dying state—he is neither a source of comfort nor of counsel. John's guilt leaves him in a horror-stricken state: "He was afraid lest she [Lucy] should die while he was asleep and he should awake to find her spirit standing over. He was equally afraid of her reproaches should she live" (132). Lucy must entrust her daughter, Isis, with her requests for certain death rites— a responsibility that Isis proves too young to enforce. Isis can only watch as, contrary to Lucy's orders, her pillow is removed from under her head as she draws her last breath (133).

While John is clearly a divinely called figure, he does not fare much better than Lucy. He is not granted the insight or the strength to save himself. His love for Lucy cannot withstand the power of the local conjurer, An' Dangie Dewoe, who provides Hattie the resources to lure him from Lucy. When John awakens from the conjurer's spell, Lucy has died, he has married Hattie, and he has no recollection of how it all transpired. In the aftermath of Lucy's death, after a night away from home and Hattie, John awakens at Zeke's house as if he had come out of a haze. John realizes that he has no memory, no recollection of what has transpired between Hattie and him (143). His recollection is too late: Lucy has died dejected and anguished, and Hattie has interjected herself as his wife, the wife of the most respected preacher in Sanford. John attempts to make things right with Lucy by saving to buy a marker for her grave. This act of homage to Lucy perhaps saves John from immediate destruction, but his fall is imminent.

Making the purchase of a "remembrance-stone" for Lucy his priority, John recognizes the primacy of the obligation of the living to the dead. While Hurston does not contextualize the cultural practice that informs John's determination, his sense of duty echoes African-rooted belief that reciprocity must be maintained between the living and the dead. Hurston's awareness of this cultural legacy is evident in her nonfictional as well as her fictional works. In her well-known anthropological study, "Hoodoo in America," Hurston speaks to the matter of relations between the living and the dead among Africans and their New World descendants: "The dead, and communication with the dead, play traditionally a large part in Negro religions. Wherever West African beliefs have survived in the New World, this place of the dead has been maintained . . . and among the Negroes of the North American continent the power of the dead to help or harm is common tenet even among those who have discarded hoodoo" (319). John's prayer to Lucy, pleading with her to loosen him from his curse, clearly captures traditional African belief that the living must show reverence for the dead.

Lucy appears to John in a dream that he reads as a divine message. In this dream he is once again the great snake conqueror. Having rescued Lucy from the threatening snake, John's old boss, Alf Pearson, appears. He advises John as he had years earlier in real life: he tells him, "Distance is the only cure for certain diseases" (183). Interpreting these words as a call for his departure, John leaves Sanford and is granted a new life in a nearby town. With a new wife, a new church, and new wealth, he vows in earnest to be true to his new wife, but his good intentions cannot stand against temptation. Having been restored to respectability and leadership, John's new wife encourages him to return to the place of his disgrace and show how well he has recovered. During what seemed his triumphant return to Sanford, however, John succumbs to the temptation of a young woman. When he awakens to the full realization of his fall, he packs up and hurriedly heads home, hoping to put distance between himself and his latest indiscretion.

Once again, distance is not enough to save John from himself, and this time his frenzied rush leads him onto the path of an oncoming train, and his death. While Hattie may have been the human source of John's curse during his marriage to Lucy, his final fall suggests that John met a fate he could not alter. Perhaps here we see the authority of the snake/ancestor: when the youthful John kills the legendary snake in his Alabama hometown, he assumes this to be a great victory. It catapults his reputation with Lucy and in the community. It is the snake that reappears decades later in John's dream, however, prompting his move from Sanford and his seeming rise to glory again. Is this mythical snake symbolic of "the wisdom of the serpent" invoked by the conjurer in one of numerous accounts of conjuration recorded by Hurston in "Hoodoo in America" (341)? The snake seems to foretell the circularity of John's experience: he is offered repeated opportunities to reconcile himself with the community, with God, with family, but John is self-consumed and too easily blinded by the glitter and structures of the material world.

In Florida, John and Lucy had found a land warm and fruitful like the homeland of their African ancestors. In this town inhabited and run by blacks, they found a cultural and spiritual community where they could set their roots. Ironically, however, in this place that Lucy felt was a return to home, she was further stifled by John's misplaced pride and his reckless womanizing. While some scholars would argue as Anthony Wilson that John's sexuality is symbolic of his more African-centered vision of the sacredness of the flesh and the spirit (65), Gary Ciuba argues that John "lives by neither Christian belief nor the faith of his African ancestors" (127). Ciuba explains this assertion with the following analysis of John's actions: "He deserts Lucy in childbirth, abandons his infant daughter as she nearly dies of typhoid, strikes his wife, and threatens to kill her if she ever practices the marital double standard that he exploits. Such unnaturalness to kin violates the holy spirit of natural supernaturalism" (127). Perhaps the more accurate reading of John Pearson lies somewhere between Wilson and Ciuba's positions. John's struggle is symbolic of his community's struggle—to maintain a black worldview in an ever encroaching white modern world. While one might read his sexuality as the expression of an African-rooted belief in the body as a gift from God, John's exploits may be alternatively read as a commentary on the ills of excessive self-interest. John is central to the spiritual world of his community; as preacher he lives the African ideal of the individual's duty to community. He delivers to the church community the spiritual nourishment they seek, and his style of preaching maintains the interactive and emotional worship practices that tie the community to their African ancestors. On the other hand, however, John's reckless self-interest symbolizes the fallout of American individualism and materialism.

Lucy is the inner voice that might have saved John. She is the source of his public success, even though she lives in his shadow. She is the great thinker and seer. Her guidance and warnings to John reveal a woman of great insight, but John is unable to act on her wisdom, and ironically, she is never able to tap into this spiritual gift to free herself. In a climactic episode for Lucy and John, he tells the deathly ill Lucy that she has been a stumbling block in his life. Lucy reminds John that he has come to think too highly of himself, and she warns him that no man is beyond the reach of a humbling experience. Their exchange of words leads John to strike Lucy, a low to which he had promised never to sink. John is the greater physical power; however, "Lucy, far more self-aware and perceptive than John, harnesses the power of vision so successfully that her visions live on after her death" (Clarke 603). John knows instantly that he has crossed the line, and Lucy's prophetic warning portends John's fate: "De hidden wedge will come tuh light some day, John, Mark mah words. Youse in de majority now, but God sho don't love ugly" (129). Lucy prepares for death after this battle, and not until after her death will John come to know the identity of the hidden wedge (Hattie and the conjurer) and the severity of his punishment.

Lucy Pearson engages in a war of words with John, but unlike her literary successor, Janie Starks, Lucy does not triumph in this world. Unlike Hurston's most celebrated heroine, Janie, Lucy Pearson dies never having stepped out onto the horizon. *Their Eyes Were Watching God* (1937) offers a central character who is sometimes reminiscent of her fictional predecessor, Lucy Pearson. Like Lucy, Janie lives in the shadow of her husband. Unlike Lucy, however, Janie frees herself from her husband's stifling hold and it is he, not Janie, who dies soon after their climactic battle of words. When Joe attempts to embarrass Janie about her age, she turns the insult back on him. For the first time in their relationship, Janie reveals to Joe that she sees him as he really is, not as he has constructed himself. She acknowledges that she is nearly forty, but that he is already fifty. Giving herself a thorough lookover, Janie tells Joe that at forty she is a good-looking woman, while he looks every bit of his age and more. Her words devastate Joe, for her public retaliation "had robbed him of his illusion of irresistible maleness that all men cherish" (*Their Eyes* 75). This was a life-changing moment: Joe Starks knew that "[w]hen he paraded his possessions hereafter, they would not consider the two together. They'd look with envy at the things and pity the man that owned them" (75). Joe answered Janie's words with a blow that sent her away, but Janie was clearly the victor. This victory was confirmed with Joe's death shortly afterward and Janie's subsequent shedding of her old self.

With Joe's death Janie begins anew her journey to self-realization—a journey that had been halted by twenty years of marriage. Joe's death marks the end of Janie's subjugation not only to Joe but to her grandmother's distorted vision of womanhood that set Janie on the road to self-denial. Nanny arranged Janie's marriage to Logan Killicks because she believed he would provide respectability and financial security for Janie. However, Nanny's decision kills young Janie's vision of marriage and paradise. In the episode that introduces Janie as a young girl, Hurston paints the portrait of an Eden-like world spoiled not by the temptation of the serpent, but rather the manifestation of God him/herself—Nanny. Janie is coming of age in the warm, colorful, blossoming world of her west Florida home. It is a paradise of sunshine, of new life emerging, and of lessons to be learned. Janie wants to know, to understand the secrets of love and life. Her curiosity is particularly piqued by the blossoming pear. The captivating image of the pear tree in bloom symbolizes the mystery of life, but it also echoes Janie's own blossoming stage. Like the pear tree, Janie "had glossy leaves and bursting buds," but more importantly "she wanted to struggle with life" although she cannot fathom how to begin (11).

Janie is not unlike the biblical Eve whose sexual awakening merely epitomizes her desire for knowledge. Eve seeks to uncover the mystery of life through intimacy with Adam, and Janie in kind seeks the path to knowledge through a young man. Like God who uncovers Eve's sin and condemns her, Nanny catches Janie kissing the young, shiftless Johnny Taylor: "Thus, like God in the Garden of Eden, Nanny authoritatively imposes a death-like sentence on Janie when she insists on her marriage to a man with the chilling name of Killicks" (Weathers 203–204). She admonishes Janie and condemns the sixteen-year-old to marry Logan Killicks, an older unattractive man who in Janie's estimation looks "like some ole skullhead in de graveyard" (13). Nanny is convinced that with Logan's material wealth, Janie will be spared the demeaning and backbreaking existence faced by most black women. Despite her good intentions, Nanny has ended Janie's childhood and desecrated her youthful vision of life and love.

Janie soon leaves Killicks after her grandmother's death, but in her subsequent marriage to Joe Starks she is again forced to lay aside her desires and curiosities. For nearly twenty years, Janie is married to Joe, and she survives by separating her soul from her body. As the "shadow of herself [goes] about tending store and prostrating itself before Jody," the real Janie escapes "under a shady tree" (73). Janie lives in this spiritually dormant state until she is awakened through her verbal showdown with Jody. With her triumph over Jody, Janie begins the journey back to self. Janie's road to self-realization is marked by an awakening of her African spiritual self. She turns away from western Christian paradigms of self, a shift that echoes Hurston's conviction that "Christian explanations have never proved fully adequate for blacks, whose sensibilities are deeply rooted in folk traditions" (Hubbard). Hurston calls on paradigms and practices of black folk culture to trace Janie's emergence into selfhood. Hurston's application of black cultural conventions is not for the mere sake of nostalgia, but rather "her means of comprehending transformation" (Lamothe 158). While Daphne Lamonthe is interested particularly in Hurston's use of Vodou in the text, she posits this as a reading of Hurston's general use of folk culture. In this light we see then the novel's intricate weaving of memory, nature, community, and self as nuances of African American culture that make possible Janie's transformation.

Janie's narrative opens with the act of remembering: she must remember and revisit the past to arrive at a comprehensive understanding of her emergence into selfhood. The pear tree is a recurring nature image that anchors Janie's remembering throughout her life: "To understand herself, Janie has revisited that pear tree time and again, documenting life's experiences with references to the pear tree situated in her grandmother's garden" (Weathers 202). Her connection to the pear tree symbolizes Janie's innate sense of the importance of nature in human identity and understanding. She instinctively knows that the secrets to unfold will come to her away from the superficial world carved out of western materialism. In this regard, Janie's instincts echo the sentiments of the Akan who were the forefathers of many populations of New World Africans. In Akan cosmology, "the land was the source of not only sustenance and value but also corporate identity" (Gomez 112).

Janie often finds herself the object of scorn and criticism in the community, but it is her lack of community and thus lack of self-identity that signals her inner conflict early in the novel. Though Hurston humorously depicts six-year-old Janie as she is unable to identify herself in a photo, Janie's calamity signals her isolation. Having been raised with the young white grandchildren of Nanny's employer, Mrs. Wahburn, Janie assumes that she is white like them. When a photographer happens to take a snapshot of Janie and the white children, Janie views the resultant photo with astonishment and dismay. When the children point to Janie in the photo, they laugh at her failure to recognize herself as the dark one. She recalls the affirmation from Miss Nellie who tells her, "Dat's you, Alphabet, don't you know yo' ownself?" (9). Janie's lack of identity and place is further revealed in the pet name given her by the Washburns. According to Janie they had given her the name Alphabet because so many people had given her different names.

As a young child, Janie lacks community, and Hurston's humorous account of Janie's disturbing moment of self-discovery points to the important role of the community in the individual's understanding of self. Self-realization is dependent on the individual's relationship to community. While Janie thinks that she is like the Washburns and is one among them, the Washburns clearly see Janie as one separate from them. Alternatively, Janie's separation from the black community leaves her doubly alienated. Living on the Washburn property and wearing Washburn hand-me-downs that were noticeably finer than the clothes worn by other black children, Janie was ostracized by her black schoolmates. The alienation Janie experiences as a child follows her into adulthood. Nanny marries her off to Logan Killicks, once again offering her a world materially richer than other blacks in the community, leaving her without community. When Janie takes off with Joe Starks and arrives in Florida, she meets with her first opportunity to belong to a community. However, Joe dismisses Janie's desire to belong because, like Nanny, he attempts to mark his success with the image of Janie above and distinct from what he deemed the inferior class of laboring black women. While Janie longed to be part of those activities that brought folks together in laughter and thought, Joe decided that this kind of community gathering was beneath the dignity of his wife. So Janie had to withdraw from the porch sitting, storytelling, and signifying that was so central to life in this black Eatonville community.

The real Janie would lie dormant for years, and while Janie's moment of awakening is arguably her war of words with Joe, this turning point is presaged earlier. With the novel's early emphasis on the interdependent relationship of the community and the individual, Joe Starks is destined to fall. Ironically, Joe does not physically isolate himself from the common folks. On the premise that he is mayor and must be in touch with his constituency, Joe gives audience to and takes part in their antics. He does so, however, with an air of self-righteous superiority. This is especially highlighted in the mule-burying episode. Joe won't allow Janie to attend the funeral of the mule that he earlier liberated as a show of his power and compassion. Joe leaves the store and accompanies the townspeople to the swamp where they have a lively funeral for the dead beast. Joe returns to the store aware of Janie's displeasure, and he answers her resentment with a mocking and pompous summary of the event: "Ah had tuh laugh at de people out dere in de woods dis mornin', Janie. You can't help but laugh at de capers they cuts. But all the same, Ah wish mah people would git mo' business in 'em and not spend so much time on foolishness" (59). Joe has enthusiastically participated in the mule burying fun, but he attempts to distinguish his role as that of observer. As the model of success in the community, Joe presumes himself a smarter and better class than those he represents as mayor or conducts business with as storeowner.

As storeowner Joe's disconnect from the community is further revealed with his unsympathetic treatment of one of his regular customers, Mrs. Robbins. Mrs. Robbins frequently purchases food on credit, claiming that her husband does not feed his family sufficiently. The men on the store porch, as well as Joe himself, find her behavior outrageous and embarrassing for her husband. While Joe insists that he does not believe her complaint, he encourages her behavior through a humorous verbal exchange that ends with him assuming the role of pacifier. He tells Mrs. Robbins, "Ah know you don't need it, but come on inside. You ain't goin' tuh lemme read till Ah give it to yuh" (69). What might otherwise seem a noble deed becomes apparently otherwise as the ensuing dialog reveals. Mrs. Robbins praises Joe for his compassion until they reach the meat box where Joe marks off a cut of meat smaller than Mrs. Robbins had anticipated. When she motions as if to refuse such a small slice of meat, Joe threatens to return it to the box. Mrs. Robbins accepts the small slice of meat, and Joe adds the cost to her husband's account. Joe's stingy behavior is especially notable when juxtaposed with his treatment of the mule. He purchases a worthless mule as a show of power, but when offered the opportunity to extend a gift to those less fortunate than himself, Joe declines.

Joe is revered and even feared by fellow blacks in Eatonville. While they admire his leadership in establishing the town and orchestrating its growth, his pompousness and his self-proclaimed godlike stature sets him apart. Ironically, Joe's transposition of the commonly used exclamation, "My God," to "I god," underscores his presumption of godliness. Not unlike John Pearson in *Jonah's Gourd Vine*, however, Joe will find that he is not God. Before her departure from the store, Mrs. Robbins leaves Joe with an indirect (third person) insult: "Some folks ain't got no heart in dey bosom. They's willin' tuh see uh po' woman and her helpless chillun starve tuh death. God's goin-tuh put 'em under arrest, some uh dese days, wid dey stingy gripin' ways" (70). Her words are more than just an insult hurled at the pompous and self-serving Joe Starks: her words are a curse, warning the mighty Joe of his own imminent fall. As Janie breaks her silence answering the men's criticism of Mrs. Robbins, her words further portend Joe's end. Like Mrs. Robbins, Janie does not direct her words to Joe specifically, but she too clearly offers Joe a vision of what will become reality for him. In the guise of humor, speaking of men in general, Janie warns that they presume themselves smarter than they are and that it might be quite a surprise for them to discover that they know very little about womenfolks whom they presume to know so well.

These closing words lead to the next chapter and the narrator's account of Joe's declining health. Joe is convinced that someone, probably Janie, has conjured him. Joe dies as Mrs. Robbins had described—he is essentially under arrest. He is confined to his bed, and as Janie had predicted, he would learn how little he knew her. On his deathbed, where he could not turn a deaf ear or send her away, Joe had to hear Janie tell him of his failure with her and with others, and this time Janie tells him with a first person voice. Though Joe commands her to shut up, Janie now has control of the conversation and will have the last words: "[N]ow you got tuh die tuh find out dat you got tuh pacify somebody besides yo'self if you wants any love and any sympathy in dis world. You ain't tried tuh pacify nobody but yo'self. Too busy listening tuh yo' own big voice" (82). While Joe and Nanny kept Janie away from community, her words to Joe reveal that the experience of distance and alienation had taught her the central place of the community in the making of the self.

If *Their Eyes Were Watching God* had ended with Janie's final words to Joe, the novel's message of community would have been rather simple and clear. However, this closing episode is only the midpoint of the narrative, and by the end of her journey to self-realization, Janie will learn that the individual's relationship with community is complicated. When Janie moves down on the muck with Tea Cake, she finds community and the promise of the pear tree that had lain dormant during her marriage to Joe. Living on the muck, Janie now participates in the storytelling, the singing, the dancing, the signifying, and the overall socialization that gives life to this community. African Americans, Bahamians, and Native Americans coexist here with no deference for the pretenses of western culture. Janie and Tea Cake work in the fields together with others in their community, and they live in a village-like setting that reinforces their community ties. On the muck, Janie and Tea Cake's home becomes the center of evening and weekend life, much like Joe's store in Eatonville. In Janie and Tea Cake's home, however, Janie freely engages in these defining moments of community life: "The men held big arguments here like they used to do on the store porch. Only here, she could listen and laugh and even talk some herself if she wanted to" (128). Janie's utopic relationship with the community on the muck is shattered with the death of Tea Cake and her subsequent trial. Ironically, at Janie's lowest hour, when she needs to be comforted by the community, they betray her. She must defend herself against the charge of murdering Tea Cake, and none of her friends offer public support. In fact, many who had once been friends launch piercing accusations against her. The trial ends with Janie set free, but instead of being embraced by her community of fellow blacks, only the whites in the courtroom offer Janie solace.

The community's betrayal could arguably be read as a commentary on the absence of solidarity among blacks. Hurston, however, offers a picture of the complex nature of community, and by the novel's end, suggests that the individual must reconcile herself to the community. It is a reconciliation that serves the interest of all. Understanding this, Janie organizes Tea Cake's funeral and calls on all their friends to join her in celebrating his life. They come, "with shame and apology in their faces," and along side Janie, they deliver Tea Cake to his resting place (180). Afterward, Sop, who had led the rallying cry against Janie in the courtroom, now leads the call for Janie to be restored to the community. He announces that he holds no malice against Janie, as she was forced to kill Tea Cake to save herself from him. Janie buries Tea Cake in keeping with African spiritual traditions that call for burying the dead with reverence and great attention, in preparation for the afterlife. Hurston illustrates the survival of this pre–Middle Passage sensibility through the account of Tea Cake's burial. Janie's respect for this tradition confirms her love for Tea Cake and her innocence in his death. Sop offers final confirmation of this as he tells the others to "Look at de way she put him away" (181).

The novel's final reflection on community occurs in Janie's closing words to her friend Phoeby. Janie has returned to Eatonville facing those who sat in judgment of her, those who hoped that she had returned with a story of abuse and disappointment. She knows that the townfolks await the second-hand report of her time with Tea Cake. Although she is convinced their curiosity originates in envy and ill will, Janie authorizes Phoeby to share her story: "Ah know all dem sitters-and-talkers goin tuh worry they guts into fiddle strings till dey find out whut we been talkin' 'bout. Dat's all right, Phoeby, tell 'em" (182). With this authorization, Janie avoids further alienation. As with the community on the muck, Janie recognizes that for all its shortcomings, community shapes, defines, and grounds the individual. The community and the individual are interdependent entities that must struggle to coexist. In this coexistence each offers the other insights. Janie learns compelling maxims as she watches blacks in Eatonville and as she becomes part of the community on the muck. The seemingly mindless porch stories and humor shared at Joe's store are filled with philosophical reflections and maxims. For example, when Lige and Sam debate what keeps a man from burning himself on a red-hot stove, the inquiry originates in Sam's desire to once again bait Lige into an argument that leaves him the butt of laughter. In their verbal exchange, however, Lige and Sam explore a timeless epistemological question: How do humans arrive at knowledge? Is it through experience or through instinct? Sam and Lige do not invoke the discourse of acclaimed western philosophers; however, Hurston manipulates black southern dialect to show that this question is no more beyond the capacity of everyday folks than it is for a Kant, a Locke, or a Hume. In the larger context of the novel, this is a question that underscores Janie's journey to self-realization. Janie is in search of knowledge; she wants to understand the secret to living and loving, but she is not altogether certain how one arrives at this knowledge. The implication of the question raised by Sam thus underscores Janie's struggle.

When Janie gives Phoeby permission to share her story, she shares with the community both her legacy of learning, and she also answers Lige's unresolved inquiry of long ago. She tells Phoeby to tell the others "dat love ain't somethin' lak uh grindstone dat's de same thing everywhere and do de same thing tuh everything it touch. Love is lak de sea. It's uh movin' thing. . . . it takes its shape from de shore it meets, and it's different with every shore" (182). To those who will criticize Janie's relationship with Tea Cake, she wants them to know that the fault they find originates in their own misconceived notion that love is a constant. Janie has learned that God prescribes different formulas of loving and living for different people. There is no single model, and you don't reach the horizon by talking about it. How do we come to know, then? Do we learn through instinct or experience? Janie suggests that living is in the doing, that we learn from experience:

> [T]alkin' don't amount tuh uh hill uh beans when yuh can't do nothin' else. . . . It's uh known fact, Phoeby, you got tuh go there tuh know there. Yo' papa and yo' mama and nobody else can't tell yuh and show yuh. Two things everybody's got tuh do fuh theyselves. They got to go tuh God, and they got tuh find out about livin' fuh theyselves. (183)

Janie has both learned from the community and brought it enlightenment. She understands that the relationship between the individual and the community is central to the survival of both, but it is a dynamic relationship that is not without its strains and disillusionment. Janie was hurt and disillusioned by the Eatonville community that was unwilling to accept her relationship with Tea Cake, and she was further disillusioned by the black community on the muck that wanted her convicted of murder. Janie returns to both communities, however, reconciling differences and confirming her place among them.

Unlike Nanny and Joe, Janie desires to be part of the community rather than to stand above or apart from it. This desire to belong is a force that informs Janie's road to self-realization. Tea Cake's significance in Janie's reawakening is not simply that of the traditional love mate of sentimental fiction. Tea Cake shows Janie the path to community and belonging. When he returns from his adventurous day away after their wedding, Janie assures him that she wants to live in the world of folks and laughter. She does not want to meet with the isolation she had known as Joe's wife. With the assurance that Janie would not think badly of his lifestyle and his companions, Tea Cake introduces Janie to the life she had envisioned years ago under the pear tree. It was the trip to the horizon: the sunshine, love, laughter, adventure, and sharing that she had previously been denied.

Janie's path to community is also the path to self, but this journey does not take place serendipitously. *Their Eyes Were Watching God* is a narrative of remembering, and it is memory that empowers Janie at critical junctures in the novel. As Janie begins to think about the story she must tell Phoeby, she realizes that she must call on memory to gather all the parts that will make the story clear. To fully explain the story of her experience with Tea Cake, Janie tells Phoeby that she must "give . . . de understandin' to go 'long wid it" (7). This takes Janie to the beginning—she must remember or revisit her childhood, because the story of Janie's relationship with Tea Cake originates in Janie's childhood. Janie must start with the story of Johnny Taylor and the pear tree, because the desires born here lay dormant until Tea Cake reminds her of her childhood visions. Janie's remembrances of her grandmother in slavery, the rapes suffered by both her grandmother and mother, and the absence of both her mother and her father provide Phoeby a more profound picture of Janie's childhood years. The importance of community and belonging felt by Janie are compelled by her childhood feelings of abandonment and alienation. As Janie remembers and shares her story with Phoeby, she relives those experiences, allowing her to connect the past with the present.

When Janie watches Joe die, she pities the person he had become and the hard way he had to die. However, with Joe gone, Janie can turn her attention to herself. She remembers the young girl and the vision that had been smothered for so long: "Years ago, she had told her girl self to wait for her in the looking glass. It had been a long time since she had remembered" (83). Janie does not find the little girl. She is gone; however, the adult Janie still remembers the vision, and she begins again the search for the horizon. It is the adult Janie who can now remember Nanny and more clearly discern her destructive influence. In fact, now as an adult, Janie is able to face her real feelings about her grandmother. She realizes now that "[s]he hated her grandmother and had hidden it from herself all these years under a cloak of pity. She had been getting ready for her great journey to the horizons in search of *people*; it was important to all the world that she should find them and they find her" (85). Remembering and fully understanding her grandmother's influence, Janie can move forward. She has lived Nanny's stifling vision, and she now prepares to return to her own.

Janie concludes her story, telling Phoeby about the package of garden seeds Tea Cake bought but did not live to plant. She had given away all his other possessions to his friends on the muck, but she kept the seeds. The seeds remind Janie of Tea Cake, and she vows to "plant them for remembrance" (182). Tea Cake is gone, but he is not dead. The power of remembering will keep him alive. When Janie realizes this, the feeling of loneliness and despair leave her. With the image of Tea Cake "prancing around her where she was," the horrible memory of his death is flushed from Janie's mind. It is this living memory of Tea Cake that will prevail and preserve Janie, for "[h]e could never be dead until she herself had finished feeling and thinking" (183). Janie's ontological view echoes African belief systems that maintain the interconnectedness of carnal and spiritual beings and their ability to cross boundaries of existence, time, and space. Janie is thus confident that Tea Cake is present. Her assuredness is as sound as that of the Bahamian, Lias, whose departing words to Tea Cake and Janie during the storm conveys his expectation to see them in death: "If Ah never see you no mo' on earth, Ah'll meet you in Africa" (148). Lias expresses a concept of death that dates back to the first Africans forced to cross the Atlantic into American slavery. Many African slaves in America looked forward to a death that they maintained would deliver them again to their African homeland. Countless Africans threw themselves overboard while in passage, and others killed themselves upon arrival so that they could return home. Generations after the arrival of the first Africans, Lias reminds readers that this cultural longing did not die with slavery, and that it is an expectation that connects blacks throughout the Americas.

While Hurston frames the opening chapters of *Their Eyes Were Watching God* in biblical allusions, she concludes the novel affirming the place of African spirituality in African American culture as well as its centralness to her protagonist's enlightenment. Young Janie is introduced in language and imagery that recalls the biblical Garden of Eden, but the story of Hurston's protagonist will not mirror that of the fallen Eve. Janie is castigated and scorned like Eve in the Garden, but she will not meet Eve's fate. She will find the secret to life that she seeks, and she will not be condemned to life long suffering.

Janie's shift from an Anglo Christian cosmology is not evident through an explicit proclamation or moment of epiphany. Until Joe's death, the narrative offers no mention of Joe and Janie's involvement in church; however, in the aftermath of Joe's death we are told that Janie "quit attending church like she used to" (105). Sam tells Phoeby that the pastor suspects Tea Cake is keeping Janie away so that he can lay claim to the money she would be offering in church (106). Tea Cake does not consort with Janie on his beliefs about Christianity, but his influence draws Janie away from the church and into a new vision of life. This is suggested in an episode when Janie finds herself consumed with thoughts of Tea Cake. At this early stage in their relationship, Janie knows little about Tea Cake. She is struck, however, by Tea Cake's likeness to her childhood vision of life unfolding. In part, her description paints Tea Cake as the answer to years of female longing for unanswered love. In Janie's mind Tea Cake "looked like the love thoughts of women. He could be a bee to a blossom—a pear tree in the spring" (101). Tea Cake is more than the conventional heroic male suitor of sentimental fiction, however. Janie associates Tea Cake with her vision of the ideal love union, but that vision moves beyond the carnal. Tea Cake appears mythical in Janie's description of him "crushing scent out of the world with his footsteps" (101). He is a majestic figure—"a glance from God" (102). His mythical stature is even more evident in his death. Janie buries this "son of Evening Sun" in a style reminiscent of the ancient Egyptians, the sun worshippers who buried their kings in preparation for a glorious afterlife. Dressed in fine clothes, with a brand new guitar by his side, Tea Cake is marched to his resting place, in a procession that resembled the ride of "a Pharaoh to his tomb" (180).

Looking like a glance from God, Tea Cake is the vision, the presence that directs Janie's attention away from the church. With Tea Cake as her earthly guide, Janie returns to the visions of her childhood that hinted at a metaphysical interdependency of nature, God, and living. Janie returns to the picture of the blossoming pear tree with its suggestion of new life and new possibilities. She and Tea Cake go down on the muck where they experience directly the gifts of God that come from the earth. They live a simple existence, feeding themselves in large part by their own labor. They hunt wild game, and they fish. They work in the fields, planting and then harvesting the ready crops. They befriend the Bahamian workers, and as the local blacks and Bahamians develop a relationship of mutual trust and respect, their lives are reminiscent of their ancestors prior to the Middle Passage: "Many of the Americans learned to jump and liked it as much as the 'saws.' So they began to hold dances night after night in the quarters, usually behind Tea Cake's house" (146).

It is not mere coincidence that the end of Tea Cake and Janie's idyllic existence begins when they disregard warnings of impending danger signaled by those closest to the land. Choosing the promise of the white man's dollar over the Indians' warning of the raging storm, Tea Cake and Janie find themselves in danger that will ultimately lead to the end of their paradise. After watching the Seminoles leave for higher ground and animals scurrying to safer ground, Tea Cake and Janie remain with those who are led by their desire to make money: "Beans running fine and prices good, so the Indians could be, *must* be, wrong. You couldn't have a hurricane when you're making seven and eight dollars a day picking beans" (147). Even when the Bahamian, Lias, offers them a ride out with his uncle who insists that they must leave before the onset of the storm, Janie and Tea Cake choose to stay and weather the storm. Janie has momentarily lost sight of the lesson of the blossoming pear tree; she and Tea Cake risk the gift of life for material gain.

The workers who remain have cast their lot with the white bosses who defied the natives' warning, but by nightfall their confidence will begin to falter: "The folks in the quarters and the people in the big houses further around the shore heard the big lake and wondered. The people felt uncomfortable but safe because there were the seawalls to chain the senseless monster in his head" (150). Tea Cake, Janie, and Motor huddle together as they soon become aware that the white man's authority and technology are no match for nature. As the storm gains strength the six turn their eyes from white authority and fix their sights on God. They stared at the door knowing that "[t]he time was past for asking the white folks what to look for through that door" (151). In the hurricane that rages Janie, Tea Cake, Motor, and the other blacks who had chosen to stay understand that they are about to witness God in all his might. They knew that they were not just watching a storm: "their eyes were watching God" (151). Ironically, Hurston has her "characters watch God in darkness," suggesting that God does manifest himself to people and that his presence is manifested in darkness as well as light (Clarke 609). Tea Cake and Janie survive the storm, but they have unknowingly paid a fatal price for their dismissal of the Seminoles' warning. When a rabid bog bites Tea Cake during their trek through the raging stormwaters, Tea Cake's days are numbered. As he grows mad from the effects of rabies, the muck is no longer the idyllic world that he and Janie had known. Death sweeps in and Janie is alone again, but the loneliness does not prevail. Janie's final lesson is that while death marks the separation of bodies, it does not sever the bonds of the spirit. She no longer has Tea Cake in carnal form, but his spirit remains with her.

Janie's determination to plant the seeds that Tea Cake left further underscores the novel's emphasis on the African spiritual concept that spirit resides in all matter and is regenerated in different forms. Tea Cake will live again in the plants that emerge from the seedlings. Life is regenerative and circular: there is no ending. This, too, is underscored in the repeated moments in the narrative that require Janie to think new thoughts for new beginnings. Although the narrative opens with a proclamation of beginning, that is, "So the beginning of this was a woman" (1), this is only one of many beginnings in the text. As Janie reaches critical moments in her life, particularly those marked by endings, she then enters upon a new beginning. When Nanny admonishes Janie for her sentimental notions of marriage, Janie dejectedly goes home to Logan fully knowing that her childhood dream had been killed. Despite Janie's low state, she maintains a regenerative vision of life and possibilities—she still believes that "God tore down the old world every evening and built a new one by sun-up" (24). Similarly, when Janie leaves Logan, she realizes that the end of this life is the beginning of another. She would reach back to her childhood vision and "old thoughts"; however, for her new journey "new words would have to be made and said" (31). Janie again finds herself in need of "new thoughts" and "new words" when she and Joe take separate bedrooms and their relationship begins its ending (78). With Joe's death, Janie again embarks upon a new beginning, this time marked by the birth of her relationship with Tea Cake. It is a beginning that once again requires "new thoughts" and "new words" (109). With Tea Cake dead, in what seems the end of all her childhood thoughts, Janie will embark upon a new beginning. Tea Cake is gone, but life will begin again, and Janie will witness this as she plants the seeds and watches the flowers emerge.

The novel ends with the portrait of Janie at peace and satisfied. She has arrived at this state by shedding layers of Anglo Christian notions of being and alternatively reimagining herself and the world through an African spiritual lens. Janie's return to Eatonville after Tea Cake's death illustrates her understanding of the complicated interdependency of the community and the individual. She is not blind to the faults of its sometimes small-minded and mean-spirited members, but Janie's short time on the muck has confirmed for her the necessary connectedness of individuals. In both the South Florida community on the muck and her Eatonville hometown, Janie meets with scorn as she experiences two critical moments of loss. Although the Eatonville residents are aware that Joe had treated Janie badly, they want Janie to continue life as Mrs. Mayor even after Joe's death. They scorn her for dating Tea Cake, who, in their estimation, is a man beneath her social status. Like Joe, they want to see Janie maintain the image of the idle, privileged outsider among them. Perhaps their desire originates in a need to hold Janie as a public icon, a reminder that blacks, too, can achieve the markers of white privilege and success. Janie has other ideas, however, and her will is influenced in part by the daily sharing of stories and humor she has witnessed but been denied participation. Although she has been relegated to spectator, the underlying themes in the tales and laughter at these porch gatherings prompt self-reflection in Janie that saves her from giving over fully to her subjugated and isolated existence. She has thereby maintained a lifeline to the hopefulness of the young Janie Crawford under the pear tree. As spectator, Janie appreciated the bonds of kinship and belonging secured on those porch settings. This imprint informs her experience of community on the muck and her return to her Eatonville home.

Janie returns to Eatonville, bringing a story and a message for the community. Just as she understands the weakness that fueled betrayal by her South Florida community, she also understands that the mule-like existences led by those in Eatonville leave them similarly blinded by despair and fear. Her understanding saves her from feelings of hate and a desire to withdraw. In South Florida and Eatonville, she returns to the community because she understands that place and people are elements of the self. The young Janie Crawford who was unaware that she was black was far worse off than Janie Woods. Janie Woods knows that belonging brings both laughter and pain, but it is nevertheless the means of knowing the self.

Janie's transformative journey to self symbolizes the spiritual transformation of Africans who, in the New World, were forced to reimagine themselves in a world shrouded in whiteness. *Their Eyes Were Watching God* marks the fruition of this long journey in black women's literary fiction. Shedding the shroud of white religiosity that shackled her grandmother (ancestors) and her youthful self, Janie turns to an African spiritual worldview and embarks on the road to recovery. It is through an African-derived understanding of the power of memory, community, and nature, and the unending relation between the living and the dead, that Janie emerges into the heroic self at the novel's end. With Janie's triumph, *Their Eyes Were Watching God* represents the resolution of African-Christian tensions unresolvable in the earliest works of fiction by black women. Moreover, as a triumphant black heroine, Janie paves the way for some of our most celebrated contemporary black heroines—most notably Alice Walker's Celie (*Color Purple*), Toni Morrison's Sethe (*Beloved*), Paule Marshall's Avey (*Praisesong for the Widow*), and Gloria Naylor's Cocoa (*Mama Day*). With these contemporary fictional black heroines, Africanity is no longer silenced or desecrated; instead, as with Janie, Africanity emerges as the spiritual source that defines and shapes black life.

WORKS CITED

Chandler, Karen M. "Nella Larsen's Fatal Polarities: Melodrama and Its Limits in *Quicksand*." *CLA* 42.1 (September 1998): 24–47.

Ciuba, Gary. "The Worm against the Word: The Hermeneutical Challenge in Hurston's *Jonah's Gourd Vine*." *African American Review* 34.1 (2000): 119–133.

Clarke, Deborah. "'The Porch Couldn't Talk for Looking': Voice and Vision in *Their Eyes Were Watching God*." *African American Review* 35.4 (2001): 599–613.

Defalco, Amelia. "Jungle Creatures and Dancing Apes: Modern Primitivism and Nella Larsen's *Quicksand*." *Mosaic* 38.2 (June 2005): 19–35.

Gomez, Michael A. *Exchanging Our Country Marks: The Transformation of African Identities in the Colonial Antebellum South.* Chapel Hill: University of North Carolina Press, 1998.

Hubbard, Dolan. "'. . . Ah Said Ah'd Save de Text for You': Recontextualizing the Sermon to Tell (Her) Story in Zora Neale Hurston's *Their Eyes Were Watching God*." *African American Review* 27.2 (1993): 167–178.

Hurston, Zora Neale. "Hoodoo in America." *The Journal of American Folk-Lore* 44.174 (October–December 1931): 318–417.

———. *Jonah's Gourd Vine*. 1934. Ed. Henry Louis Gates, Jr. New York: Harper & Row, Publishers, 1990.

———. *Their Eyes Were Watching God*. 1937. Ed. Henry Louis Gates, Jr. New York: Harper & Row, Publishers, 1990.

Jenkins, Candice M. "Decoding Essentialism: Cultural Authenticity and the Black Bourgeoisie in Nella Larsen's *Passing*." *MELUS* 30.3 (Fall 2005): 129–54.

Lamothe, Daphne. "Vodou Imagery, African-American Tradition and Cultural Transformation in Zora Neale Hurston's *Their Eyes Were Watching God*." *Callaloo* 22.1 (1999): 157–175.

Larsen, Nella. *Quicksand*. 1928. In *Quicksand and Passing*. Ed. Deborah E. McDowell. New Brunswick, NJ: Rutgers University Press, 1991. 1–135.

Montgomery, Georgene Bess. *The Spirit and the Word: A Theory of Spirituality in Africana Literary Criticism*. Trenton, NJ: Africa World Press, 2008.

Weathers, Glenda B. "Biblical Trees, Biblical Deliverance: Literary Landscapes of Zora Neale Hurston and Toni Morrison." *African American Review* 39.1–2 (2005): 201–212.

Wilson, Anthony. "The Music of God, Man, and Beast: Spirituality and Modernity *in Jonah's Gourd Vine*." *Southern Literary Journal* 35.2 (2003): 64–78.

Index

African carryovers in the New World, 8

African Christianity. *See* black Christianity

A.M.E. Church. *See* African Methodist Episcopal Church

African Methodist Episcopal Church, 12, 51

African spirituality: ancestors, 7, 8, 10, 14, 18, 21, 24, 48, 56, 67, 76, 153, 156; animals, 17; black women, 11–14; burial, 14, 17; community, 8, 10, 11, 14–15, 15–16, 23, 75; dance, 17, 45; death, 17–18, 48, 49, 62; divinities, 14, 16, 19, 55; dogs, 17, 49, 56; life and death, 17; memory, 11, 14–15, 16; nature, 16, 55; pre-Middle Passage, 11; ring shout, 7–8; sacred and secular, 9, 21; serpent, 12; snake, 17, 57, 153; spiritual possession, 31, 46; spiritual and material beings, 8, 17, 18; spiritual interveners, 18–19; sun, 49; thunder and lightning, 55; trees, 17, 73; water and baptism, 16, 17, 55

"An Address Delivered Before the African Female Intelligence Society of America". *See* Stewart, Maria

"An Address Delivered Before the African Masonic Hall". *See* Stewart, Maria

Baker, Harriet, 11

Baldwin, James, 13

Bambara, Toni Cade, 13–14

Banneker, Benjamin, 3, 7. *See* Keckley, Elizabeth

Bible: blacks and biblical typology, 4; blacks in, 3; Biblical allusions, 60; Cain, 2, 4, 27; Ham, 2, 24n1

black migration, 101

black Christianity, 5, 7, 20, 22, 28, 44, 51, 65, 67, 95, 101, 103, 104, 107, 108, 121, 135

black church, 44

black modernism, 128

black novel, 68

black oral culture, 43

black women and Christianity, 11, 62

black women's spiritual narratives, 2

Bondwoman's Narrative. See Crafts, Hannah

Brandon, George: three stage process, 21–22; formative period, 22; persistent period, 22–23; transformative period, 23

Brown, William Wells, 65, 70

call and response, 7. *See* Fauset, Jesse

Christian Recorder, 69

Christianity, 101

Comedy, American Style. See Fauset, Jesse; Hopkins, Pauline

conversion narrative, 22, 44, 59–60, 66, 77

Crafts, Hannah: *Bondwoman's Narrative*, 22, 69, 70–77; ancestors, 76; black

About the Author

Elizabeth J. West is an associate professor of English at Georgia State University. She received her Ph.D. in English with a certificate in Women's Studies from Emory University. Her research and teaching focus on representations of gender, race, class, and spirituality in early American and African American literary works. She has published articles in anthologies and in *CLA, MELUS, JCCH, Womanist, Black Magnolias,* and *South Central Review*. She was an invited speaker and discussant for the 2009 Summer Transnational American Studies Seminar (sponsored by the German Academic Exchange Service) at the University of Mainz (Germany). She was a 2002 AAUW Research Fellow and a ROOTS 2003 NEH Summer Seminar Participant (6/2–7/11 Virginia Foundation for the Humanities and University of Virginia). She has served as a Special Delegate for the Modern Language Association, and she is currently assistant treasurer for the College Language Association.